Trading In Sync With Commodities

Introducing Astrology To Your Financial Toolbox

Trading In Sync With Commodities

Introducing Astrology To Your Financial Toolbox

Susan Abbott Gidel

Pines Publishing, Inc.

Copyright © 2018 Susan M. Gidel.

Published by
Pines Publishing, Inc.

ISBN: 13:978-0-9766820-2-8
eISBN: 13: 978-0-9766820-1-1

Cover and Interior Design: GKS Creative, Murfreesboro, TN

All Rights Reserved. No part of this publication may be reproduced, stored in a retrieval system or transmitted in any form or by any means, electronic, mechanical, photocopying recording, scanning or otherwise. Nor may it be stored in a retrieval system, transmitted, or otherwise copied for public use—other than for "fair use" as brief quotations embodied in articles or reviews—without prior written consent of the publisher.

All information in this publication—written and visual—is merely the personal opinion of the author and is not to be construed as financial advice, nor relied upon as such. Please contact your broker or financial advisor for trading and investment advice. Past results are not necessarily indicative of future market behavior.

Designations used by companies to distinguish their products are often claimed by trademarks. In all instances where the author or publisher is aware of a claim, the product names appear in Initial Capital letters. Readers, however, should contact the appropriate companies for more complete information regarding trademarks and registration.

All astrological horoscope charts that appear in this book are created from Sirius v2.0 with kind permission from Cosmic Patterns Software. www.astrosoftware.com

All price data and price charts that appear in this book are courtesy of Barchart.com. www.barchart.com

Publisher's Cataloging-In-Publication Data
(Prepared by The Donohue Group, Inc.)

Names: Gidel, Susan Abbott, 1956-

Title: Trading in sync with commodities : introducing astrology to your financial toolbox / Susan Abbott Gidel.

Description: [Morrison, Illinois] : Pines Publishing, Inc., [2018] | Includes bibliographical references.

Identifiers: ISBN 9780976682028 | ISBN 9780976682011 (ebook)

Subjects: LCSH: Astrology and personal finance. | Stocks. | Commodity exchanges.

Classification: LCC BF1729.F48 G54 2018 (print) | LCC BF1729.F48 (ebook) | DDC 133.58332024--dc23

Dedicated to Ed Abbott, the original inspiration for my lifelong fascination with what makes market prices change every day.

Thanks, Dad.

Susan Abbott Gidel

Table of Contents

Acknowledgements ix

Introduction xiii

Chapter 1 Astrology 101 1

Chapter 2 Commodities 101 19

Chapter 3 How You Sync Up with the Markets 38

Chapter 4 The Importance of First-Trade Data 49

Chapter 5 How Markets Sync Up with Planets 54

Chapter 6 Agriculture 79

Chapter 7 Currencies 93

Chapter 8 Energy 109

Chapter 9 Interest Rates 123

Chapter 10 Metals 136

Chapter 11 Stock Indexes 153

Chapter 12 Outlook 2018-2020 177

Chapter 13 How to Introduce Astrology to Your Financial Toolbox 200

Appendix Dates of Potential Highs and Lows 2018-2020 205

Astrology Glossary 213

Bibliography 217

Resources 221

Acknowledgements

My writing desk looks into my back yard, and I am constantly reminded that "It's all good!" by the metal sign hanging on the garage. What that means to me is that even the tough stuff in life has a purpose in order to propel me down my life's path. So, in that category, I'm grateful to previous day-job employers who saw fit to go bankrupt or fire me so that I would have time to study astrology in the way that I needed to study it, and to finally realize that my life's path is in combining my passion and expertise for writing, the commodity markets and astrology in a way that not only satisfies my own curiosity, but also can help others. This book is the result of the full-time focus I have been able to afford it, and is the foundation for the work I will do the rest of my life.

As a self-published author, I'm grateful for the support team that has been attracted to this project. At the top of the list is Sara Connell, my writing coach, accountability check and cheerleader. It's often easy to blow off deadlines you've committed to only with yourself, but having meetings on the calendar with Sara and a pre-meeting copy deadline helped immensely in sticking to the timeline I wanted to achieve. That she and I are on the same page spiritually made our working together even more special. In addition, her understanding of self-publishing challenges and her network of designers and distributors made answering questions and making decisions much easier.

I'd also like to thank my own network of friends with professional writing, editing, design and public relations insights for their help and advice. These include: Susan Taylor, who read every word to make sure all the commas and apostrophes were in the right places and that the words made sense; Ginger Szala, who I can always count on to make sure I am being accurate; Guy Swartz, who is generous with his support and willingness to help me speak design in the current vernacular; and Patricia Campbell, who never met a launch party she didn't like.

In the astrological community, my first thanks must go to my first formal teachers—Ena Stanley and Julene Louis of the International Academy of Astrology. I can only hope to attain a small percentage of the knowledge they have about astrology, which they have always shared generously and without fail. In addition, they provided the first open window toward my professional development by urging me to teach a course on financial astrology at my alma mater as well as gain online lecturing experience at the school. Much admiration and appreciation also go to my longstanding informal teacher and mentor, the late Barbara Schermer, who kept my astrological fire burning one reading at time over the course of the 19 years she was my personal astrologer. I so wish Barbara were here to share the joy of this accomplishment.

Throughout this project, I have been extremely fortunate to have help that I have needed come into my life just as I have needed it. I'm grateful to the Universe for the synchronicity of encounters with Gary Kamen, Al Dina, Bob Dieli and Barbara Schmidt-Bailey that sent me down paths leading to "aha" insights and information that were invaluable in my understanding of the depth of work that needed to be done and the correcting of otherwise embarrassing errors.

Also in the synchronicity category are my friends and fellow astrologers, Joni Schultz and Sandy Rueve, who on the same day helped make it clear that it was time for me to write this book. Joni, a former student, posted the following meme on Facebook: "If you don't see the book on the shelf you want, write it," just as I had been lamenting the lack of information about commodities and astrology in one of my online financial astrology classes. That evening, Sandy hosted one of her infamous New Moon Circles that helped me set an intention for this project and consecrate it with a tangible talisman. Thank you both, very much. I'm glad you helped me listen.

I am ever and always grateful for the work that has been done, published and shared by the community of financial astrologers who have spent entire careers studying the markets through this lens. Many thanks go to the following astrologers, from whom I have learned so much via their books, newsletters, lectures, workshops and, in many cases, personal conversation: Grace Morris, Christeen Skinner, Gloria Stathis, Ray Merriman, Bill Meridian, Michael Munkasey, Madeline Gerwick, Norm Winski, Arch Crawford, Jeanne Long, Barbara Koval, Mary Downing, Carol Mull, Lcdr. David Williams, Louise McWhirter, and W.D. Gann.

Finally, my gratitude and thanks go to my husband, Jerry Gidel, who understands the significance of this work to both me and the financial community, and supports and encourages it wholeheartedly.

Introduction

As a young editor at *Commodities* magazine, I was the resident expert on W.D. Gann as we covered a revival of his methodologies in the late 1970s and early 1980s. I edited the articles that traders and brokers submitted for publication, and attended conferences to learn more and vet potential sources for future articles. I quickly became fascinated with Gann and his approach to trading.

I got myself a three-foot long roll of official Gann charting paper—orange with eight squares to the inch—and began plotting December corn prices by hand every day on the chart taped to my office wall. (Choosing December corn as my experiment subject was a no-brainer. I grew up on a corn and cattle farm in Northwestern Illinois and had a summer internship as a wire reporter covering the corn market at the Chicago Board of Trade.) I found daily price data going back in time to create weekly and monthly Gann charts of December corn prices. With a red pencil, I dutifully drew 45-degree lines from important highs and lows on all of them. I watched prices hit support and resistance at the corners of my December corn Gann square.

And then, as I watched the bull market of early 1981 keep climbing up my office wall, approach the December corn all-time high of $4.00 per bu., set in 1974, hit resistance against a red 45-degree line on the chart, and head toward the upper left corner of the Gann square, I told my Dad it would be good time to sell his corn. He sold his crop that year on the day in April that December 1981 futures hit the high for the year at $3.96. By harvest, prices had fallen to $2.83.

Three decades later, as I was finishing four years of formal astrological study, I finally figured out what I was doing way back when with all my December corn charts and Gann techniques. I was using astrology to stay in sync with the market!

The Gann angles come from the degrees of astrological aspects. The chart paper with eight squares to the inch relate to the 8th harmonic, which divides the 360-degree horoscope wheel into eight sections, and adds importance to the 45-degree angle. The anniversary dates Gann watched were his name for what astrologers call solar returns. The start of the Gann square—at the lowest price for a particular contract month—set the vibe for how that contract month resonated individually, just as an individual horoscope chart does.

I have concluded that W.D. Gann was a financial astrology pioneer, and imagine that what inhibited him from openly proclaiming what was behind his methods was, among other things, the threat of imprisonment if convicted of fortune-telling in New York in the early 1900s. Honestly, I was thrilled to figure out why I was so attracted to Gann's work those many years before. And, I was thrilled to know I was on *my* path of understanding what made the markets move, something that has continually fascinated me throughout my career.

TRADING IN SYNC GROUND RULES

Throughout this book, I will be using my own set of ground rules (assumptions, biases) that I've come to rely on over the years as both a student of astrology and market observer. It's only fair that you know where I'm coming from.

First, in casting a horoscope chart, I am a Western astrologer. I use the tropical zodiac, in which each sign correlates to a certain time of year, starting with 0 degrees Aries at the spring equinox in March. Of the numerous ways to divide a 360-degree wheel into 12 houses, I use the Placidus calculation system simply because that's what I grew up on as a student and I'm used to seeing my own chart that way. I use the "modern" planets of Uranus, Neptune and Pluto that are not able to be seen by the naked eye because I think they have value in financial astrology. Pluto is still a planet in my book.

(In contrast, if I were an Eastern astrologer, I'd be using the sidereal zodiac that tracks planets by their physical position in the sky. In 2160 BCE, ancient astrologers observed 0 degrees of the constellation Aries on the eastern horizon at the spring equinox. The 29th degree of Pisces was there by 0 CE. Now, because of precession of the equinoxes[1], the constellation Pisces at about 2 degrees is on the eastern horizon on the spring equinox. This will shift to the 29th degree of Aquarius in 2160, the beginning of what I consider to be the Age of Aquarius.)

Second, my go-to resources for planetary information, transits and horoscope chart creation include:

- Sirius 2.0 software from Cosmic Patterns Software, Inc.
- The American Ephemeris, 1950-2050 at Midnight, by Neil F. Michelsen and Rique Pottenger
- Tables of Planetary Phenomena, Second Edition, by Neil F. Michelsen; revisions by Rique Pottenger
- The Astrolabe World Ephemeris, 2001-2050 at Midnight, by Astrolabe, Inc.

Third, and most of all, I believe that "things," like markets, events, and companies, resonate to their natal birth horoscope charts just like people do. To understand a market, event, or company from when it first started via the horoscope for that day, time, and place is to understand it at its core. The natal horoscope also lets you understand the sensitive planetary positions for that market, event, or company that may be activated in the future as the planets traverse the sky.

DEFINITIONS AND CLARIFICATIONS

1. Astrologers call any type of horoscope a "chart." So, please consider the context when I'm talking about a "chart," to understand if it is a horoscope chart or a market price chart.

---

1 "The Precession of the Equinoxes." Ancient Wisdom.com. 18 February 2017. http://www.ancient-wisdom.com/precession.htm#what is precession.

2. "Natal" and "birth" are used interchangeably to describe the horoscope chart of any type of event, be it the beginning of a life, a company, a country, or an event. I try to stick to "first-trade" for commodity markets, but might sometimes use "natal." The majority of commodity markets simply have a first-trade chart. However, for stock index futures, I do find value in tracking both the natal horoscope of when the index was first published as well as the first-trade of its associated futures contract.

   If this work inspires you to look at individual stocks from an astrological point of view as well, there are three points of time that likely will come into play. For companies whose stock is listed on an exchange, it is good to get in the habit of differentiating among the "incorporation" chart (when it gained legal status as a company), the "IPO" chart (when the initial public offering occurred), and the "first-trade" chart (when the stock opened for trading on an exchange). The incorporation chart seems to be most helpful in forecasting what would be considered "fundamental" news for the company, while the IPO and first-trade charts are more attuned to stock price movement.

3. Please consider "you" as used in describing astrological basics to represent not only an individual person, but also a market, event, or company, depending on context.

4. The "glyphs" for each planet, sign, and aspect are included in the following sections for your reference when looking at a horoscope chart. These glyphs are astrological shorthand, and essential to getting all the information you need into a horoscope wheel on a single page. As you become more comfortable with them, you'll find yourself using them exactly like shorthand, where instead of writing out "Mercury in Libra opposite Saturn in Aries" you write it as ☿♎☍♄♈. But, don't kill yourself over it. It will come naturally as you learn more about astrology (and get tired of writing out all those words…). Think of them like trading symbols for markets and contract months. Instead of E-mini S&P 500 December 2018, you know that ESZ18 says the same thing.

MARKET-SPECIFIC PLANETARY TRANSITS

The transiting planets not only aspect each other, but they also form aspects with the natal horoscope charts of people, companies, and markets. The difference from the mundane aspects that affect everyone is that the transiting planets are triggering energy specific to the natal planet, sign, and house when they form aspects with individual horoscope charts. This makes the transiting aspects 100% personal to you, a company you're following, or a market you're trading. The key to making it work is accurate birth, incorporation, or first-trade data—date, year, time and location.

The last half of this book focuses on the position of transiting planets at the time of significant highs and lows in six commodity futures markets, one in each major sector—soybeans, gold, crude oil, S&P 500, 10-year T-note and the euro currency. The premise that planetary transits play a key role at times of market extremes not only comes from astrological traditions that watch for significant events in a person's life at these times, but also from a standard practice of using transits in the evaluation of stock market trends.

I have not seen something similar done with commodity markets available publicly. My guess is that attempts have proven of little interest, likely because true, reliable first-trade data is so hard to come by in the commodity markets. Indeed, even the first-trade data from the federal regulator is not necessarily accurate. This book attempts to correct that situation.

GENERAL ASTRO TRADING TIPS

Far more time, attention, research, and study have been paid to applying astrology to the stock market than the commodity markets. And that's not surprising. The stock market is the recognized engine of a country's economy, with a long history of investment by a broad range of both institutions and individuals. In contrast, the commodity futures markets are derivative instruments with high leverage and high risk that only the most sophisticated should trade.

My deepest thanks and gratitude go to the financial astrologers who have come before me and done extensive work with the stock market and published their findings. The collection of insights throughout this book are inspired by their work as it applies to natal horoscope charts of companies, individual stocks, and in some cases where noted, a specific commodity. Many thanks to the following astrologers and their published works: Mary Downing, Jeanne Long, Bill Meridian, Ray Merriman, Grace Morris, Carol Mull, Michael Munkasey, Georgia Stathis, LCdr David Williams, and Norm Winski.

GET TO KNOW YOUR MARKET

This applies to any type of trading you do, and argues for focusing on a handful of markets you come to know well. In stocks and commodities both, focusing on a single sector so that there is spillover knowledge across the individual markets is valuable. But, at any rate, start with a single market and get to know it inside and out before you add another.

MARKET BEHAVIOR VS. THE NEWS

Once again, knowing your market well enough to react instantly to news is important. For using astrological inputs for trading, be sure to understand how your market behaves during the following:

- Transits of planets across the first-trade chart's angles
- Lunations (phases of the Moon)
- Eclipses
- Retrograde and direct motion of the ruling planet
- Solar arc progressions (a projection technique based on advancing the natal chart by one day per month or one day per year)

TRANSIT REPORTS TO ALL PLANETS IN THE FIRST-TRADE CHART

This is the nitty gritty of astrological analysis, and requires astrological software. What you're looking for are dates when transiting planets are making exact aspects to important planets and the angles in your market's first-trade chart. The importance of the aspect will depend on the planets involved and the strength of aspect as described previously. A single aspect could have short-term effect, while multiple aspects can be expected to have a longer-term effect.

What you no doubt will discover is that there are certain days in a year that have several big, important aspects clustered together. Those are the ones to put on your calendar, mark as Red Letter Trading Days, and not go on vacation.

ASTROLOGY AS JUST ONE TOOL IN THE TOOLBOX

I've said it before and I will say it again. Astrology is not the be-all, end-all trading tool. It is simply yet another technical tool that may or may not fit in with the other indicators you watch and find valuable to your trading. What astrology has going for it is that it can pinpoint timing, down to the minute, years in advance. I believe it also is good for understanding long-term, overarching economic trends.

MY WISH FOR YOU

After I got my diploma from the International Academy of Astrology in 2014, I developed and began teaching a nine-week online course there—Introduction to Financial Astrology. My favorite weekly class is the one on the commodity markets, and every time I taught the class I would get to that week's homework and reading assignments only to lament that there *were* no reading assignments because there were no books about commodities and astrology. Then I'd joke that maybe that meant I should write one.

On February 9, 2016, it was commodities week for my financial astrology class. I made my typical comment about lack of reading assignments and that maybe I should take that as a sign that I should write a book (Sign One). Later that day, one of my former students, Joni Schultz, posted this meme on Facebook: "If you don't see the book you want on the shelf, write it." (Sign Two). And, it was the day of a new moon, signaling a great time for new beginnings (Sign Three).

That evening, I was part of a New Moon Circle hosted by friend and fellow astrologer Sandy Rueve of Intention Beads, to set an intention and create a clay bead talisman aligned with the energy of that particular new moon. The new moon was in Aquarius and aligned with my natal horoscope's Venus—the money planet—in my 2nd house of how I earn a living.

My intention that night was: "I say what is important *for me* to say." Meaning that I am called to write a book that perhaps few in the world can write. That I am perhaps unique in being able to combine my expertise in writing, commodity markets, and astrology into the book that you are reading right now.

My wish for you is that you come along on my journey of exploration into understanding how astrology works in the commodity markets and find value in whatever is important to you, be it knowledge, understanding, or a new tool to help you trade and invest better. What you read here is just the beginning of what will occupy my time and attention for the rest of my life. I do hope you'll stay tuned for upcoming episodes and an ever-unfolding story.

Susan Abbott Gidel
Chicago, Illinois
February 4, 2018

CHAPTER 1

Astrology 101

To use astrology as part of your financial toolbox, you have to learn a little bit about the basic building blocks and the lingo. Not a lot. Just enough to understand the concepts as we move on to learning about big-picture economic cycles and what might trigger a change in trend in a market's first-trade chart.

This chapter walks you through the need-to-know basics of the 10 planets, the 12 zodiac signs, the 12 houses in a horoscope chart, and the important transits that can trigger reaction in a natal horoscope chart. Please see the Introduction for background on my approach to astrological analysis.

GETTING STARTED

In each of the following sections, you'll learn the basic characteristics of the important components in astrological analysis. I encourage you to refer to them often as you begin to apply your knowledge of astrology to the markets and what type of energy is in play.

A common, easy way to think of the planets, signs, houses and transits is to imagine them as part of a stage play.

- The planets are the actors.
- The zodiac signs are the costumes and identities the actors assume.
- The horoscope houses are the stage sets where the action takes place.
- The transits are the outside visitors who join the actors on stage or in the audience.

PLANETS

Modern astrologers follow 10 planets, three more than the ancient astrologers of Babylonia who tracked only those they could see with the naked eye, with the Saturn the last visible planet. They include:

Luminaries—Sun and Moon
Personal planets—Mercury, Venus, and Mars
Social planets—Jupiter and Saturn
Transpersonal planets—Uranus, Neptune, and Pluto

You also might hear astrologers talk about the inner planets and the outer planets. Inner planets are the luminaries and the personal planets because they all move fast enough to affect life on a daily basis. The outer planets are Jupiter though Pluto, which move through the zodiac more slowly and have longer effects during a transit to a natal chart.

LUMINARIES—SUN AND MOON

The Sun and Moon are the two most important planets in the horoscope. The Sun represents the core identity of the person, market, or company. The Moon represents emotional makeup and inner workings.

Sun ☉

The Sun is how you shine in the world and who you are at your core. It rules the sign of Leo and its natural house rulership is the 5th house that governs creativity and speculation. Its keywords include: bright, shining, leader, and self-expression.

Moon ☽

The Moon is how you feel on the inside and how you respond emotionally. The Moon rules the sign of Cancer and its natural house rulership is the 4th house that governs family, roots, and real estate. Its keywords include: reflective, emotional, and insightful.

Table 1.1 Luminary Rulerships

	Personal	Business	Mundane	Markets
Sun	Core identity, self-expression	CEO, owner, men in company	Head of state	Gold, corn, orange juice
Moon	Response, feeling, intuition	Public image, employees, women in company	The people, national mood, waterways	Silver, water

PERSONAL PLANETS—MERCURY, VENUS, AND MARS

The personal planets—Mercury, Venus, and Mars—are close enough to Earth that their movement affects us on an individual level. That's because they go through all the zodiac signs about every one to two years.

Thus, Mercury, Venus, and Mars touch (transit) each planet in our natal horoscope chart every one to two years. In contrast, it takes Saturn nearly 29 years to go around the zodiac and touch each planet directly. Pluto, with an orbit of 248 years, doesn't even get halfway around a horoscope chart in a person's lifetime.

Mercury ☿

Mercury is the fastest-moving planet, and goes around the zodiac in about a year (including its retrograde periods). Mercury is the zodiac's messenger, and it rules communication, commerce and trading. It is the ruler of two zodiac signs, Gemini and Virgo. Its natural houses are the 3rd (Gemini) and the 6th (Virgo). Mercury's keywords include: communication, thought, and movement.

Mercury turns retrograde, i.e., appears to be moving backward in the sky as seen from Earth, typically three times per year for about three weeks at a time. When Mercury is retrograde, communications, technology, and travel plans can be disrupted unexpectedly. Thus, it is best to be extremely careful in placing trading orders that may be prone to communication mistakes either by phone or computer in order to avoid errors. Also, be alert for glitches in online markets and online trading platforms during these periods.

Venus ♀

Venus is the planet that rules money, love, and beauty. Like Mercury, it sticks tightly to the Sun and takes about a year to go around the zodiac. However,

Venus goes retrograde the least of any of the planets, only once about every two years. Venus also rules two zodiac signs, Taurus and Libra. Its natural houses are the 2nd (Taurus) and 7th (Libra). The keywords for Venus include: money, love, beauty, and harmony.

Mars ♂

Mars, the red planet one further away from the Sun than Earth, orbits the Sun in 687 days and takes about two years to go around the zodiac. It is the planet of aggression and action. It rules the first sign of the zodiac, Aries, and its natural house is the 1st. Keywords for Mars include: fiery, impulsive, aggressive, and warrior.

Table 1.2   Personal Planet Rulerships

	Personal	Business	Mundane	Markets
Mercury	Communication, thought	Communication, commerce	Retail trade, writers	Stock indexes
Venus	Harmony, love, beauty	Banking, mergers, design	Artists, culture	Copper, sugar, cattle, wheat
Mars	Energy, aggression	Motivation, strategy, action	Military, fires, disputes	Iron, coal, steel, diamonds

SOCIAL PLANETS—JUPITER AND SATURN

Jupiter and Saturn are called the social planets because their orbits move through the zodiac at a slow enough pace to influence society as a whole. Jupiter takes about 12 years to move through the signs, so spends about one year in each. Saturn has about a 29-year trip around the zodiac, so spends about 2 ½ years in each sign.

Together, Jupiter and Saturn are one of the most important pairs of planets for financial astrology because of their connection to the business cycle. They meet in the same degree of the same sign (a "conjunction") every 20 years or so. The Jupiter/Saturn conjunction typically is seen as the start to a new business cycle. The most recent conjunction was in May 2000, two months after the dot-com craze peaked; the next one is on the winter solstice of 2020 and is an especially significant game-changer that I'll discuss in more detail in Chapter 12.

Jupiter ♃

Jupiter—at 2 ½ times the size of all the other planets combined—is by far the galaxy's biggest. That's why when Jupiter is involved in a chart or a transit astrologers say that it expands or exaggerates whatever it is influencing. My first astrological teacher and mentor, Barbara Schermer, described Jupiter as the "Cosmic Santa Claus." It's a great way to think about Jupiter, which wants nothing but good for whatever it touches. The ancient astrologers described Jupiter as the "greater benefic," with Venus as the "lesser benefic." In the markets, Jupiter's touch can mark a top because it's as good as it gets. Jupiter rules the sign of Sagittarius, and is the natural ruler of the 9th house. Keywords include: expansive, optimistic, and exploratory.

Saturn ♄

Ah, Saturn, the planet with rings. Our taskmaster and lesson-teacher, Saturn takes about 29 years to move through the zodiac, teaching us the life lessons to be learned in each house and sign. Your first "Saturn return," when Saturn is back where it started when you were born, is a significant life passage into adulthood. Your second Saturn return, around age 59, is when it is time to become the wise one, based on what you learned by applying Saturn's lessons the second time it visited each of your natal planets during ages 29-59.

The ancients described Saturn as the "greater malefic," with Mars as the "lesser malefic." Saturn is the Debbie Downer of all the planets, and a Saturn transit to planets in a market's horoscope chart can put pressure on prices. Saturn rules the sign of Capricorn and is a co-ruler of Aquarius. It is the natural ruler of the 10th house. Keywords include: restrictive, limiting, and oppressive.

Table 1.3   Social Planet Rulerships

	Personal	Business	Mundane	Markets
Jupiter	Expansion, achievement, success	International, marketing, visionary thinking	Bankers, judges, clergy, wholesale merchants	Oats
Saturn	Structure, limitation, containment	Management, structures, buildings, real estate	Government, elderly, conservatives, collapses	Coffee, Deflation

Susan Abbott Gidel

TRANSPERSONAL PLANETS—URANUS, NEPTUNE, AND PLUTO

The transpersonal planets have influence over generations because of how slowly they move through the zodiac—84 years for Uranus, 165 years for Neptune, and 248 for Pluto. These planets are not visible to the naked eye, and each was discovered via a telescope. Uranus and Neptune often are associated with Jupiter and Saturn in various economic cycles, while Pluto focuses on transforming the areas indicated by its current sign and ruler of that sign. In terms of sign rulership, this trio is considered "modern," as opposed to "ancient," which belong to the seven visible planets.

Uranus ♅

Uranus, the closest to Saturn of the three, was discovered on March 13, 1781 by William Herschel, a British astronomer. King George III was so impressed that he named Herschel as Court Astronomer. Uranus is the trickster planet, producing surprising, unforeseen events. A gaseous planet with a blue hue, Uranus is typically involved when something happens "out of the blue." When it hooks up with Mars, watch out for accidents. Uranus is the modern ruler of Aquarius (along with ancient ruler Saturn), and is associated with the 11th house. Keywords include: change, unusual, sudden, and electric.

Neptune ♆

Neptune was discovered on September 23, 1846, and two astronomers who had done the math about where it should be eventually were recognized as co-discoverers. Working independently, John Couch Adams of Britain and Urbain Le Verrier of France shared the credit after a German astronomer, Johann Gottfried Galle, used their calculations to find the planet with his telescope.

Neptune is the master of illusion and delusion. It is the modern ruler of Pisces, along with the ancient ruler of Jupiter. Because Neptune rules spirituality, it is most closely associated with the 12th house, the last house of the zodiac. Keywords include: dreamy, foggy, and unclear. In the markets, Neptune is associated with the oil and debt markets.

Pluto ♀

Pluto was discovered on February 18, 1930 by Clyde Tombaugh, an American astronomer working at Lowell Observatory in Flagstaff, Ariz., founded by astronomer Percival Lowell. The planet's name was chosen in part because the first two letters were Lowell's initials.[1] Pluto was demoted to "dwarf planet" by the International Astronomical Union on August 24, 2006, but that has not dampened its use by astrologers. Pluto is the modern ruler of the sign Scorpio (with Mars the ancient ruler), and is associated with the 8th house. Keywords include: transformation, power, and deep.

Table 1.4 Transpersonal Planet Rulerships

	Personal	Business	Mundane	Markets
Uranus	Sudden change, liberation, rebellion	Internet, technology, innovation	Explosions, electrical grids, political agitators, aeronautics	Electricity, copper
Neptune	Illusion, imagination	Mergers, reorganization, debt	Socialism, idealism, pollution, oil, pharmaceuticals, inflation, debt	Crude oil, soybean oil, inflation, commodity indexes
Pluto	Transformation, renewal	Power, money, mass production	Secret societies, debt, underground minerals, revolutionaries, political extremists, gangsters, and banksters	Cocoa, hogs, T-bonds

SIGNS

The 12 zodiac signs get their names from the constellations that the ancient astrologers/astronomers witnessed in the night sky. In addition, the characteristics of these signs also come from the ancients' observations of the type of behavior that occurred when those constellations were prominent.

Because of the precession of the equinoxes, the constellations no longer match up physically with the time of year with which they were associated. However, Western astrologers who use the tropical zodiac—which is tied to the seasons—keep the zodiac in their traditional time frames, starting with Aries at the spring equinox.

---

1   "Clyde Tombaugh." Wikipedia.com. 15 April 2017. <https://en.wikipedia.org/wiki/Clyde_Tombaugh>.

The zodiac signs are grouped into two categories that add further flavor to their base characteristics:

TEMPERAMENT ELEMENTS—FIRE, EARTH, AIR, WATER

Life's four elements—fire, earth, air, and water—apply to the zodiac signs in order to provide insight into the temperament of a person, business, government or market. Fire signs can have a hot temperament and be unwilling to compromise, yet can get things going. Earth signs are grounded and take a steady-as-she-goes view. Air signs are intellectual, but can be spacey. Water signs are emotional and sensitive, and literally can go with the flow.

- Fire—Aries, Leo, Sagittarius
- Earth—Taurus, Virgo, Capricorn
- Air—Gemini, Libra, Aquarius
- Water—Cancer, Scorpio, Pisces

QUALITIES—CARDINAL, FIXED, MUTABLE

These designations are related to the four seasons. The four zodiac signs that mark the start of each season are Cardinal signs and have the quality of initiating. The second month/sign of each season is Fixed, when the season's essence peaks. The final month/sign of each season is Mutable, where the season is winding down and preparing to transform into the next.

- Cardinal—Aries, Cancer, Libra, Capricorn
- Fixed—Taurus, Leo, Scorpio, Aquarius
- Mutable—Gemini, Virgo, Sagittarius, Pisces

Aries ♈

The first sign of the zodiac, Aries is associated with being first and winning. Aries is aggressive and likes to make forward movement. Aries marks the spring equinox, around March 20 each year. It is Cardinal Fire, ruled by the planet Mars, and associated with the 1st house.

Taurus ♉

The second sign of the zodiac is Taurus, starting about April 20 each year. Taurus is when spring really kicks in, with flowers blooming and grass growing. Ferdinand the Bull always comes to my mind when I think of Taurus—strong, yet docile, and loving beautiful things. Taurus is Fixed Earth, ruled by the planet Venus and associated with the 2nd house.

Gemini ♊

The sign of the twins, Gemini is quick and changeable, which is suitable for the last month of spring as the weather gets ready to transform into summer. Gemini—also associated with being two-faced or undecided—begins around May 20. Naturally associated with the 3rd house, Gemini is Mutable Air and ruled by the planet Mercury.

Cancer ♋

Cancer marks the summer solstice, around June 20. The sign of the crab is not crabby at all. Rather, Cancer is protective and will defend to the death, which comes from the crab's hard shell and pincers as its protective mechanisms. Cancer is considered nurturing because it is ruled by the Moon. Cancer is Cardinal Water and associated with the 4th house.

Leo ♌

The sign of the lion, Leo marks mid-summer when it begins around July 20. Think lion when you think of Leo—king of the jungle, a big roar and a big, tousled mane of hair. Leo is showy and in charge, ruled by the Sun. It is Fixed Fire and associated with the 5th house.

Virgo ♍

The sixth sign of the zodiac is Virgo, starting around August 20. Virgo represents the qualities of the Vestal Virgins, who were helpers, served others, and kept the home fires burning. Virgo is detail-oriented, ruled by Mercury. Virgo is Mutable Earth and associated with the 6th house.

Libra ♎

The Scales of Justice are the symbol for Libra, and are a reminder that Libra represents balance and fairness. Starting at the fall equinox around September

20, when day and night are equal, Libra is Cardinal Air. Libra is ruled by Venus and associated with the 7th house.

Scorpio ♏

The scorpion's tail delivers a sting when confronted, and Scorpion traits include some of the zodiac's least savory—manipulative and secretive. On the flip side, Scorpio likes to research and delve deep to get answers. In either case, intense is a good keyword. Scorpio, starting around October 20, is Fixed Water. It is co-ruled by Mars (ancient) and Pluto (modern) and associated with the 8th house.

Sagittarius ♐

It's almost an about-face when the zodiac moves into Sagittarius from Scorpio on about November 20. Sagittarius stands for optimism and exploring to satisfy an unquenchable thirst for knowledge. Sagittarius is Mutable Fire, ruled by Jupiter. It is associated with the 9th house.

Capricorn ♑

The tenth sign of the zodiac is Capricorn, the goat, which climbs to the top of the horoscope chart—the 10th house—with unfailing determination. Ruled by Saturn, think status quo, tried-and-true, and organized structure with this sign. Capricorn, marking the winter solstice around December 20, is Cardinal Earth.

Aquarius ♒

Get it out of your head right now that Aquarius should be a water sign because of its first four letters. Nope, Aquarius is Fixed Air and co-ruled by Saturn (ancient) and Uranus (modern). Think eccentric, free spirited, and humanitarian when you think Aquarius. The sign begins around January 20 and is associated with the 11th house.

Pisces ♓

The final sign of the zodiac is Pisces, with a glyph that represents two fishes that relates well to the spiritual aspect of the sign. Pisces is Mutable Water, and its job is to tie up everything learned in the previous 11 signs to assimilate and transform to get ready for the next new beginning when Aries starts. Pisces begins about February 20 and is co-ruled by Jupiter (ancient) and Neptune (modern). It is associated with the 12th house.

HOUSES

As mentioned at the beginning of this chapter, the 12 houses of the horoscope chart—conveniently matching up with the number of zodiac signs—are the stage sets where the actors (planets) in their costumes (signs) are performing. Each house pertains to a certain segment of life, business or the world, and the planet(s) in that house natally or by transit act out their parts accordingly.

You might think that a 360-degree horoscope wheel divided by 12 houses would create 30-degree slices of pie. But, not necessarily. Two methods of dividing the horoscope (whole sign and equal houses) do so, but there are a couple dozen other ways to determine house cusps (the degree of each sign that divides one house from the next) based on complex mathematical formulas that were developed to solve one problem or another that astrologers saw, most often with the lopsided-size houses that occur when the horoscope is drawn for a place at extreme latitude.

Most Western astrologers use the Placidus or Koch house system. And, indeed, planets can move houses when switching house systems. I find valid insights using either Placidus or Koch, and even whole sign houses. But I tend to stick to Placidus because that's what I learned from the beginning of my studies.

No matter how you slice the horoscope pie, though, the following table will help you understand the segments of life, business, and the world (mundane) that apply to the house you are examining. For watching what might be affecting the commodity markets (particularly the stock indexes), I lean most heavily on the mundane descriptions. If you were looking at an individual company or stock, then the business column would be most relevant.

The 1st house of the horoscope starts at what would be 9 o'clock on a clock face and ends at 8 o'clock. The rest of the houses go around the wheel counter-clockwise, e.g., the second house starts at 8 o'clock and ends at 7 o'clock on the dial.

Table 1.5   House Rulerships

House	Personal	Business	Mundane
1st	Personality, physical body, appearance	Business objectives, shareholders, company personnel and morale	National identity, the populace
2nd	Money, values, possessions, resources, self-esteem, earning ability	Revenues, earnings, liquid assets, disposition of investments	Finances, treasury, resources (natural and human)
3rd	Communication, writing, speaking, social media, short journeys, grade school, siblings	Magazines, newsletters, social media, telephones, networks, customer service, trade volume	Roads, communications infrastructure, primary education, neighboring nations, states, provinces, cities
4th	Home, family of origin, family land, roots, soul, hidden parent	Real estate, tangible assets, office space, condition of buildings, property hazards, direct competition	Land, history, family policies, the opposition party
5th	Children, creativity, sports, speculation, hobbies, love affairs, social life	Management teams, income from invested capital, speculation, conventions, seminars, workshops	Children, entertainment industry, sports and recreation, the higher house of government (e.g., Senate)
6th	Service, health, skills, co-workers, pets, healers, fitness, diet	Workers, labor unions, health insurance plans, routines, inventories, fixtures, and furnishings	Working class, farmers, armed forces, labor unions, health care, private hospitals
7th	One-on-one relationships, partnerships, marriage, open enemies	Trade agreements, mergers, relationships with other organizations, lawsuits, legal affairs	Treaties, alliances, foreign relations
8th	Death, taxes, sex, other people's money	Insurance, credit, donations, losses/gains from closure, loans, board of directors	Banking, foreign debts, insurance, military aggression or treaties, mortality
9th	Higher education, long journeys, adventure, philosophy, religion, higher courts, publishing	Advertising and public relations, foreign activities, code of ethics, contracts, all legal affairs	Ambassadors, higher education, courts, religious institutions
10th	Career status, reputation, authorities, honors, shaping parent	President/chairman, national reputation, pubic image, power, general business conditions	Head of state or government unit, the party in power, national reputation

11th	Friends, groups, organizations, hopes, goals, group cooperation	Friendly organizations, political and community connections, long-range goals, intangible assets, club activities	Legislative bodies (Congress, Parliament, assemblies), other clubs and associations
12th	Karma, secret enemies, self-sacrifice, suffering, alcohol/drugs, hospitals, prisons, churches, charities	Hidden enemies, research and development, trade secrets, sabotage, labor troubles, secret negotiations	Charities, prisons, secret police, spies, public hospitals, general infrastructure, sewers

TRANSITS

The horoscope chart based on someone's birth, a company's incorporation, or a market's first trade is a snapshot of where the planets were in the sky at that date, time and place. But, it is only a snapshot. The planets keep moving constantly, and when a moving planet makes a geometrical connection—an aspect—to a planet in the birth chart, it is called a "transit."

These transits stimulate a planet/sign/house in the natal chart to varying degrees based on the strength of the geometrical connection. So, watching transits can alert you to when something might happen in your life, your business, or the markets. In our analogy about stage plays, transits are the new characters that come on stage and interact with the main players, changing the story's dynamics.

Based on watching transits to my own birth chart, the natal charts of other people, and first-trade charts of markets, I'm convinced that transits set off a natural resonance or vibe that we respond to, whether consciously or unconsciously. For example, when gold futures peaked on September 6, 2011, the transiting Sun, Moon, Venus, Mars, Jupiter, and Saturn all were connected in important ways to the first-trade chart of the market. (See Chapter 10.) When the U.S. stock market topped in 1987, five planets had moved into the sign of Virgo within the previous few days. (See Chapter 11.)

The cool thing about astrology is that we can look ahead to see what transits are coming up in the market we trade and might trigger important points in that first-trade chart that could signal a change of trend.

DEFINING ASPECTS

"Aspects" are the geometrical distance between two planets by zodiac degree and sign. In a 360-degree horoscope with 12 zodiac signs, each sign has 30 degrees, and each degree has 60 minutes.

Ptolemy, the 1st century CE Greek mathematician, astronomer, and astrologer, defined what are considered to be the "major" aspects used today. These Ptolemic aspects include:

- Conjunction—0 degrees
- Opposition—180 degrees
- Square—90 degrees
- Trine—120 degrees
- Sextile—60 degrees

The conjunction, opposition (dividing the circle by 2), and square (dividing the circle by 4) are considered "hard" aspects that bring tension and confrontation to the connected planets. The trine (dividing the circle by 3) and sextile (dividing the circle by 6) are called "soft" aspects that provide cooperation.

The aspects resulting from dividing the 360-degree circle by numbers other than 2, 3, 4, or 6 typically are called "minor" aspects, but I am not a fan of using that word to describe them because they can have significant influence in a chart, so let's just call them "other" aspects.

In the markets, the 8th harmonic (dividing the circle by 8) is particularly interesting if you are a fan of W.D. Gann, and brings attention to the 45-degree aspect (semi-square) and the 135-degree aspect (sesquiquadrate). These are uncomfortable, tension-filled aspects that often bring change to relieve the tension.

Conjunction ☌

Two planets are conjunct when they are at the same degree and same minute of the same zodiac sign, e.g., 14 Libra 45. (This is the way to write a location of 14 degrees and 45 minutes of Libra. In each sign, there are 30 degrees, and each degree has 60 minutes.)

The strongest of the aspects, a conjunction brings the full power of each planet to bear on the other, and they work in tandem for the same goal. Of course, sometimes you'll see three or more planets conjunct, and that only increases the intensity. I use an "orb" of ± 8 degrees to define a conjunction, and up to 10 degrees if the Sun or Moon are involved.

Opposition ☍

Two planets are opposite one another when they are 180 degrees apart in the sky, e.g. one at 14 Libra 45 and the other at 14 Aries 45. I use an orb of ± 6 degrees to define an opposition.

The opposition is like a see-saw. Each planet has its own idea about what should happen and how, and the challenge is to find balance between the two. In transits, oppositions are also about culminations, and marking a maximum. For example, the full moon each month is an opposition of the Moon and Sun, when the Moon reflects the most light.

Square □

When two planets are square to one another, they are 90 degrees apart in the sky by zodiac sign, e.g., one at 14 Libra 45 and the other at 14 Capricorn 45. I use an orb of ± 6 degrees to define a square.

Squares are about tension. Like the opposition, each planet has its own idea about what to do and how, but compromise is more grudging with a square. Each planet gives in a little, but isn't happy about it. Still, the tension does make something happen.

Note that the signs associated with each quality—Cardinal, Fixed, Mutable—are square to one another.

Trine △

Planets are trine when they are 120 degrees apart in the sky by zodiac sign, e.g., one at 14 Libra 45 and the other at 14 Aquarius 45. I use an orb of ± 6 degrees to define a trine.

Planets work together easily when they are trine, and virtually no effort is required to make the situation work out. Both planets are agreeable and willing to let the other express itself the way it wants.

Note that the signs associated with each element—Fire, Earth, Air, Water—are trine to one another.

Sextile ✶

A sextile is half of a trine, and notes a 60-degree separation in they sky by zodiac sign, e.g., one planet at 14 Libra 45 and the other at 14 Sagittarius 45. I use an orb of ± 2 degrees to define a sextile.

Opportunity is the keyword for a sextile. Like a trine, the planets are willing to work together, but only if some outside factor comes in to take advantage of the connection. Otherwise, the sextile planets are just as happy to wave to each other and go on their merry ways.

Semi-Square ∠ and Sesquiquadrate ⚼

A semi-square is half of a square and notes a 45-degree separation in the sky by zodiac sign, e.g., one planet at 14 Libra 45 and the other at 29 Scorpio 45.

A sesquiquadrate is a square plus a semi-square and notes a 135-degree separation in the sky by zodiac sign, e.g., one planet at 14 Libra 45 and the other at 29 Aquarius 45.

I use an orb of ± 2 degrees to define a semi-square and a sesquiquadrate. Both behave like squares in that the two planets involved are at odds and have tension between them. Interestingly, these two aspects can be like a square on steroids if the aspect is exact, i.e., exactly the same degree and exactly the same minute.

USING ASPECTS

Aspects are used in three ways: (1) to delineate the connections between planets in a natal chart; (2) to describe the connection between a transiting planet and a planet in the natal chart; and (3) to describe the connection between two transiting planets.

- In natal chart delineation, the faster planet is listed first in an aspect, e.g., Mercury square Saturn.
- For transits with a natal chart, the transiting planet is listed first and the natal planet second. So, it could still be Mercury square Saturn if transiting Mercury were coming up to make a 90-degree angle to natal

Saturn. But, it also could be the reverse—Saturn square Mercury—if transiting Saturn were making a 90-degree angle to natal Mercury.

- For connections between transiting planets, the faster planet is listed first in an aspect, e.g., Saturn trine Uranus.

NATAL CHART ASPECTS

A big part of telling the story of the natal horoscope chart is describing the energy of how the planets connect by aspect at the moment in time captured by the snapshot of the sky at whenever the life, company, or market first came into being.

It's rare that a planet has no aspects to any other planet, in which case it can be seen as a loner or misfit. And, at the other end of the spectrum, one planet can be connected by aspect to several others. Often, those connections form patterns that have their own names, like T-square (two planets opposite one another, each square to a mutual third planet) or Grand Trine (three planets, each separated by a trine). I use the orbs noted above for determining natal chart aspects, with a little bit of wiggle room if called for given the chart's layout.

It is the astrologer's job to meld the three big points in any natal chart—Sun, Moon, and Ascendant (the zodiac sign at 9 o'clock on the chart)—with the aspects to provide a holistic view of the natal chart's character as well as challenges and areas of ease. This delineation provides the background to further work that then overlays the transiting aspects and other astrological forecasting techniques.

TRANSITING ASPECTS

Watching how the planets in the sky move in relation to a natal chart is the fun part of doing astrology. It's like watching different size cogs on the back of a watch each move at their own pace and then make the time on the watch move when they all happen to click at the same time.

I find that transiting aspects are the strongest when they are within 2 degrees of being exact. And, stronger still if the transiting planet is getting closer to the natal planet (e.g., at 12 degrees vs. natal 14 degrees) rather than getting further away (e.g., 16 degrees vs. natal 14 degrees). In astrology lingo, the former is called "applying," and the latter is called "separating." The closer to exact the aspect—meaning that the transiting planet has the same degree and same minute of the natal planet—the stronger the connection.

My other main observation about transits is that big changes happen in life or to a company or a market when conjunctions or oppositions are involved. The other, smaller transits provide color to be sure, but it's been my experience that most substance occurs with a transiting conjunction or opposition because those two aspects signify a new beginning or a culmination, respectively.

As you'll see in Chapters 6-11, which show transits vs. first-trade charts for six different commodity markets, the significant changes in trend typically have a significant transiting conjunction or opposition in play with a significant planet in the market's first-trade chart.

CHAPTER 2
Commodities 101

My first job as a newly minted agricultural journalist in 1978 was with *Commodities Magazine*. My farm background and summer internship as a wire service reporter writing daily commentary about the corn market at the Chicago Board of Trade were a perfect fit for a magazine covering the commodity futures markets. At the time, soybean futures were by far the biggest market in the industry. Financial futures—a half-dozen currencies along with U.S. GNMAs and Treasury-bonds—had been trading for only one to six years and were blips in comparison to the ag markets that had been trading in Chicago and New York since the mid-1800s. Clearly, "commodities" meant physical goods like grains, livestock, sugar, gold, or copper.

In just five years, though, financial futures had taken hold. Interest rate futures were booming because of the need to hedge against double-digit borrowing rates. Stock index futures, which debuted in 1982, were made possible by the incredibly freeing innovation of cash settlement, which allowed for settlement of a futures contract to be made in cash rather than physical delivery. Exchanges were popping up the world over to provide futures trading in their own domestic financial instruments and stock market barometers. As I was celebrating five years on the job and two years in our first-ever Chicago office, we changed the publication's name to *Futures Magazine*.

Everyone in the industry happily adopted the more-sophisticated sounding name of "futures" rather than "commodities." It opened doors much more easily as brokers and exchanges pitched using futures as a hedge against cash market risk to banks, corporations of any kind, and investment advisors.

Still, there was some sort of taint. The Chicago-centric industry, home to the two largest futures exchanges in the world—the Chicago Board of Trade and Chicago Mercantile Exchange—was not mainstream in any sense of the word. The industry promoted leveraged products with limited lifespans that few people understood. It had (and still has) a federal regulator separate from the one that regulated the securities industry, which meant that your stock broker was prohibited from offering futures as a product without additional testing and licensing. It was best known for its portrayal in the hit 1983 movie, "Trading Places," which told the story of market manipulation in the orange juice futures market. And, let's face it, the hub of futures trading was not in New York, where futures markets were clearly second-class citizens to stocks in terms of prominence, influence, and career aspiration for young MBAs.

Fast forward to the 21st century. In 2000, I became the Director of Marketing at Lind-Waldock, the premier retail brokerage firm in the futures industry. A big part of my job was to understand the mindset of the individual trader so that we could market our brokerage services effectively—particularly to those securities traders who might like to try stock index futures, which were now by far the most popular contracts. I had CNBC on in my office all day, every day for the next 11 years, listening to the talking heads and their guests discuss the markets. We commissioned marketing research studies on our clients and our prospective target markets. And, what I concluded was that we were in the "commodities" business, not the "futures" business, no matter how much we said and believed otherwise.

It simply didn't matter that stock index, interest rate, and currency futures—financial futures—far outshined traditional ag, metal, and energy futures in annual trading volumes. Twenty years after the industry had embraced "futures," the perception outside the industry was that if a product traded on a commodity exchange, not a stock exchange, it was a commodity. Everyone my futures brokerage firm was targeting with marketing messages (including 30-second ads on CNBC) very likely already had a stock brokerage relationship. Because of the bifurcated regulatory agencies, if they wanted to trade "futures," they needed a relationship with a commodity broker. So, of course, they thought of the "futures" markets as the "commodity" markets.

All of which is to say that I embrace that distinction. I am completely down with the idea that commodity markets—whether they are physical things or financial instruments—trade on commodity exchanges.

So, if you're interested in trading futures on the E-mini S&P 500 or the Euro FX currency or the U.S. 10-year T-note or crude oil or soybeans or gold, you're interested in the commodity markets. No matter the underlying market, a commodity is a leveraged product with certain contractual obligations that are appropriate only for those who understand the risk and are willing to accept it.

WHAT ARE COMMODITY FUTURES?

Commodity futures grew out of mercantile practices of the mid-1800s in Chicago, where buyers and sellers of grain and other products would gather to exchange cash for goods. Based on the research I have done for this book, I can say with confidence that the first futures contract—in the form we recognize as such today—began trading at the Chicago Board of Trade on October 14, 1865, nearly 20 years after the exchange organized.

I settled on this date because it is the first trading day after members voted to adopt a new set of Rules and Regulations that included for the first time together: (1) the requirement that both buyers and sellers post 10 percent margin when initiating a market position; and (2) the requirement to deliver upon a contract's expiration. In support of the latter, this set of rules was the first to ban "privileges" (put and call options today) as a recognized business transaction between members.[2]

At its beginning in 1848, the Board of Trade was organized to bring the city's merchants and businessmen together to promote commercial activity, do business

---

2 Chicago Board of Trade records: Series I – Organizational records, Special Collections and University Archives, University of Illinois at Chicago. "Rules, Regulations and By-Laws, of the Board of Trade, Chicago, Ill. Adopted October 13th, 1865," 14-15.

with one another and establish commercial codes of conduct. Initiated by Thomas Richmond, who owned grain elevators, and W.L. Whiting, the city's first grain broker, the original 82 members included leading businessmen, such as William Ogden (railroad mogul and Chicago's first mayor) and Gordon Hubbard (meat packer), whose names you'll see now on downtown Chicago streets.

The Board of Trade had close ties to the Chicago Chamber of Commerce, and was seen as the leading organization to promote economic trade in the young city, incorporated in 1833. Interestingly, the Board of Trade was organized two years before the St. Louis Merchant's Exchange. At the time, St. Louis was the Midwest's major city because of its dominance in trade done via steamboat on the Mississippi and the Ohio Rivers, which connected the Midwest to the East Coast. Indeed, in 1848, the population of St. Louis was nearly 56,000, almost triple that of Chicago's 20,000. But, transportation progress in Chicago that began in 1848 started shifting that prominence, and by 1870, Chicago and St. Louis both boasted populations near 300,000.

As the furthest western point along the southern edge of the Great Lakes, Chicago also had been an obvious destination choice for shipping products from the East Coast. This became particularly so after the Erie Canal debuted in 1825 and connected the Atlantic Ocean to the Great Lakes via the Hudson River. Once the Illinois & Michigan Canal was completed in 1848, Chicago had its first link from the mouth of the Chicago River to the Mississippi. The canal cut shipment times to the East substantially. For example, two shipments of sugar from New Orleans were sent to Buffalo, New York on the same day. One went north to Chicago via the river system and canal and then across the Great Lakes. The other went by the traditional route—by sea to New York and then by river/canal to Buffalo. The canal route beat the sea route by two weeks.[3] Chicago's destiny as a transportation hub was sealed.

Railroads, also newly arrived in 1848, cemented Chicago's new role as a transportation hub because there was great interest in getting rail lines to California, where gold had just been discovered. The Galena and Chicago Union Railroad (later renamed the Chicago & Northwestern), run by Board of Trade member

---

3   Taylor, Charles H., History of the Board of Trade of the City of Chicago, Vol. 1 (Chicago: Robert O. Low Company, 1917) 136.

William Ogden, had 10 miles of track completed that year (with another 29 under construction) and began transporting wheat and hides into the city on the train's first run to the end of the line and back. Two years later, in 1850, the first out-of-state train arrived from Detroit, by which time the Galena and Chicago had 50 miles of track laid to Elgin and Aurora.

Railroads were springing up as fast as they could be built, and all of them in Illinois connected to the Chicago terminus. By 1853, the Chicago and Mississippi Railroad made Chicago's first rail connection to the Mississippi River at Alton, just north of St. Louis. In just three years more, in 1856, there were seven railroads that reached from Chicago to the Mississippi, from Alton north to Galena—all of them able to carry grain from Illinois, Iowa, and Wisconsin directly to Chicago. In addition, the new, highly touted Illinois Central Railroad ran the full length of the state—all 375 miles from Chicago to Cairo, where the Mississippi and Ohio Rivers converged.

Farmers settling land in Illinois, Iowa, and Wisconsin and beyond were keen on having a railroad nearby in order to get their crops to the best market for grain—Chicago. In 1854, nearly 2,500 miles of railway were connected to Chicago, and 12.9 million bushels of grain were shipped from Chicago that year, more than any other city in the world. It was the year Chicago first claimed it was the "greatest primary market in the world." [4] No doubt, this cash market dominance supported not only the growth of futures trading, but also that the price of grain in Chicago established a world benchmark. As a result, throughout most of the 20th century, the Chicago Board of Trade was the premier commodity futures exchange in the world.

COMMODITY FUTURES CONTRACTS

Commodity futures are contracts on any type of underlying market that have four specific contract characteristics—an obligation to buy or sell an underlying product at a specific price at a specific time in the future. In addition, to trade commodity futures typically requires no more than 10 percent of the contract's full value as margin, hence the leveraged aspect of the product.

---

4   Ibid. 197.

1. OBLIGATION TO BUY OR SELL

When you take a position in a commodity futures contract, you are making a commitment to buy or sell the underlying product when the contract expires. It is not an option, it is an obligation. No need to fear getting soybeans dumped on the front lawn, though. Nearly all traders exit their original position before expiration. Some producers or users of the underlying product might stick it out to the end and make or take delivery.

2. SPECIFIC UNDERLYING PRODUCT

Each contract specifies a certain quantity (and sometimes quality) of the underlying product so that everyone is trading with the same, standardized set of terms. For example, in soybeans, the contract calls for 5,000 bu. of #2 yellow soybeans. The largest of the gold contracts is for 100 troy oz. of gold. In the S&P 500 stock index futures market, the contract is valued at $50 x the S&P 500 index level.

3. SPECIFIC PRICE

Price is the only variable in a commodity futures contract, and it is set when a trade is made between buyer and seller on a government-regulated commodity futures exchange. If you were to hold the contract to expiration, this is the price you would pay or receive for the specified product.

4. SPECIFIC TIME IN THE FUTURE

Futures contracts have a shelf life, and expire at a specific time in the future, at which point they cease trading and no longer exist. Whatever you trade, be sure you understand when the contracts expire. If you are holding a position at expiration, you are obligated to deliver or accept delivery of the terms of the contract in full. Probably not something you want to do. Wiser to exit the trade with an equal and opposite position beforehand.

Expiration dates typically are in the last half of the contract trading month, a carryover from the earliest of trading days when delivery was more common and both parties needed time to physically move goods. Today, for example,

E-mini S&P 500 contracts expire on the morning of the third Friday of March, June, September, and December.

CONTRACT MONTH SYMBOLS

Futures traders use a long-established series of symbols to designate each of the 12 possible delivery months, ranging from F through Z. Why not start at A? I have no clue, and I've never seen an explanation of how these contract month symbols came about—but I'd love to find out!

January	F
February	G
March	H
April	J
May	K
June	M
July	N
August	Q
September	U
October	V
November	X
December	Z

In combination with the market's designated contract code, e.g., CL for light, sweet crude oil, or ES for the E-mini S&P 500, traders use a shorthand to convey which product, contract month, and contract year they are trading. For example, ESU18 stands for the September 2018 contract of the E-mini S&P 500.

Some contract codes reveal a contract's trading genealogy. For example, the contract code for soybeans, ZS, indicates it is traded electronically and not in an open-outcry pit. When soybeans first started trading at the Chicago Board of Trade in 1935, the symbol was S, which only made sense because corn was C, wheat was W, and oats was O. After the electronically traded E-mini S&P 500 launched in 1997 and had immediate success, the rush was on to list electronic versions of open-outcry contracts that easily could offer around-the-clock trading. These contracts traded side-by-side (i.e., both open for trading at the same time during certain hours) for several years. To make sure that customer orders were going to the right venue, the electronically traded contract had a different contract symbol, e.g., ZS for electronically traded soybeans vs. S for open-outcry soybeans. That's why the contract symbol today for soybeans remains ZS, even though open-outcry trading in the grains (and most all CME Group products in Chicago and New York) ended on July 6, 2015.

TYPES OF COMMODITY FUTURES MARKETS

Commodity futures markets sort themselves into big buckets that group similar types of products together. Historically, it was common for a single exchange to be dominant in a certain sector, e.g., the Chicago Board of Trade and grain or the New York Mercantile Exchange and energy. Traders commonly refer to the type of markets they trade by these sectors, and describe themselves as a currency trader or a grain trader, for example.

AGRICULTURAL

The agricultural markets typically describe markets in which there is constant, renewable production and consumption of a food source. The grain markets are those planted and harvested annually, along with the meal and oil products resulting from soybean processing. Livestock markets include live cattle (on the hoof) and lean hogs (processed yield after slaughter), as well as dairy cow products, milk, and cheese. The "softs" are a bit of an odd name and are kind of a catch-all category. They include four of the oldest futures markets in New York—cotton, coffee, cocoa, and sugar—all of which were trading by the early 1900s, as well as relative newcomer orange juice, which started in the 1960s. Lumber, which isn't soft at all and trades in Chicago, tends to get lumped into this category for lack of a better one.

- Grains--Corn, oats, soybeans, soybean oil, soybean meal, wheat (several varieties)
- Livestock—Cattle, hogs, milk, cheese
- Softs--Coffee, sugar, cocoa, orange juice, cotton, lumber

CURRENCIES

Currency futures markets were the first financial futures ever traded, opening on May 16, 1972 at the International Monetary Market (IMM), a newly formed division of the Chicago Mercantile Exchange. Why the CME, home to livestock trading? Because of the exchange's ambitious chairman, Leo Melamed, and his connection with free-market champion and Nobel Prize economist Milton Friedman, just down the road at the University of Chicago.

Just nine months earlier, on August 15, 1971, the United States quit tying the U.S. dollar to the price of gold, effectively ending the Bretton Woods agreement of fixed-exchange rates established post-WWII in 1945. Earlier in 1971, Friedman was expecting that Bretton Woods would collapse, but had been denied the ability to short the British pound in the currency market that existed between banks—the cash Interbank market—because he was not a bank and had no commercial interest in the pound. Melamed, who smelled big opportunity in listing futures markets on what were now variable, floating exchange rates, asked Friedman in November if he would support the idea of currency futures. Friedman was all for it, and was paid $7,500 by the CME for a feasibility study titled "The Need for Futures Markets in Currencies."[5] Delivered in December 1971, Friedman's study opened doors and minds across the country and around the world.

Seven currency markets opened at the IMM on that first trading day, all of which were quoted in how many U.S. dollars it took to buy one unit of the foreign currency. For example, a quote of 1.50 in the British pound meant that one pound cost $1.50. Because the U.S. dollar remains the primary reserve currency internationally, the largest FX (foreign exchange) contracts are dollar-based. Note that some of those original currency futures markets, such as the Deutsche mark, ultimately were delisted once the euro became the single European currency for member nations on January 1, 1999. The U.S. Dollar Index futures contract tracks the value of the dollar against a basket of currencies.

---

5   Melamed, Leo. "The Birth of FX Futures." CME Group. 11 May 2017. <https://www.cmegroup.com/education/interactive/fxproductguide/birthoffutures.pdf>.

Major futures markets include:

- Australian dollar
- British pound
- Canadian dollar
- Euro FX
- Japanese yen
- Swiss franc
- U.S. Dollar Index

ENERGY

Energy futures markets took hold at the New York Mercantile Exchange, which listed the first such product—fuel oil (later re-launched as heating oil) in the mid-1970s. The oil crisis of the 1980s and global deregulation meant energy prices became much more volatile, and users saw value in locking in their costs with the new crude oil and gasoline futures markets at NYMEX. Originally listed as unleaded gasoline, that contract now specifies RBOB gasoline, which stands for Reformulated Blend Stock for Oxygen Blending. The fuel oil contract still uses HO as its contract symbol, but is now based on ultra-low-sulfur diesel fuel (ULSD). Both changes were made to reflect new product standards stemming from environmental regulations.

Major markets include:

- Crude oil (light sweet, Brent)
- RBOB gasoline
- ULSD fuel
- Natural gas

INTEREST RATES

After currency futures debuted in 1972 and the Chicago Board Options Exchange became the first exchange for listed put and call options in 1973, new product development was in full swing at both Chicago futures exchanges. And, the attention was on the ultimate commodity—money. How to put a price on money? By trading the cost of interest to borrow it.

The first interest rate futures contract, in 1975, was on mortgage rates from the Government National Mortgage Association (GNMA). Futures on U.S. Treasury bonds—which ultimately would become the CBOT's most heavily traded contract—launched in 1977. Meanwhile, the CME was developing products on the short end of the yield curve, and had great success with the 90-day T-bill (1976) and Eurodollars (1981).

Although early trading attracted some attention, the interest rate futures markets didn't explode with activity until the U.S. Federal Reserve announced on the evening of Saturday, October 6, 1979, after an unscheduled FOMC meeting that day, that it would abandon using the Fed funds rate as a tool to control the money supply. Instead, it would fight rising inflation by managing the volume of bank reserves in the system, which was expected to result in more volatile interest rates.[6]

As a result, banks and companies saw the benefit in hedging their exposure with U.S. T-bond futures almost immediately. Indeed, shortly after the Fed's announcement, Salomon Brothers made news by using T-bond futures to hedge part of a $1 billion IBM bond offering.[7] What's more, this financial futures revolution prompted exchanges all over the world to introduce similar futures contracts on their own domestic financial instruments, such as the Japanese government bond or the U.K. long gilt.

Major interest rate markets include:

- Eurodollar (interest rate on U.S. dollars held overseas)
- U.S. 5-year Treasury notes
- U.S. 10-year Treasury notes
- U.S. Treasury bonds

---

6   Medley, Bill. "Volcker's Announcement of Anti-Inflation Measures." FederalReserveHistory.org. 13 May 2017. <https://www.federalreservehistory.org/essays/anti_inflation_measures>.

7   Falloon, William D. Market Maker: A Sesquicentennial Look at the Chicago Board of Trade (Chicago: Board of Trade of the City of Chicago, 1998) 230.

METALS

Metals futures markets date to the earliest days of trading in New York, when the National Metal Exchange formed in 1883. Fifty years later, near the end of the Great Depression, four New York exchanges trading metals, raw silk, hides and rubber merged to become the Commodities Exchange, or COMEX, which is now a part of the CME Group of designated contract markets.

Eventually, the metals markets dominated at COMEX, be they precious metals, like silver, or industrial, like copper. Thus, COMEX had the edge when four U.S. exchanges listed gold futures on December 31, 1974, the day before U.S. citizens could once again own gold in unlimited quantities. Owning more than five ounces had been a crime punishable by fees and jail time since April 5, 1933 by President Franklin D. Roosevelt's Executive Order to free up supplies so that the Fed could access enough gold to support the U.S. dollar.[8] Because the price of gold currently is in the thousands of dollars, contract sizes at COMEX and other global exchanges range from 10 oz. to 100 oz. to provide affordability for any type of individual or institutional trader.

Major metals futures markets include:

- Gold
- Silver
- Copper
- Platinum
- Palladium

STOCK INDEXES

Trading futures on the stock market—and enticing stock traders to come over to the futures market—was the big endgame for futures exchanges across the United States. The innovation of cash settlement, introduced with the Eurodollar futures contract in late 1981, solved the problem of how to "deliver" a basket of individual stocks to fulfill a futures contract. This opened the floodgates for

---

8   "Executive Order 6102." Wikipedia.com. 13 May 2017.
<http://en.wikipedia.org/wiki/Executive_Order_6102>.

stock index futures development not only in the United States, but in any country that had an established stock market.

In the United States, stock index futures trading began in April 1982. The first contract to open was on the Value Line stock index at the Kansas City Board of Trade. But, the one that took off from the get-go and remains dominant (in its electronically traded version, the E-mini S&P 500) was the Standard & Poor's 500 at the Chicago Mercantile Exchange. The CME wisely had researched the institutional marketplace to find that the S&P 500 was the most widely used benchmark for stock performance, and then licensed use of the index name from Standard & Poor's. Meanwhile, crosstown rival Chicago Board of Trade spent 15 years in an almost constant legal battle trying to introduce a contract that mimicked the Dow Jones Industrial Average before Dow Jones eventually agreed to license its name to the product in 1997.

Ever hear the S&P 500 futures market called the "spoos"? It comes from the first contract month listed on the S&P 500, for September 1982 delivery. The contract symbol was SPU, pronounced "spoo." Traders talked about trading the "spoos" early on, and the nickname stuck to indicate trading in the S&P 500 generally, not just the September contract.

Major stock index futures contracts include:

- E-mini S&P 500 and Standard & Poor's 500 –Capitalization-weighted index of the top 500 companies listed on the New York Stock Exchange or The Nasdaq Stock Market.
- Dow Jones Industrial Average—Price-weighted average of 30 blue-chip stocks listed on the New York Stock Exchange or The Nasdaq Stock Market.
- Nasdaq-100—Capitalization-weighted index of 100 of the largest domestic and international non-financial companies listed on The Nasdaq Stock Market.
- Nikkei 225—Price-weighted index of 225 blue-chip companies listed on the Tokyo Stock Exchange.
- FTSE 100—Capitalization-weighted index of the top 100 market-cap companies traded on the London Stock Exchange.

- DAX—Capitalization-weighted index of 30 blue-chip stocks listed on the Frankfurt Stock Exchange.
- EURO STOXX 50—Capitalization-weighted index of 50 blue-chip stocks across the Eurozone.

UNIQUE FEATURES VS. STOCKS AND ETFS

Futures contracts are a unique product in the financial world that take some getting used to if you are most familiar with stocks and exchange-traded funds (ETFs). What futures, options (on both futures and stocks), stocks and ETFs have in common is that they all are traded on federally regulated exchanges, to ensure a level playing field for all investors.

CONTRACT TERMS

In futures, the contract is simply that buyer and seller agree to be obligated to buy or sell at the contract's expiration; in options, the buyer has the right (but *not* the obligation) to buy or sell at expiration. With stocks and exchange-traded funds (ETFs), however, ownership is transferred at the time of the trade.

TYPE OF CONTRACT

Futures, options, and ETF contracts all are standardized, with no limit on how many contracts can be created. In contrast, the number of shares available to trade on any stock is set by the company.

TIME FACTOR

In futures and options, contracts expire and cease to exist at a specific point in time. Stocks and ETFs exist into perpetuity and never expire.

MARGIN

We'll discuss the nuances of margin more in the next section, but for now, know that margin in futures is a good-faith deposit to ensure that the buyer or seller will make good on the contract. In stocks and ETFs, margin is a down payment on the purchase. In options, only the seller posts good-faith margin; the buyer pays for the option in full at the time of the trade.

LEVERAGE

Likewise, more details about leverage will be found in the next section. The overview is that futures are extremely leveraged, thus risky. Stocks and ETFs can be leveraged no more than 50 percent, based on the amount that can be margined. In options, leverage varies by the type of position, e.g., outright buy/sell or any variety of time or volatility spreads.

SHORT SELLING

Selling short (taking an initial short position) is easy in both futures and ETFs because it is the same process as buying. Decide which side of the market you want to be on and place your order. To avoid a mass sell-off in stocks, rules exist that make it more difficult to take a short position. In addition to finding a party to lend you money to short a stock, you also have to wait for an uptick (a higher price than the previous tick) in the market to place the sell order. In options, the hard part about shorting is deciding which option and strike price to trade, based on price, volatility, and time to expiration.

Table 2.1 Trading Instrument Comparisons

	Futures	Stocks	ETFs	Options
Contract terms	Agreement to perform	Conveys ownership	Conveys ownership	Gives buyer right, not obligation
Type of contract	Standardized unit, no limit on number	Shares in company, only number issued	Standardized, no limit on number	Standardized, no limit on number
Time factor	Contracts expire	Perpetual	Perpetual	Contracts expire
Margin	Good-faith deposit ensures performance	Down payment on ownership	Down payment on ownership	Buyer pays premium; seller posts margin
Leverage	High. 2%-15% of contract value	Limited. 50% of share price	Limited. 50% of contract value	Varies by position
Short selling	Simple. Same process and margin as going long	Complex. Requires uptick and borrowing shares to sell	Simple. Buy and sell process is same	More complex when determining which option to use

Source: Lind-Waldock. The Complete Guide to Futures Trading (New York: Wiley, 2005) 5.

MARGIN AND LEVERAGE

The regular practice of trading on margin is the main distinguishing characteristic of the futures markets vs. stocks. For starters, the way the word "margin" is used is a big point of confusion. In stocks when you trade on margin, it means that you are borrowing up to 50% of the total purchase price from your broker.

In futures, margin is a good-faith deposit that you will make good on your obligation to buy or sell. To either buy or sell, you typically put up about 10 percent of the contract's full value in order to take a position. For example, if gold is trading at $1,200 per oz. and margin required by the exchange is 10 percent, then you would need to post $12,000 in your futures trading account to take a one-lot position in a 100-oz. contract with a contract value of $120,000.

The leverage available in futures is directly related to margin. In the gold example, if the initial margin requirement is 10 percent of the contract's value, then that means that you are leveraged 10:1. Say you owned 100 ounces of gold outright. Your wealth would go up $1,000 for every $10 move up in the price of gold. The same would be true if you were long one 100-oz. gold futures contract. The difference is that you'd need to $120,000 to own the physical gold but only $12,000 to own the futures contract. So, with leverage, you get the same benefit (or risk) as owning outright with a greatly reduced financial commitment.

Another way to grasp the concept of leverage is to compare the ROI you get in owning outright vs. holding a futures contract. Your $1,000 profit on the $120,000 you spent to own gold is a return on investment of less than one percent. However, a $1,000 profit on $12,000 spent to own a futures contract is a return on investment of 8.3 percent.

The most important thing to grasp about leverage in the futures markets is that it cuts both ways. You can lose money just as quickly as you can make it. And, because you're trading on margin, if the market goes against your position, you are required to post additional margin money in order to keep holding the position—even if that is more than what is in your trading account or more than you have in the bank. This unlimited risk is what gives futures its hot-potato reputation—and with good reason. No one should trade futures who cannot afford to lose all the money devoted to the venture—and more.

WHO TRADES FUTURES?

The people who trade futures mostly fall into one of two groups—speculators or hedgers. Speculators take risk in hopes of reaping a reward. Hedgers lay off risk associated with a commercial venture of some sort to protect their rewards. A third category, non-hedgers, identifies those who use futures as a wholesale-type product.

But, no matter your role in the market, there is still a human at the core of the trading decision (even algos) who is motivated by the emotions of fear and greed. And, that's why I'm writing this book about using astrology as part of your financial toolbox. Astrology can provide insight into how and when those emotions are stirred in an individual trader, in a company, and in our collective society.

I'm absolutely convinced that each of us is sensitive to the movement of the planets in the sky. I've seen it in events that happened in my own life before I knew anything at all about astrology, as I looked back and studied my own horoscope chart. And, I've seen it in the lives of friends and clients who had no knowledge of astrology. The energy of the planets simply expresses itself in certain ways at certain times, whether we are aware of it or not. The challenge is how to be aware and use the energy pro-actively for its highest good rather than simply react unconsciously. In my book (literally, ha!), astrology is the tool that can help.

SPECULATORS

Speculators trade because they want to make money. They have an opinion about where prices might go next and place a trade that would make money if they are right. They are the risk-takers. They also are the grease that keeps the market wheels turning because they typically trade in smaller size and more often than the hedgers, so allow for bigger orders to be digested without causing market heartburn.

- Arbitrageurs—Trading several related markets to keep them in balance relative to one another.
- Individual investors—In it to win it.

- Market-makers—Active participants willing to take either side of the market in order to ensure a current bid/ask at a reasonable spread. In the days of open outcry, these traders were called "locals." In today's electronically traded markets, market-makers come in the form of algorithmic traders and high-frequency traders, both of whom rely on computers to place orders.
- Commodity Trading Advisors—Professional money managers in the commodity futures world, licensed by the federal regulator. They trade money for individual clients or funds in exchange for fees.

HEDGERS

The commodity futures markets evolved out of the need to serve hedgers—producers of a product and end-users of a product. Each has inherent exposure to price risk. For example, a farmer who raises soybeans is at risk that prices will drop and reduce his revenue. A company that makes the vegetable oil you buy at the grocery store is at risk that the price of soybeans will rise and increase its production expenses. Each can hedge that risk in the futures market by taking the opposite position to their cash market situation. The farmer would *sell* futures to lock in a sale price for his natural long cash position; the vegetable oil company would *buy* futures to lock in a purchase price for its natural short cash market position.

Indeed, hedgers were the main focus for futures contracts since the first days of the Board of Trade. As time went on, exchange officials embraced the idea that a successful futures contract required a design that kept hedgers in the market because of its economic utility as a risk-management tool, which in turn would attract speculators.[9]

- Commercial users—These are producers and end-users of physical commodities. They come in every stripe and flavor, from farmers and mining companies to crude oil refiners and food manufacturers. If your day-to-day business exposes you to the risk of commodity price movement, you are a hedger.

---

9   Falloon, William D. Market Maker: A Sesquicentennial Look at the Chicago Board of Trade (Chicago: Board of Trade of the City of Chicago, 1998) 235.

- Financial lenders and borrowers—Institutions, companies and municipalities that lend money at one interest rate have risk that rates could rise and they aren't earning the going rate. On the flip side, those who borrow and pay interest take the risk that rates could drop and they could be paying less. In global operations, these risks can become three-dimensional when you add in the risk of fluctuating foreign exchange rates.

NON-HEDGERS

For the longest time, the trading world was split down the middle between speculators and hedgers. Then along came exchange-traded funds, introduced in the United States in 1993, first as stock market proxies and later as a security product on commodity markets. More than 100 ETFs use futures markets as part of their product design, the largest of which is United States Oil Fund (USO) that is 100 percent invested in the light sweet crude oil futures contract at NYMEX.[10]

- ETF issuers—Companies that create exchange-traded funds that use futures contracts in the design. The issuers do not have price risk exposure to the market, so are neither speculators nor hedgers. Rather, they are middlemen who simply access the market.
- Spread traders—Some traders focus only on the price differential between two contracts, e.g., July soybeans and November soybeans. They maintain varying positions in both to keep the relationship between the two contracts within historical norms, in hopes of making a profit.

---

10   "Futures-Based ETF List." ETF Database. 15 May 2017. <http://etfdb.com/type/commodity/exposure/futures-based/>.

CHAPTER 3

How You Sync Up with the Markets

If you're a trader, you've no doubt heard of legendary financial trader W.D. Gann, not only for the vast fortune he made by trading stocks and commodities in the first half of the 20th century, but also for the mysterious methodology behind his stunning success. He introduced technical analysis tools known and used today as Gann Angles and Gann Squares.

If you're an astrologer, you'll be interested to know that Gann was one of the earliest financial astrologers, even though he avoided using the word astrology in any of his nine books, his two stock and commodity trading courses and countless newsletters written over 50 years in the business. Rarely elaborating beyond describing his methodology as based on "natural laws," Gann left it to others to discover how he incorporated astrology, numerology and other disciplines into his market forecasting. (Personally, I think he refrained from being on the record about astrology because "fortune-telling" was a punishable crime in New York in the early 1900s. Indeed, his contemporary Evangeline Adams was arrested three times from 1911 to 1923, including one that went to trial, in which she was acquitted.)

Here's what the cryptic Gann had to say about picking which markets to trade:

> "My own experience in trading and my analysis of the cause of effects enabled me to discover the reason for these things. For many years Mex Pete was one of my particular pets. I could always make money in it. My forecasts on it were so accurate that people all over the country who subscribed to my market letter called me the 'Mex Pete Specialist.' I was able to catch its moves up and down over 90 per cent of the time just the same as if I had been making the fluctuations myself.
>
> Now there must be some cause for this, as nothing just happens. Everything is the result of a cause. When you find that a stock does not seem to work well for you, leave it alone. Quit trading in it, and stick to the ones that favor you. I could explain to you the cause for this, but it is not necessary, and many of you would not believe it."[11]

When I first read this passage, written by Gann nearly 100 years ago, it dawned on me that in order to find "ones that favor you," I should start comparing the horoscope charts of traders to the horoscope charts of the markets they trade. It's called "synastry" by astrologers, and is a common practice when looking at the relationship between two people from an astrological perspective. The connections between the two charts reveal the couple's strengths, weaknesses, and how they relate to one another.

So, why not traders and their markets? Like Gann, you want to be one with your market so that you understand at a gut level how prices might behave. And, there's no better way to find out if you're compatible with your market than by comparing your natal horoscope charts.

HOW SYNASTRY WORKS

To understand how synastry works with markets, I find it best to think of the market as a person. You have chemistry with certain people where you just click and become BFFs or spouses. The same is true with markets, and you gravitate toward some more than others. I like corn, you like soybeans. Different strokes

---

11   W.D. Gann, <u>Truth of the Stock Tape</u>, 1923. (Pomeroy, Wash.: Lambert-Gann Publishing Co., Inc., 1976) 75.

for different folks. But, whether it's a person or a market, your horoscope's connection with the other natal horoscope is likely to reveal the reasons why you're attracted. The more connections between two horoscope charts, the more you click.

ASPECTS

I look first for "conjunctions" between two planets, one on each chart, where they are within about five degrees of each other (although as wide as 10). These conjunctions can be in the same zodiac sign (e.g., 23 Capricorn and 28 Capricorn), or in signs next to one another (e.g., 28 Capricorn and 3 Aquarius). Conjunctions are the strongest contact between any two charts and indicate that the pair involved is pulling in the same direction.

The second strongest connection is an "opposition," where a planet on one chart is directly opposite a planet on the other chart by 180 degrees, plus/minus about five to seven degrees. To be opposite a planet at 28 Capricorn, the other planet would be at 28 Cancer; to be opposite 3 Aquarius would be 3 Leo. Like the name implies, oppositions have opposing points of view, but work to find balance and compromise. Oppositions can also indicate the full, maximum expression of a relationship, just as the full moon (Moon opposite Sun) is the maximum amount of light in the Sun/Moon relationship that began when they were together in the sky two weeks earlier at the new moon.

The next two aspects to consider are the square (90 degrees) and trine (120 degrees). The square brings tension while the trine brings ease. In our 28 Capricorn example, a square would be at 28 degrees of other Cardinal signs, including Aries, Cancer, and Libra. A trine with 28 Capricorn would be with 28 degrees of other Earth signs, including Taurus and Virgo.

Sextiles (60 degrees) round out the big five aspects, and are nice to have in a synastry chart, but not the basis for a solid working relationship. Interestingly, though, a sextile can be a clue to look for a formation called a "yod," or Finger of God, between the two charts that is quite significant.

A yod is formed among three planets—the two separated by 60 degrees (the sextile) each are connected to the third planet by an aspect of 150 degrees (quincunx or inconjunct) to form a narrow triangle. A yod telegraphs to watch for important happenings between you and your market (big trading day, lesson learned, etc.) when transiting planets hit the point of the triangle or the point directly opposite.

PLANETS

Next, take a look at the planets that are making the connections. I like to look at them through the lens of the trader because the trader is one who is taking action. For example, if your Mars (action, warrior) were conjunct your market's Sun (core identity), you would likely be a pretty aggressive trader of that market, trying to advance for a win at any cost. If your Mercury (communications, trading) were conjunct the market's Sun, you'd be attuned to its news and be inclined to take short-term trades.

In contrast, when you're doing a synastry analysis of two people, you'd want to look at the connections from both directions. For example, my Sun conjunct your Mars means I bring attention to your work. Looking at it from the other direction, your Mars conjunct my Sun means you kick my butt to get going and do something. Sun conjunct Sun is a mutual admiration society, and so on. Check in again with Chapter 1 for an overview of each planet's character and its role in the cosmos to get a feel for how your planet might behave in connection with your market's planet.

Of all the planets involved, pay most attention to aspect connections between the Sun and the Moon in your chart and the Sun and the Moon in your market's chart. How do your Sun and Moon connect to planets in your market's chart? What planets in your chart connect to your market's Sun and Moon? The Sun and Moon are by far the two most important planets in any horoscope chart because they represent the whole entity—Sun for the core nature and Moon for emotional makeup. Don't have any Sun/Moon connections? It's probably time to look for another market to trade.

WHAT MAKES A GOOD TRADER

Your natal horoscope holds the keys to understanding your potential as a trader based on clues regarding skill set and wealth potential. Your horoscope also can help you understand what type of trading you gravitate toward. For example, if you want to make a career of trading or trade for a company, then analyzing the 10th house of career would be important. However, if you're trading with play money on the side, the 5th house of speculation would be the primary one to focus on.

In either case, though, the horoscope's "money houses" of 2, 5, 8, and 11 are important to examine. The 2nd house shows the skills that we employ to earn a living. The 5th house emphasizes speculation and gambling. The 8th house is "other people's money," as in inheritance, debts, taxes, and trading with someone else's money. The 11th house is lucky money, like the lottery, or windfall gains/losses.

The planets in these houses as well as the planets ruling the beginning cusps of these houses (the house ruler) are important actors in your money story as a trader. So, too, is your natal Moon, which reveals the all-important emotional make-up you bring to your trading. Is your Moon in cool-as-a-cucumber Capricorn? Or trigger-happy Aries? Natal moons in difficult signs or in difficult aspect to other planets in your chart could mean that trading might present challenges.

VESTA AND THE ANGLES

One of the best tips on trading acumen came to me from London-based financial astrologer Christeen Skinner. She has noticed over the years that good traders tend to have the asteroid Vesta close to one of the natal chart's four "angles,"—the ascendant/descendant axis that runs from the 9 o'clock to the 3 o'clock position on the chart, and the midheaven/IC axis that runs from 12 o'clock to 6 o'clock.

In mythology, Vesta was the sister who kept the home fires burning. It represents what we hold sacred and our commitment. The angles on a chart are the four most important degree areas representing how we respond as self vs. others and publicly vs. privately. Major life events typically occur when one of the natal chart's angles is activated by transiting planets. In sum, I think Vesta on one of your chart's angles indicates that you bring focus, attention, and commitment to your chosen path.

Wouldn't you know it? Gann has Vesta at 2 Gemini in his 10th house, within 8 degrees (conjunct) his midheaven at 25 Taurus, indicating that he not only had the potential to be a good trader, but also be well known for it (Figure 3.1).

Figure 3.1 W.D. Gann Natal Vesta Conjunct Midheaven

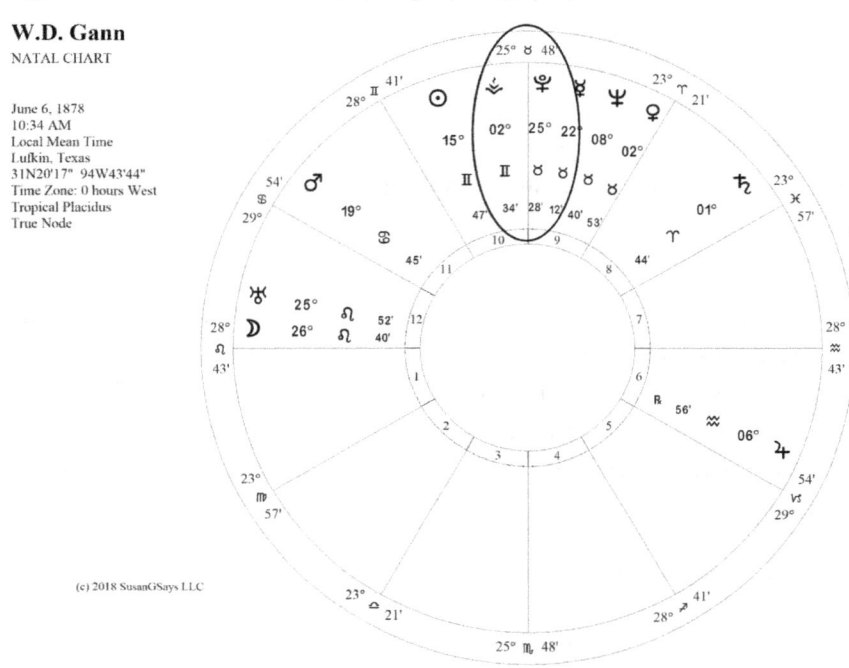

SYNCING UP WITH YOUR MARKET

Based on Gann's writings, I believe he used synastry between his own natal horoscope and the charts of the companies and markets he traded to determine which ones he should focus on and which he should avoid.

So, let's see if Gann and his "pet stock" had any synergy between their astrological horoscopes. We start by finding birth data for Gann and the company's stock listing. Gann was born on June 6, 1878 at 10:34 am in Lufkin, Texas.[12] His favorite stock, Mexican Petroleum Company of Delaware, began trading on the New York Stock Exchange on April 20, 1912.[13] (Just as an aside, Mex Pete began trading at the end of an extremely emotional week on Wall Street, five days after the Titanic sank.)

---

12 "W.D. Gann." Astro-Databank. http://www.astro.com/astro-databank/Gann,_W.D.
13 "New York Stock Exchange—Saturday, April 20, 1912." The New York Times. 21 April 1912, p. 92.

Then, we start looking for connections between the two natal horoscope charts (Figure 3.2). Most obvious is that Gann's natal Venus is conjunct Mex Pete's first-trade Sun (A), which means he is capable of making money by trading this stock. Second in importance is that Gann's natal Sun is conjunct the market's natal Moon and opposite the market's natal Jupiter (B). Not only did Gann tap into the market's emotional status (Moon), he also was able to see the market's full potential (Jupiter).

Next, I like that Gann has two planets conjunct Mex Pete's first-trade ascendant and midheaven. Gann's natal Mars was conjunct the market's ascendant (C), indicating that it was easy for him to take action as something important affected it. His natal Saturn was conjunct the market's midheaven (D), so he had discipline with trading the stock. Vice versa, Gann's natal Mercury was conjunct the market's natal Saturn (E), so he was able to pull the trigger even when prices were under pressure.

Figure 3.2 Synastry Strong Between W.D. Gann and Mex Pete

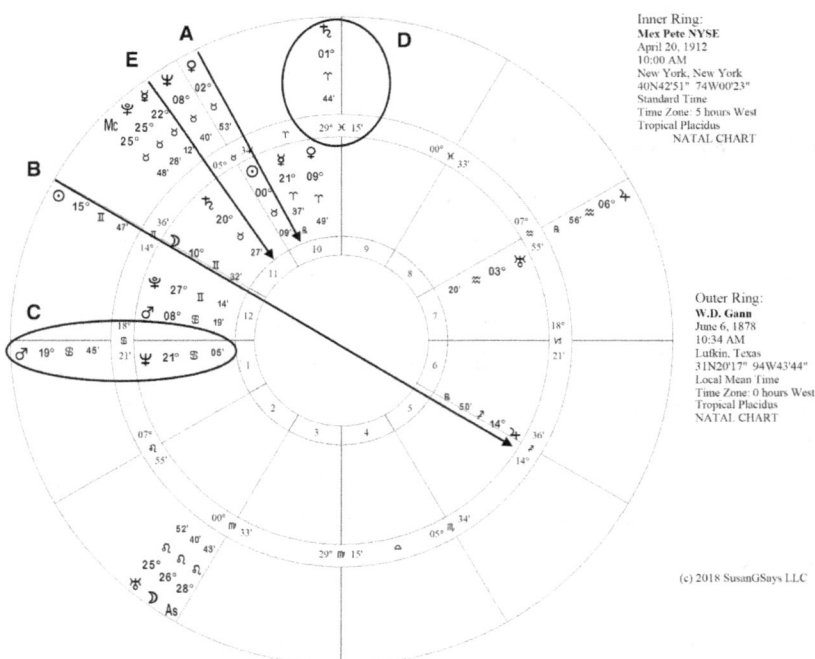

GANN AND WHEAT FUTURES

Gann was famous for making very precise forecasts that picked both time and price objectives. One of the most cited is his prediction that the September 1909 wheat contract at the Chicago Board of Trade would reach $1.20 per bushel before it expired.

On the contract's expiration day (September 30, 1909), it was trading at $1.08 per bushel at 12 noon, and prospects for his prediction looked dim. Indeed, the contract had traded in a range of $1.00 ¾ -$1.07 ¾ from September 22-29.[14] The *Ticker and Investment Digest* article that brought Wall Street's attention to Gann's trading prowess reported: "It is common history that September wheat surprised the whole country by selling at $1.20 and no higher in the very last hour of the trading, closing at that figure."[15]

First, let's look at Gann's synastry with the wheat futures market at the CBOT (Figure 3.3). I believe the first-trade chart for wheat futures to be October 14, 1865 at 11:00 am in Chicago. That is the first time trades were made under a new set of exchange by-laws that defined what we know today as a futures contract. (See Chapter 1 for more detail.)

---

14 Chicago Board of Trade records: Series I – Organizational records, Special Collections and University Archives, University of Illinois at Chicago. "Annual Report 1909." 78.

15 Gann, W.D. <u>W.D. Gann Commodities Course.</u> Reprint of article "William D. Gann: His Remarkable Predictions and Trading Record" in December 1909 issue of <u>The Ticker and Investment Digest</u>, N.p., Lambert-Gann Publishing Co., n.d., 163-166.

Figure 3.3 W.D. Gann's Strong Connections to Wheat Futures

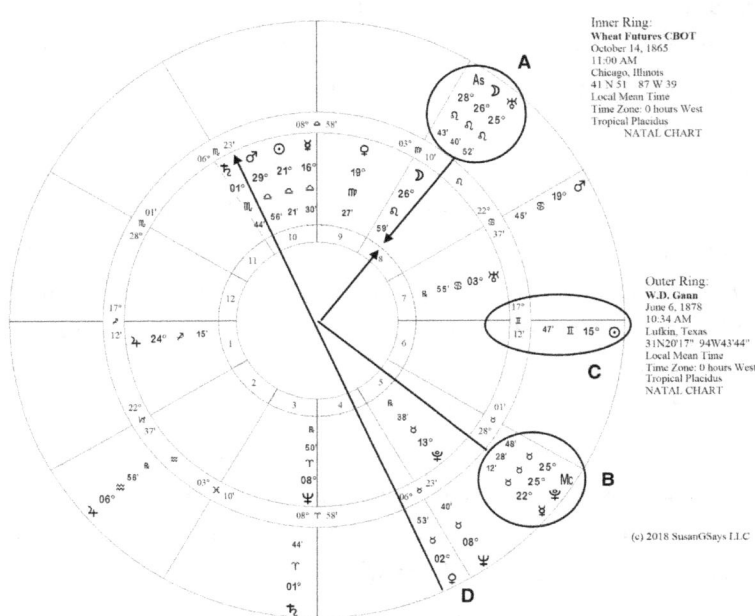

The strongest connection in the two charts is that both natal Moons are at 26 degrees of Leo (A). That means that Gann was extremely sensitive to the emotions of the wheat futures market, a simply great connection with any market that responds to the ups and downs of human emotion. In addition, Gann's natal Uranus is conjunct his own Moon and that of the wheat market. He likely got intuitive "aha" insights about wheat because of this connection.

Second, Gann's strong natal Mercury/Pluto is at a 90-degree angle to the wheat market's natal Moon and his own natal Moon (B). This relationship brings a certain amount of tension that keeps his trading prowess (Mercury/Pluto) on its toes with his emotions.

Third, Gann's natal Sun is within 2 degrees of the wheat market's descendant (C), one of the four "angles" in any chart that are especially sensitive to planetary activation. Finally, Gann's Venus (strong in its own sign of Taurus) is opposite the wheat market's natal Saturn and Mars (D).

SEPTEMBER 1909 WHEAT

Now let's take a peek at what Gann might have been anticipating when he made his famous call for September 1909 wheat futures to expire at $1.20 per bushel.

Astrologically, there are three interesting connections between the close of trade on September 30, 1909 and the first-trade chart for wheat futures (Figure 3.4). First, transiting Mercury is conjunct wheat's natal Mars (A), indicating that trading could be aggressive. Also, the transiting Moon in Aries is opposite the wheat market's natal Mars (in the ruling sign of Mars) and Sun (B), supporting the idea of aggressive, emotional trade at the close. Third, the transiting Sun is within 2 degrees of the market's natal midheaven (C), bringing both culmination and attention to the market.

Figure 3.4 September 1909 Wheat Expiration Connects with First-Trade Horoscope

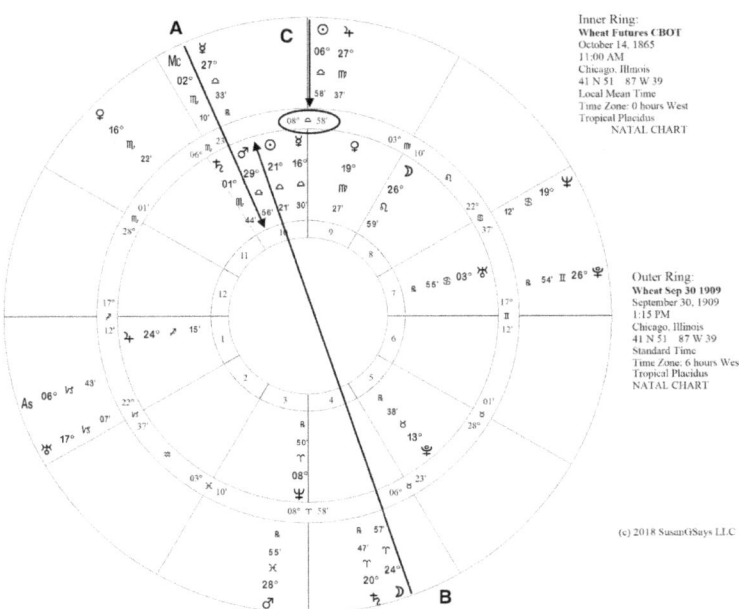

Although these connections are significant, they don't explain why $1.20 was Gann's price call. Once again, astrologically, 120 is the number of degrees in a

trine aspect and equal to one-third of the horoscope wheel, so perhaps that was one feature he liked about the price of $1.20. However, I suspect that because Gann was so attuned to "price equals time," that there was some time factor of 120 days or 120 weeks or 120 months from some previous high or low in wheat that was the real driving factor. I'll save that digging for another day, or leave it to the Gann experts to fill me in.

CHAPTER 4

The Importance of First-Trade Data

Obtaining reliable, accurate first-trade data for commodity futures contracts is the most difficult part of doing astrological analysis on these markets. Period.

Perhaps that's why no one has written about analyzing first-trade horoscope charts of commodity futures markets before (at least publicly, to my knowledge). And, perhaps this is why I am the one to do it. I've been in the commodity futures business my entire career, so I understand the quirks and where the data might be available—and I'm an astrologer.

STOCKS VS. COMMODITIES

When I first started applying what I knew about astrology to the commodity markets, I took my cues from the extensive work and research that has been done on astrology and the stock market. In stock analysis, it is standard operating procedure to obtain and use the horoscope charts of both when the company was incorporated (or began business) as well as when its stock was first listed for trade on a stock exchange. The incorporation chart helps you identify times of import to the company, while the first-trade chart is more attuned to trading insights. Some financial astrologers also look at the time of an initial public offering (IPO), which is typically about a day ahead of the first trade. The IPO is not the same as the first trade, even though many tend to use the terms interchangeably.

Another benefit for stock astrologers is that the time to use for most U.S. stock first-trade charts is easy to find—the New York Stock Exchange (de facto opening for all U.S. stock exchanges) has had just two times for the opening bell since 1877—10:00 am and 9:30 am, the latter only since 1985.

Not so with commodity markets. Back in the day, there were nearly a dozen individual commodity exchanges, each establishing a unique opening bell time for the markets it offered. Some started at 7:20 am. Some at 9:05. Some at 9:30. Some at 10:00. Others at other seemingly random times. Plus, on commodity exchanges, it often was the case in the heyday of new product development in the 1970s and 1980s that the first day of trading for a new product launch occurred at a time different than what would ultimately be its normal trading hours in order to accommodate a pre-opening ceremony of some sort. It also allowed floor traders ample time to begin trading in their regular pits and then come over to the support the new contract.

TIME OBSESSION EXPLAINED

Make no mistake, all astrologers are obsessed with finding the exact time something happened down to the minute. It's because an accurate first-trade time is the only way to establish accurate points for the four most sensitive points in the chart—the angles at 9, 12, 3 and 6 o'clock positions. Sure, you can get a lot out of a chart with just the day, month, and year. But, the all-important position of the Moon will not be correct as it moves about 1 degree every two hours. More importantly, the angles won't be correct—and they move 1 degree every few minutes. And, as you'll see in the next section, those five astrological degree positions—the four angles and the Moon—are critical in order to convert them into price levels that might provide support and resistance on a price chart.

When I got the idea to write this book in 2016, I thought getting first-trade data would be a breeze. I had a great list from the Commodity Futures Trading Commission (CFTC), the federal regulator, that I'd saved in my file cabinet

Trading In Sync With Commodities

since 1983 when I was a journalist covering the markets. It's 12 single-spaced pages that have not only the date that contracts had been approved by the CFTC for trading, but also the first-trade date. Finding the time a contract first traded? OK, a little more difficult, but that's what exchange records are for, right? Wrong. All wrong.

MY SILVER LINING STORY

Here's how I discovered the truth about my oh-so-valuable CFTC list.

About the same time in 2016, before I'd done much research for this book, a client was interested in the silver market, so I started comparing his natal horoscope chart to that of silver futures at COMEX, which my CFTC list said launched on July 5, 1933. I didn't know the exact opening time, so used 10:00 am just to get started. But, the chart synastry between my client and the silver market was almost non-existent. Strange. So, I started comparing the natal silver futures horoscope chart with the horoscope charts of the big highs and lows in the market. Still nothing clicked astrologically as I expected it should.

I figured I must be off by a few days or something, so I started digging into the online archives of *The New York Times*. It took awhile, but I ultimately discovered that silver futures were first launched by the National Metal Exchange on June 15, 1931 at 10:00 am—more than two years earlier than the "official" records show![16,17]

The July 5, 1933 date that the CFTC declared was the start date was when the newly formed COMEX (that merged the National Metal Exchange with three others for rubber, silk and hides) opened for the first time on its brand new trading floor at 81 Broad St.[18] I assume the history writers at COMEX somewhere along the line figured that July 5, 1933 was the first time silver futures started at that exchange. Technically accurate, but not astrologically accurate.

I re-ran the synastry charts of my client and important highs and lows against

---

16 "Market Opens Here For Silver Futures," *The New York Times*. 16 June 1931.
17 "Rules Formulated For Silver Trading," *The New York Times*. 14 May 1931.
18 "Commodity Board in New Home Today," *The New York Times*. 5 July 1933.

the 1931 launch date for silver futures. Ahhhh. It all fell into place and made sense to this financial astrologer. I'm beyond grateful for this very early lesson learned. (P.S. I chose to research gold futures for this book, but will be doing similar analysis for silver futures in upcoming supplements.)

AN IMPERFECT HISTORY

Here's what I think has happened. The CFTC was created in 1974, so its list includes about a century's worth of information that I have to assume came directly from its predecessors, the Commodity Exchange Administration (1936) and Grain Futures Administration (1922),[19] as well as the exchanges, which have lost accurate dates and times to the shadows of their own record-keeping, staff comings and goings, historical recollections, physical relocations, and natural disasters.

Besides the wrong year in silver, I also have discovered typos on the CFTC list that result in incorrect dates. For example, the CFTC says soybean meal futures were listed on August 19, 1951. But, the contract actually opened 10 days later, on August 29, 1951, according to the exchange's monthly newsletter update to members that summer. I'm going with what the exchange reported in real time.

However, the biggest disconnect of all to me is that the CFTC list says that corn, wheat, and oat futures began at the Chicago Board of Trade on January 2, 1877—nearly 40 years after the exchange was founded, which simply makes no logical sense. Indeed, even the exchange itself acknowledges that futures contracts existed in the 1860s.[20] It's just that recorded statistics on those contracts began on that date with the opening of trade in 1877, so that's what is reported as the start date.

The bottom line is that I can't trust the CFTC for accurate first-trade data (although I have confirmed that many of the dates are correct), and by extension, any federal regulator the world over. And, I can't trust exchange websites, which

---

19   "History of the CFTC." Commodity Futures Trading Commission. 25 May 2017. <http://www.cftc.gov/about/historyofthecftc/history_precftc>.

20   "Chronology of Key Dates in CBOT History." News Release. Chicago Board of Trade. April 29, 1983.

simply regurgitate the sometimes erroneous information passed along over the course of time.

What I do trust is my own digging into the publicly available archives of exchanges, regulators, newspapers, newsletters, and magazines. Anything I consider reliable that can show me a date and time in black and white. I'd even take a written diary from a trader, or internal memos at brokerage firms, or press releases stashed away in a reporter's files.

JOIN TEAM COMMODITY TIMES

I'd love nothing more than to collect and publish the definitive list of first-trade dates and times for every futures contract on the planet—even the now dead, but once popular ones like pork bellies, potatoes, and onions. It would be the ultimate resource for astrological research on the commodity futures markets. But that is thousands of contracts across dozens of exchanges.

Together, though, we could make that happen.

My request to you is that if you have definitive, written evidence of when any futures contract in the world was first traded, please send it my way by emailing me at: TeamCommodityTimes@yahoo.com. I promise to publish the information in a timely way and recognize your contribution to the cause.

Go Team Commodity Times!

CHAPTER 5

How Markets Sync Up with Planets

You've got your favorite market. You know that you sync up with it based on comparing your natal horoscope charts. Now, it's time to figure out how your market syncs up with the planets that are constantly moving in the sky, what astrologers call "transiting" planets.

This is the bread-and-butter of how to begin adding astrology to your financial toolbox. Figuring out how your market vibrates with the planets, their position, and their motion. And, the really cool thing about astrology is that you can know the dates—and even times, to the minute—to be on the lookout for market-moving vibration any number of days, weeks, months, years, and decades into the future.

CONVERT HOROSCOPE INTO PRICES

One of the first things you can start watching are horoscope-generated prices that may be important support and resistance points. I know it sounds far-fetched and completely whacko to think that a zodiac position like "17 Aries" can be a price. But, it makes perfect sense once you get the hang of it.

Start with the knowledge that a complete circle is 360 degrees, and each zodiac sign is 30 degrees. Then, convert each zodiac sign into its numerical place in the 360-degree total. For example, the start of the zodiac is Aries and the second sign is Taurus. Aries = 0 and Taurus =30, and so on through to Pisces, the last size of the zodiac, which equals 330.

Aries	0
Taurus	30
Gemini	60
Cancer	90
Leo	120
Virgo	150
Libra	180
Scorpio	210
Sagittarius	240
Capricorn	270
Aquarius	300
Pisces	330

Next, add the number of degrees for the natal planet's position to the degrees of the sign. For example, a planet at 17 Aries would convert to a price of 17 (0 + 17), but a planet at 17 Taurus would be a price of 47 (30 + 17).

Voila! You've converted your market's natal planetary positions into prices! To get higher prices, simply add multiples of 360 to the original set.

SAMPLE CONVERSION

I find it easiest to put all this data in a spreadsheet, with formulas set up to add 360 to the total of the previous column. Then, just enter in the initial data point and you've got the entire spreadsheet filled in.

Here's how I converted the soybean first-trade chart data into a price spreadsheet.

I look at the first-trade horoscope chart for soybeans so I'm getting the exact zodiac position that goes into the spreadsheet. I start with whatever planets or angles are in Aries so that the numbers are always increasing.

Figure 5.1 Soybean Futures First-Trade Horoscope

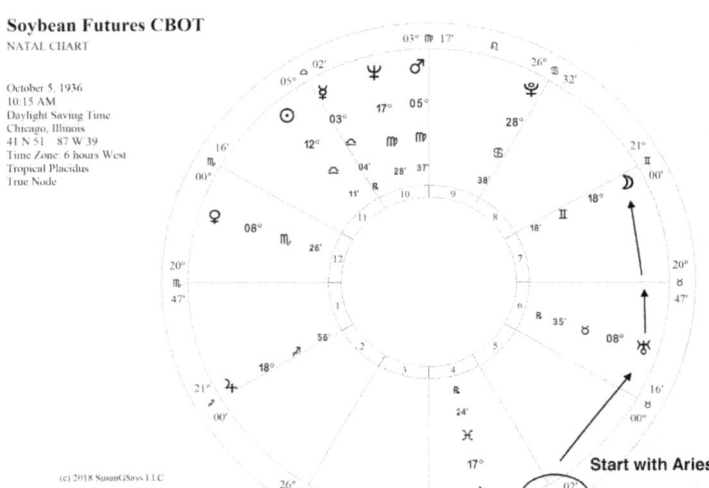

In the soybean first-trade chart, nothing is in Aries, so we move on to Taurus. Uranus is at 08 Taurus 35, so it goes on the first line in the spreadsheet simply as 08 Taurus (Table 5.1). Then, convert that to a price of 38 (Taurus = 30 + 8 degrees). Do the same for each planet as well as each of the angles--Ascendant (1st house cusp), Descendant (7th house cusp), MC (10th house cusp; stands for *Medium Coeli*, Latin for middle of the sky), and IC (4th house cusp; stands for *Imum Coeli*, Latin for bottom of the sky). You'll also note that I make a note "rx" for planets that are retrograde in the spreadsheet, just as a handy reference more than anything else; retrograde has no bearing on price conversion.

Trading In Sync With Commodities

Table 5.1 Soybean Horoscope Price Conversion

Market	Soybean Futures									
1st Trade	October 5, 1936, 10:15 am, Chicago									
Source	CBOT Monthly Letter to Members									
Price unit	Cents per bushel									
Planet	Position	Conversion	360	720	1080	1440	1800	2160	2520	2880
Uranus	08 Taurus	38	398	758	1118	1478	1838	2198	2558	2918
Desc	20 Taurus	50	410	770	1130	1490	1850	2210	2570	2930
Moon	18 Gemini	78	438	798	1158	1518	1878	2238	2598	2958
Pluto	28 Cancer	118	478	838	1198	1558	1918	2278	2638	2998
MC	03 Virgo	153	513	873	1233	1593	1953	2313	2673	3033
Mars	05 Virgo	155	515	875	1235	1595	1955	2315	2675	3035
Neptune	17 Virgo	167	527	887	1247	1607	1967	2327	2687	3047
Mercury rx	03 Libra	183	543	903	1263	1623	1983	2343	2703	3063
Sun	12 Libra	192	552	912	1272	1632	1992	2352	2712	3072
Venus	08 Scorpio	218	578	938	1298	1658	2018	2378	2738	3098
Asc	20 Scorpio	230	590	950	1310	1670	2030	2390	2750	3110
Jupiter	18 Sag	258	618	978	1338	1698	2058	2418	2778	3138
IC	03 Pisces	333	693	1053	1413	1773	2133	2493	2853	3213
Saturn rx	17 Pisces	347	707	1067	1427	1787	2147	2507	2867	3227

PRICE UNITS

Prices can be in whatever units make sense to the market you're trading. In grains, I use cents per bushel; in gold, dollars per ounce. In the crude oil table (Chapter 8), prices are in dollars and cents per barrel—and can have significance with either one or two numerals behind the decimal point. For example, the all-time high of $147.27 (1472 or 1473) in July 2008 is between the Mars price of 1465 and the Venus price of 1483. But, the all-time low of $9.75 in April 1986 was just a nickel higher than the Jupiter price of 970, which also could be seen as a price of $97 if you used just one decimal place in the Jupiter price.

CAVEAT EMPTOR

Please, please, please use this technique as simply another tool in your price-projection toolbox, not the final word. Like all things in both technical analysis and astrology, the more signals congregating in a certain area, the stronger the signal. So, add this horoscope price conversion spreadsheet to other price-projection techniques like Fibonacci percentages, head-and-shoulders breakouts, or flagpole measurements. (Personally, in the modest amount of work I've done with Gann squares and December corn, I've been really impressed with how the market responds to prices on a properly built Gann square.)

For example, in the soybean conversion table, the all-time high of $17.94 ¾ in September 2012 was 7 cents beyond the Saturn price conversion at 1787. The 1973 high of $12.90, which stood for 35 years, was 8 cents less than the Venus price conversion at 1298. Both close (and close enough to count). At the other end of the spectrum, the 1988 summer drought high of $10.99 ½ is nowhere close to anything on the conversion spreadsheet. One that did hit it on the nose was the May 1997 high of $9.03 ½, which aligned with the price conversion for Mercury of 903.

Also interesting are clusters of planets, which make clusters of prices. In August 1991, the soybean low of $5.14 neatly split the difference between the MC conversion price of 513 and the Mars price of 515.

ASTROLOGICAL RULERS OF COMMODITY MARKETS

Ancient astrologers in Babylonia and Egypt were the first to associate certain planets and certain zodiac signs with certain objects and behaviors based on their observations. These "rulerships" have been handed down over the millennia and help astrologers today look for clues about why something is happening or might be happening.

These rulership associations often are based on the planet's physical makeup or a zodiac sign's characteristics. An easy example to understand is gold. It is ruled by the Sun, which is bright, shiny, and yellow. Other obvious connections are between the sign Taurus (the bull) and cattle, and between the Moon (silvery) and silver.

Table 5.2 is my current compilation of rulerships by commodity. It is drawn largely from the bible of such lists, "The Rulership Book," by Rex E. Bills. However, it remains a work in progress as I continue my own learning and observation about how the markets respond to movement by the planets and influence of the signs. Indeed, some entries have two planets or signs listed in order to keep them on the radar.

Note, also, that this table focuses on the planet and sign rulers associated with the underlying physical commodity. It's a whole 'nother ball of wax when we start looking at the ruler of a specific commodity futures market.

Commodity ruler and commodity futures chart ruler are different. That's because the individual futures market ruler is linked to the zodiac sign that was on the eastern horizon when it first started trading, i.e., the ascendant. Both rulerships are good to know and good to follow for upcoming market clues. We'll get to that later in this book in the individual market chapters.

Table 5.2   Commodity Rulerships

Commodity	Ruling Planet	Ruling Sign
Cattle	Saturn	Taurus
Cheese	Moon	Cancer
Cocoa	Venus	Libra
Coffee	Mars	Aries
Copper	Venus, Uranus	Taurus, Libra, Aquarius
Corn	Sun	Leo
Cotton	Venus	Taurus
Crude oil	Neptune, Pluto	Pisces, Scorpio
Currencies	Venus	Taurus
Gasoline	Neptune	Pisces
Gold	Sun	Leo
Heating oil	Neptune, Pluto	Pisces, Scorpio
Hogs	Saturn	Taurus
Inflation	Neptune, Jupiter	Pisces
Interest rates	Jupiter, Venus	Sagittarius, Taurus
Lumber	Saturn	Capricorn
Milk	Moon	Cancer
Natural gas	Neptune	Pisces
Oats	Mercury	Virgo
Orange juice	Sun	Leo

Platinum	Neptune, Uranus	Aquarius
Silver	Moon	Cancer
Soybeans	Mercury	Virgo
Stock indexes	Mercury	Gemini
Sugar	Venus	Libra
Wheat	Venus	Taurus

HOW TO USE RULERSHIPS

The whole point of associating commodities with planet and zodiac sign rulerships is to become alert to astrological shifts that might affect the markets.

The following tips on rulership indicators come from the writings of several financial astrologers I've studied; I appreciate their hard work in developing these ideas and sharing them publicly. They include: Mary Downing, Jeanne Long, Bill Meridian, Ray Merriman, Carol Mull, LCdr. David Williams, and Norm Winski.

RULING SIGNS

There are two tips here about how knowledge about a planet's ruling sign might provide some market movement insight.

- Look for a change of trend when Mars enters a commodity's ruling sign.
- Moon's North Node is supportive when in it is in the market's ruling sign; leaving that sign equals a top.

1. MARS ENTERS RULING SIGN

Mars entering Leo, for example, would put you on alert for a change in trend in the corn, gold, and orange juice markets because Leo is the ruler of those commodities. The key phrase is "change of trend," which always is frustrating as opposed to just being able to say definitively if the market is going to go up or down. But, it's the shift in energy that's important. You have to be able to figure out which way the trend is going. The examples below show how

Trading In Sync With Commodities

Mars moving into gold's ruling sign of Leo played out in 2013 and 2017—but certainly not all situations are this good.

Gold trend change with Mars in Leo August 29–October 15, 2013

This was a pretty ideal Mars in Leo for the gold market. Cash gold topped at $1,433 per oz. the day before Mars moved into Leo on August 29, 2013 and bottomed at $1,259 on the last day Mars was in gold's ruling sign on October 15 (Figure 5.3). Gold lost $174 per oz. during this six-week change in trend (equal to $17,400 per 100-oz. futures contract), and ultimately bottomed at $1,182 on the last day of the year for an additional $77 loss.

Figure 5.2   Gold Prices Drop with Mars in Leo

Source: Barchart.com

Gold trend change with Mars in Leo July 21-September 5, 2017

In 2017, Mars moving into Leo resulted in a bullish change of trend vs. the bearish trend change in 2013. In 2017, the gold market bottomed on July 10 (11 days before the Mars ingress) at $1,211 and topped on September 8 (three

61

days after Mars left Leo) at $1,362 (Figure 5.4) for a move of $151. The market rallied an even $100 per oz. during the time Mars was in Leo, or $10,000 per 100-oz. futures contract.

Figure 5.3   Gold Prices Rally with Mars in Leo

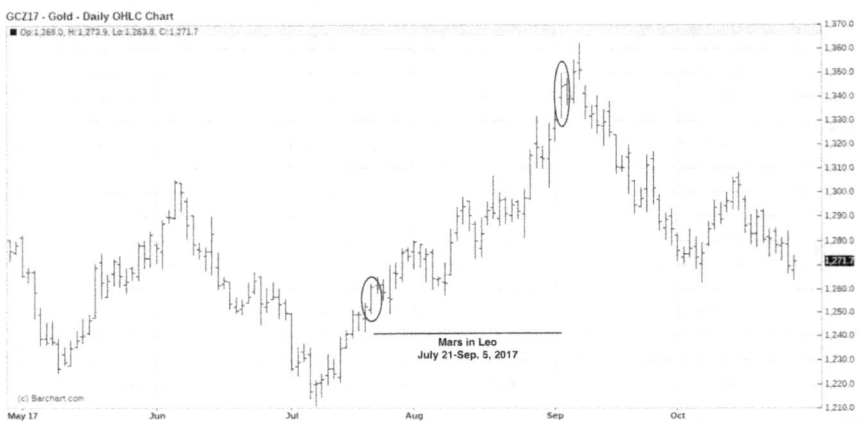

Source: Barchart.com

2. RULING PLANETS

- Usually bearish (prices fall) when the ruling planet of a commodity goes retrograde.
- Usually bullish (prices rise) when the ruling planet of a commodity goes direct.

Retrograde and Direct Motion

Watching for the retrograde/direct motion of a commodity's ruling planet is an easy way to be on the alert for a bullish or bearish trend change. In the two examples below, I looked at crude oil's ruler, Neptune. Despite that Neptune is retrograde for about five months each year, its retrograde/direct dates show interesting correlation with changes in market direction in some years, but certainly not all.

Trading In Sync With Commodities

Crude oil downtrend with Neptune retrograde June 9-Nov. 15, 2014

This is a pretty good example of how prices behaved as expected during Neptune's retrograde period. Nearby light, sweet crude oil topped on June 13, 2014 at $107.68 per barrel, four days after its ruling planet turned retrograde, and it was a steady downward move to $43.58 on January 29, 2015. However, notice that when Neptune turned direct in mid-November, the market stabilized for a few days, but did not have a change in trend.

Figure 5.4   Crude Oil Prices Drop with Neptune Retrograde in 2014

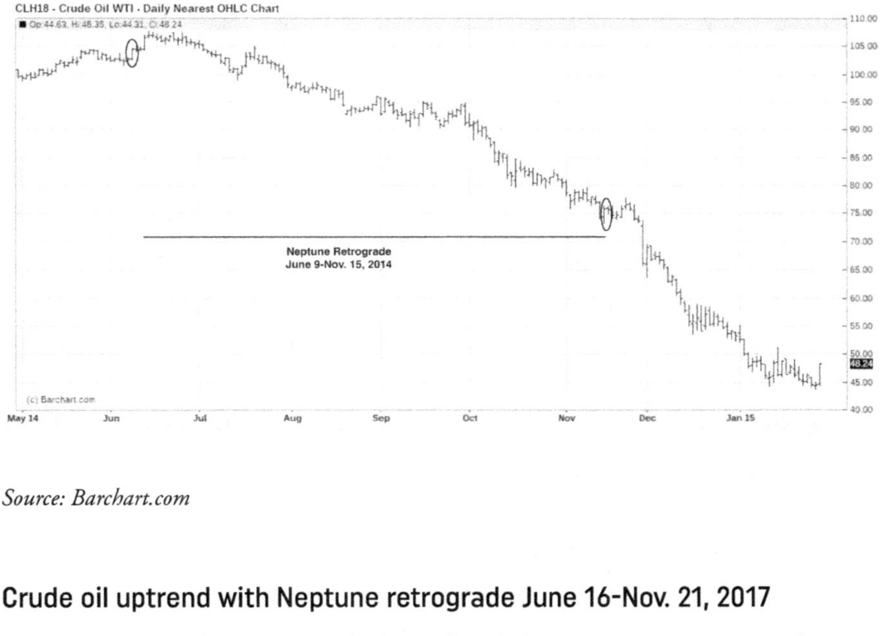

Source: Barchart.com

Crude oil uptrend with Neptune retrograde June 16-Nov. 21, 2017

In 2017, crude oil prices staged a big rally while Neptune was retrograde, starting from a low of $42.05 set five days later, on the summer solstice. By the time Neptune turned direct, prices had rallied nearly $15 per barrel to $57.22, on their way to a January 2018 high of $66.66.

63

Figure 5.5 Crude Oil Rallies with Neptune Retrograde in 2017

Source: Barchart.com

ZODIAC SIGN CHANGE

Anytime a planet changes signs (or "ingresses"), it brings a new flavor of thinking and feeling. This is when the actor (planet) changes costume or character (sign). Therefore, there is always the possibility of a change in trend as traders adjust to the new vibe.

The zodiac sign/vibe change happens the most with the planets that move the fastest and affect us personally—Moon (2 ½ days), Sun (once a month), Mercury (every three weeks), Venus (three to four weeks), and Mars (every two months). Of course, the periods can be longer when Mercury, Venus, and Mars turn retrograde and retrace their steps.

When the other planets (Jupiter, Saturn, Uranus, Neptune, and Pluto) change signs, the effect is felt more broadly by society. Jupiter is the swiftest of these five planets, and moves to a new sign annually; Saturn spends about 2 ½ years in a single sign. Uranus, Neptune and Pluto change signs once every decade or two, so the effect is long and long-lasting. For example, Pluto moved into Capricorn in January 2008, heralding the start to 17 years of transforming (Pluto) business and government (Capricorn) that kicked off with the U.S.

financial crisis of 2008. At the shorter end of the spectrum, financial astrologers commonly look to Jupiter's current sign as supportive for the companies and sectors associated with that sign. For example, Jupiter in Scorpio (October 2017—November 2018) would tend to favor scientific research, pollution control, pharmaceuticals, and bankruptcy.

INGRESSES OF THE SUN

As the planet that enables life on Earth, the Sun holds particular sway when it moves into a new zodiac sign each month. More so than any other planet, the Sun's ingresses mark shifts in temperament and tone that pervade every bit of life on our planet. Think of people you know born under different Sun signs that embody the flavor of that sign and you'll understand how the vibe can change as the Sun moves into a new zodiac sign.

The most important sign changes by the Sun are those that occur at the start of each season—Aries (spring), Cancer (summer), Libra (fall), and Capricorn (winter). These four signs are the "cardinal" signs that emote initiating, get-going-now kind of energy. Indeed, legendary trader W.D. Gann watched for changes of trend at these four ingresses, and also made it a point to watch the dates halfway between two successive signs as well as those one-third and two-thirds of the way from one Aries ingress to the next.

FIVE SIGN CHANGES AT 1987 STOCK MARKET TOP

The stock market top in August 1987, preceding the Crash of 1987 in October, is a stellar example of how planets changing signs can affect the markets (Figure 5.6). From August 21 to 24, all five of the fast-moving personal planets not only changed signs, they all moved into the same sign—Virgo, the keeper of accountability. To be fair, other astrological markers pointed to that day as one to watch as well, but certainly five sign changes in four days catches the eye. The Dow Jones Industrial Average peaked at 2722 on August 24, later crashing a record 508 points (22.6%) on October 19.

For the first time since 1987, a similar period will occur in the last half of August 2019, although the sign changes will happen over about 10 days rather than four. From August 19 to 30, 2019 those same five fast-moving personal planets—Sun, Moon, Mercury, Venus, and Mars—will once again be moving into the sign of Virgo relatively close together. Mark your calendars now!

Figure 5.6   Five Planets in Early Virgo at 1987 Top

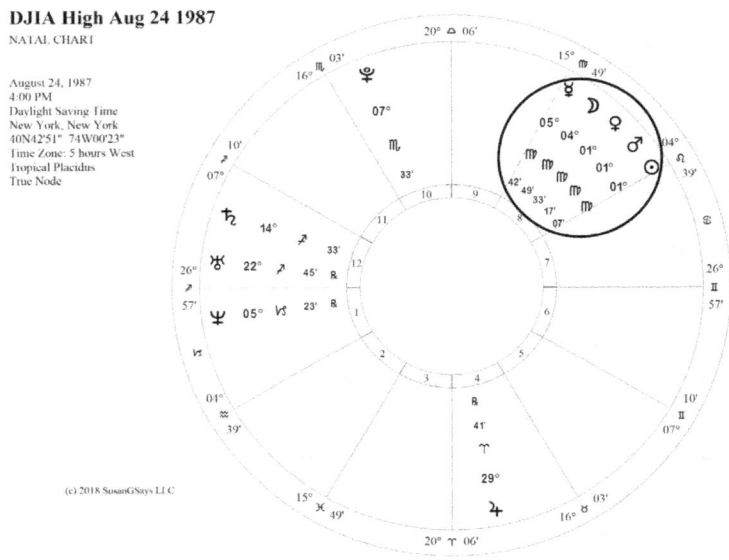

DECLINATION

Declination describes a planet's north/south distance in degrees from the celestial equator, i.e., the path of the Sun. The Sun's extremes set boundaries for declination, and are at 23 degrees 26 minutes. The Sun hits these extremes at the winter solstice in the south at the Tropic of Capricorn and at the summer solstice in the north at the Tropic of Cancer.

Planets sometimes go beyond the 23 N/S 26 border, and when they do, they are called "out of bounds." When a planet is out of bounds, it expresses its nature to the extreme. For example, an out-of-bounds Moon is highly emotional; an out-of-bounds Mars is extremely aggressive. The Moon, Mercury, Mars, and Venus are the planets most often out of bounds. Saturn and

Neptune have not been out of bounds since 1600. By definition, the Sun is never out of bounds.

A way to use out-of-bounds information would be as an additional bit of information about the current nature of a transiting planet that is activating your market's natal horoscope. Another way to look at declination is by comparing degrees between planets. If they are within one degree of each other on the same side of the celestial equator (either both North or both South), they are "parallel," and work together as if conjunct by zodiac sign. If they are within one degree but on opposite sides of the celestial equator (i.e., one North and one South), they are "contraparallel," and behave as if they are in opposition by zodiac sign.

Financial astrologer Norm Winski notes that at the all-time high in crude oil prices in 2008, transiting Uranus was contraparallel to the natal Neptune (ruler of crude oil) in the horoscope of the United States. Now, that insight took some digging!

RETROGRADE AND DIRECT MOTION

Astrologers keep close tabs on the motion of planets to know if they are moving forward in direct motion or appearing to move backward in retrograde motion. Obviously, the planets are always moving forward in space, but their speed can change based on gravitational pull from the Sun. When they slow down, it's like they hit the brakes in the right lane of an interstate and the Earth passes them in the passing lane. That's when the planets are retrograde. Later, they speed up and catch back up to Earth, moving into direct motion when they pass the Earth again on the cosmic highway.

All planets (except the Sun and Moon) go retrograde as seen from Earth. Astrologic wisdom handed down over the millennia says that retrograde planets are not operating with their normal verve. It's like they are on vacation from their normal duties, and tend to let things slide.

From a trading perspective, retrograde planets tend to be bearish because of this slacking-off tendency. However, like a change in zodiac sign, as planets "station" when they move from direct to retrograde and back again, it's time to be on the lookout for a change in trend.

Figure 5.7 is an example of both these guidelines at work in the DJIA in 2014. Although Jupiter (planet of expansion) was retrograde as the year began, the market rallied nearly 1000 points in January. It was a different story, however, when Venus (money) joined Jupiter in retrograde motion. The market dropped 1200 points during the Venus retrograde period, finding a bottom two days after the planet turned direct in the beginning of February.

In mid-April, Pluto turned retrograde and the market shifted to uptrend from downtrend. A big correction occurred in late summer on news of international defaults and shaky banks, but then the Dow recovered to make a high as Pluto turned direct in September, nearly 1400 points higher than when Pluto began its retrograde period.

Figure 5.7   Retrograde Periods Shift DJIA in 2014

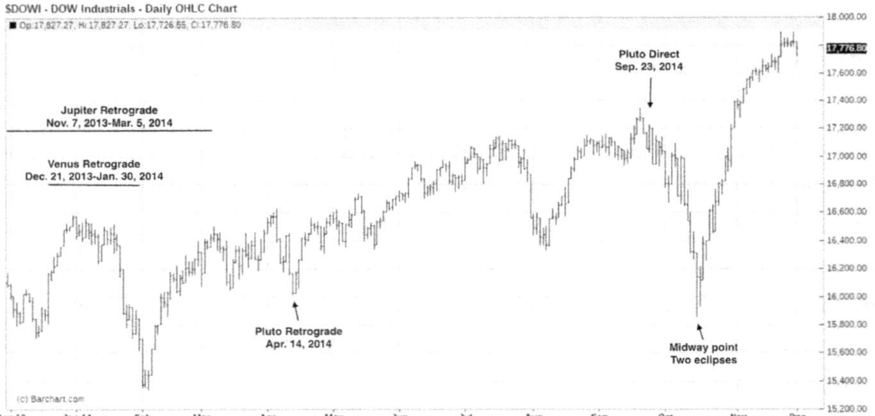

Source: Barchart.com

ECLIPSES

Figure 5.7 also includes an example of why financial astrologers pay attention to eclipses, which interrupt the normal pattern of light we see from the Sun or Moon. On the day of the lunar eclipse on October 8, 2014, the U.S. Federal

Reserve said it would not be quick to raise interest rates given the weak global economy; the DJIA had its biggest rally of the year.

However, global news soured quickly and the market lost 1150 points over the next five days, bottoming midway between the October 8 lunar eclipse and the October 23 solar eclipse with volatility that resulted in record trading volume at the CME Group. These two eclipses were part of a centuries-long pattern (a Saros Series) that began in 1870 and continues to 3114. Its meaning revolves around money and relationships, with actions likely to be impulsive, exciting, and passionate. So, market volatility was certainly likely.

ECLIPSES 101

An eclipse occurs when the Earth, Moon, and Sun are aligned, disrupting the light of the Sun or the reflection of the Moon. In a solar eclipse (at the new moon), the Moon is between the Earth and Sun, blocking the Sun's light. In a lunar eclipse (at the full moon), the Earth is between the Sun and Moon, blocking the Moon's ability to reflect the Sun's light.

Eclipses are always at the new moon or full moon, and can be considered a supercharged version of either one. What distinguishes a regular new moon or full moon from those that are eclipses is that one of the Moon's nodes (north node or south node) is also in close zodiacal alignment with the Sun. This means the path of the Moon is close to the celestial equator, the path the Sun follows in the sky.

Each eclipse is part of a family of 69-87 eclipses that span on average about 1,300 years, starting at either one of the Earth's poles and ending at the other. To keep the eclipse families straight, NASA assigns each one a Saros Series (SS) number, and these are available at the NASA website, https://eclipse.gsfc.nasa.gov/eclipse.html. Astrologers take the Saros Series (or cycle) one step further and delineate the nature of each eclipse based on the natal horoscope of the first one in the family. The theme of the first eclipse sets the tone for all the rest to follow in that family.

For example, Saros Series expert Bernadette Brady, author of *Predictive Astrology—The Eagle and the Lark*, is watching SS 117 with interest due to its connection with the English monarchy. The series began in 792 CE, 10 years before the first recognized King of England came to power. Prince William, second heir to the throne, was born on this eclipse on June 21, 1982. The entire Saros Series ends on July 23, 2036, when Prince William is 54 years old. Brady's delineation of the cycle says it is a difficult one for personal relationships and brings ideas of separation or the ending of a union.

Eclipses are special because they occur just a few times a year, typically four times total, six months apart, with a solar and lunar eclipse within two weeks of each other. However, there can be as many as five solar eclipses in a year; lunar eclipses range from zero to three in a year. There are several different types of eclipses, depending on how much of the Sun or Moon is blocked from view, and all of them should be considered powerful enough to be on your toes for a change in market tenor and movement.

THE GREAT AMERICAN ECLIPSE—AUGUST 21, 2017

The most impressive of the eclipses is the total solar eclipse in which the Moon totally blocks the light of the Sun. A large portion of the United States—in a line 70 miles wide from Washington southeast into South Carolina—witnessed a total solar eclipse on August 21, 2017. This eclipse was part of Saros 145, which advises that unexpected events could pressure relationships due to distorted or false information; health issues and tiredness also are likely.[21]

The horoscope for the Great American Eclipse, at 28 Leo 53, was directly opposite the natal Moon of the United States, which represents agitation over what it means to have freedom of opinion and the ability to explore new ideas. Just eight months into a new, contentious administration, the eclipse was symbolic in that it crossed nearly the entire country, splitting it in two.

The day of the eclipse is not the only day that experiences the eclipse energy, however. Astrologers have several methods to assess when the eclipse's peak energy will hit. For the Great American Eclipse of 2017, astrologer Ben Dykes points to March-September 2019 as the peak effect, which I discuss in more detail in Chapter 12.

It also is wise to watch when planets cross the degree of the eclipse to see the

---

21   Brady, Bernadette. Predictive Astrology—The Eagle and the Lark. (San Francisco: Red Wheel/Weiser, LLC, 1999) 308.

energy activated again. Since the preceding lunar eclipse of August 7, 2017, the United States and North Korea had been in a war of words and threats concerning the latter's escalation of nuclear arms testing. Less than two weeks after the eclipse, transiting Mars—the planet of war and aggression—hit the eclipse degree of 28 Leo 53 on Labor Day weekend, just 11 hours after North Korea tested its first hydrogen bomb. Look for this storyline to be a theme for the effects of this eclipse, particularly in the summers through 2022 as the inner planets activate the eclipse degree.

NORTH NODE MARKET CONNECTIONS

One trading hint I've seen says to watch for a change in trend when the North Node is conjunct a market's ruling planet. The North Node is in one sign for about 18 months, so this conjunction would occur just once every 18-19 years.

Not so for planets ruled by the Sun (gold, corn, orange juice) or the Moon (silver, dairy), because the North Node could be conjunct the Sun or Moon at any of the eclipses that occur each year. Typically, there is a pair of lunar/solar eclipses twice a year.

MUNDANE PLANETARY ASPECTS AND TRANSITS

Mundane planetary "aspects" are the connections between planets happening in the sky overhead that affect everyone on the planet. These aspects (conjunction, opposition, square, trine, etc.) are made by the planets as they "transit" through the sky and the zodiac signs.

Annual astrological calendars make note of each of these mundane aspects for each day of the year. Because the Moon moves through the entire zodiac every month (thus making several aspects to each of the nine other planets), it's rare to see a day without some sort of astrological aspect in play. The challenge is to separate wheat from chaff in order to find a significant aspect or a significant cluster of aspects that could affect the human psyche as a whole, which then translates into how humans might make trading decisions.

In general, aspects made by planets closest to the Sun have the most fleeting impact, while planets further away from the Sun have longer-lasting influence. Similarly, the stronger the aspect (conjunction the strongest, then typically opposition, square, trine, sextile, in that order), the more important it is to pay attention. For example, a sextile between Mercury and Venus will have far less potential market impact than a conjunction between Jupiter and Pluto. The transiting Moon plays its biggest role when it slides into position to support a larger planetary formation happening between or among other planets.

FINANCIAL SYNODIC CYCLES

Financial astrologers watch three transiting planets in particular for clues on long-term economic trends—Jupiter, Saturn and Uranus. These three interact with each other in synodic cycles that range from 14 to 45 years, the start of which is marked by when two planets are in the same degree of the same sign of the zodiac. This can be a single date or over a period of months if the planets go through a retrograde period. As you'll see in the examples below, these cycles coincide with significant shifts in the economy and the markets, which make them important for traders to follow, much like the long-term trends gleaned from monthly and weekly price charts.

I find it fascinating that cultural historian and author Richard Tarnas, in *Cosmos and Psyche*, concluded after decades of research—and no background in astrology—that societal shifts throughout history are connected to large planetary cycles like these. This is a great book for gaining a perspective on how we humans respond to the movement of the planets.

One example Tarnas points out is the triple conjunction of Jupiter, Uranus, and Pluto. In July-August 1789, when these three planets were aligned, the Bastille revolt occurred in France. Nearly 200 years later, in 1968-69, the three planets were once again aligned as other revolts occurred, including the Tet insurgency in Vietnam, the Events of May in Paris, protests in Chicago at the Democratic National Convention, and the Stonewall uprising in New York. Almost spookily, the Apollo 11 Moon landing of July 20, 1969 occurred on a day when the Moon, Jupiter, Uranus, and Pluto were conjunct.

Jupiter/Uranus

The Jupiter/Uranus cycle is the shortest of the three economic cycles, at 13.8 years. At their conjunction, Tarnas sees creative breakthroughs that "exhibit a high-spirited, celebratory, exuberant creative spirit." Two examples include creation of Beethoven's Ninth Symphony in 1817 and the Harry Potter book series in 1997. At the most recent conjunction in 2010-11, WikiLeaks published classified U.S. information and the Arab Spring uprising occurred. The next conjunction is on April 21, 2024 in Taurus.

Economically, financial astrologer and researcher LCdr. David Williams found that a 60-degree relationship (a sextile aspect) between Jupiter and Uranus is the most common aspect to mark a business cycle turning point, at 78 percent.[22] Examples of a Jupiter/Uranus sextile include: (1) August 1929-March 1930, which included the stock market crash of October 1929; and (2) March-November 2008, the height of the U.S. financial crisis. The next sextile between these two planets occurs on February 17, 2022.

Jupiter/Saturn

The two largest planets in the solar system have a 20-year cycle (19.86 years), which produces long periods of influence. Economically, Williams finds that this pair also is associated with business cycle turns, most often at the conjunction (83 percent).[23] Some examples include:

- September 9, 1921—End of WWI and start of the Roaring Twenties
- February 18, 1961—Kennedy inauguration; DJIA hits low on Feb. 20, 1961
- December 31, 1980-July 23, 1981—Interest rates rise to combat inflation
- May 28, 2000—Dot-com bubble bursts

Important markers in the Jupiter/Saturn cycle are when the two planets make

---

22   Williams, LCdr. David. <u>Financial Astrology.</u> 1982 (Tempe AZ: American Federation of Astrologers, Inc. 2004) 88.

23   Ibid.

"hard" aspects of conjunction, opposition (separated by 180 zodiac degrees), and squares (separated by 90 zodiac degrees). In the cycle beginning in 2000, these hard aspects have had significant market impact:

- Conjunction on May 28, 2000—Stock market top and dot-com bust in March 2000
- Waxing square on three dates from December 16, 2005 to October 25, 2006—U.S. housing bubble peaks, with 1.3 million foreclosures filed in 2006, up 42 percent vs. 2005
- Opposition on three dates from May 23, 2010 to March 28, 2011—Flash Crash on May 6, 2010 sends DJIA down 600 points and back in 20 minutes; Dodd-Frank signed into law July 21; U.S. Fed announces QE bond-buyback program in November 2010; Standard & Poor's downgrades U.S. sovereign debt in April 2011; and the European financial crisis
- Waning square on three dates from August 3, 2015 to May 26, 2016—Fed raises interest rates on December 16, 2015, the first hike since June 29, 2006

The next Jupiter/Saturn conjunction is on December 21, 2020 in the sign of Aquarius. This conjunction marks a paradigm shift in economic focus vs. that of the last 170 years, which I'll go into more deeply in Chapter 12.

Saturn/Uranus

This 45-year cycle is particularly interesting because the Dow Jones Industrial Average was first published near the start of the 1896 Saturn/Uranus cycle, so has shown to be responsive to the cycle's major aspects. Saturn is a planet of staying the course and playing by the rules. Uranus, the first planet beyond Saturn in space, is also the first that cannot be seen by the naked eye. It is associated with surprises and the unexpected. Thus, the Saturn/Uranus cycle is about upsetting the status quo.

The current Saturn/Uranus cycle began in February 1988 and ends in June 2032. Although the data set is extremely limited since the DJIA was first published, how the Dow has behaved at critical times in this planetary cycle is consistent:

- The DJIA makes a significant low within a few months of the Saturn/Uranus conjunction
- The DJIA moves in generally harmless fashion at the waxing square (first 90-degree aspect)
- The DJIA marks an all-time high near the Saturn/Uranus opposition. In the three examples to date, the market has corrected 36 percent to 54 percent, but then surpasses that all-time high in 5-6 years
- The DJIA makes both a significant high and then a significant low near the waning square (second 90-degree aspect)

Between the opposition and waning square is a waning trine (the second 120-degree aspect of the cycle), which financial astrologer Bill Meridian finds to be consistently the time of a peak in the business cycle.

Table 5.3 Saturn/Uranus Synodic Cycle Comparison and DJIA

	Conjunction	Waxing Square	Opposition	Waning Square
Cycle I 1897-1942	Low 5 months before	Sideways	All-time high in middle; 47% correction; 5 years to surpass	Cycle high 6 mo. before; Cycle low 9 mo. after; Down 89%
Cycle II 1942-1988	Low 5 days before	Uptrend	All-time high in middle; 36% correction; 6 years to surpass	Cycle high 32 mo. before; Cycle low 9 mo. before; Down 47%; Double tops during
Cycle III 1988-2032	Low 4 months before	Dot-com high, then sideways to lower	All-time high 1 year before; 54% correction; 6 years to surpass	TBD. Waning square February-December 2021

ASTRO TRADING CHECKLIST

Commodity traders always have taken cues from work applied first to the stock market, as any technical trader who relied on the classic *Technical Analysis of Stock Trends* by Edwards and Magee, first published in 1948, can attest. Thus, I can only assume that if it is a good idea for trading stocks that it might also be a good idea for trading commodities. To make a definitive case to that effect requires far more study by me, you, and others who would like to understand what makes the commodity markets move. While we continue together down this path, I'd like to make you aware of what other financial astrologers (recognized throughout this book) have found insightful and valuable. Please join me in using the following collection of insights as a jumping-off point for further investigation in our favorite markets:

HIGHS

1. New Moon (grain markets)
2. Mercury turns retrograde (grain markets)
3. Transiting Jupiter conjunct natal Sun in first-trade chart
4. Pluto retrograde (stock market)
5. Transiting North Node conjunct commodity market's ruling planet

LOWS

1. Full Moon (grain markets)
2. Mercury turns direct (grain markets)
3. Transiting Uranus "station," i.e., moving from direct to retrograde motion, in either direction, for a short-term trend change
4. Transiting North Node changes signs (cotton)

BULLISH

1. Eclipses conjunct/opposite the natal Sun, Venus, Jupiter, Uranus, Neptune
2. Transiting North Node conjunct Sun
3. Transiting Moon conjunct, opposite, or trine transiting Sun
4. 30 days before transiting Mars is conjunct transiting Jupiter
5. Transiting Mars conjunct transiting Mercury
6. Transiting Jupiter conjunct or trine natal Mars or natal Uranus
7. Transiting Jupiter conjunct MC of natal NYSE (1792) or natal USA
8. Transiting Jupiter trine or sextile transiting Saturn or transiting Uranus
9. Transiting Jupiter, Uranus, Sun, or Venus in trine or sextile to any natal planet in a first-trade chart

10. Ruling planet of a commodity turns direct in motion

BEARISH
1. Eclipses conjunct/opposite the natal Saturn, Pluto
2. Transiting Moon square transiting Sun
3. Transiting Mars conjunct transiting Saturn
4. Transiting Mars square transiting Neptune
5. Transiting Mars opposite transiting Jupiter
6. Transiting Saturn, Uranus, or Jupiter square or opposite one another
7. Transiting Saturn conjunct natal MC of NYSE (1792)
8. Transiting Saturn conjunct natal Moon of USA
9. Transiting Saturn conjunct transiting North Node
10. Transiting Saturn, Neptune, or Pluto square, conjunct, opposite any natal planet in a first-trade chart
11. Jupiter retrograde (DJIA)
12. Ruling planet of a commodity turns retrograde

CHANGE OF TREND
1. Eclipses to a company's natal Sun
2. Day of the eclipse or when a transiting planet hits the degree of the eclipse
3. Transiting Sun conjunct a company's natal North Node
4. New moon and full moon (short-term trend reversal)
5. Transiting Moon changes signs during market hours, and is within 24 hours of any other planetary sign change (silver market)
6. Transiting Venus or Mars "station," i.e., moving from direct to retrograde motion, either direction, for a short-term trend change
7. Transiting Mars enters a commodity's ruling sign
8. Any planetary change of sign, especially if several close together

VOLATILITY
1. Any eclipse brings unpredictability to the market
2. Transiting Moon sextile transiting Sun

SHORT-TERM TRADING (TRIGGERS)
1. Transiting Moon conjunct natal Sun, Jupiter, Saturn, Mars
2. Transiting Mars in aspect to company's natal planets

CHAPTER 6
Agriculture

Soybean Futures

October 5, 1936, 10:15 am, Chicago

Libra Sun

Soybean futures joined the grain complex of corn, wheat, and oat futures at the Chicago Board of Trade on October 5, 1936, opening at 10:15 am.[24] It had been nearly 71 years since the three mainstays of CBOT grain markets had been trading as futures contracts. The addition of soybeans to the rulebook recognized its status as an up-and-coming cash crop in the United States, having surpassed the world leaders in production—Japan and Korea—just two years earlier.

The world was changing as it came out of the Great Depression, and soybeans were becoming useful for more than soy sauce and edamame. Part of that was because technology played a role in soybean production expansion as tractors began to replace horses for field work, which led to decreasing demand for oat production. Also, seed advancements that improved yield showed soybeans to be more drought-tolerant than corn during the Dust Bowl of the early 1930s, which also attracted acres to soybeans.

On the research front, soybean industry advocates and the U.S. government were identifying new industrial uses for soybean oil as well as recommending soybean meal as a suitable protein ration for livestock. To facilitate industrial

---

24   Chicago Board of Trade records: Series III – Secretary's Records, Special Collections and University Archives, University of Illinois at Chicago, Monthly Letter to Members, August 12, 1936 and Letter to Members, September 17, 1936.

demand, ADM built the first continuous solvent extraction unit in the United States, which opened in Chicago in 1934. However, futures contracts for the soybean products did not appear until the mid-1950s.

SOYBEANS 101

Soybeans are a crop utilized by the world for their high protein level. They are processed into two products —soybean meal and soybean oil. Soybean meal is widely used in livestock rations to boost protein and increase weight gain, particularly for hogs and chickens. And, when you buy a bottle of vegetable oil or almost any prepared salad dressing at the grocery store, you're buying soybean oil.

Beans are grown mainly in the United States, Brazil, Argentina, and China (human consumption) in the same regions and climates that can grow corn. As a result, producers can choose which crop to grow. Because soybeans are legumes that produce nitrogen they release to the ground, many U.S. producers rotate the two crops annually to provide nitrogen-hungry corn extra support.

For soybean futures traders, the U.S. crop was dominant throughout the 1970s and 1980s. Then, South American production climbed steadily because of expanding meat demand and adoption of the American style of meat production that utilizes high-protein feeds for rapid weight gains. Now, in the mid-2010s, each continent's crop is nearly identical in size, providing a year-round supply of beans and year-round attention on plantings and weather.

In the futures markets, the most-traded contracts are January, March, May, July, August, and November. The November contract is considered the first one in the "new-crop" year in the United States and trades on the fundamental supply/demand factors for the crop planted in that year's spring. In turn, that makes the August contract the last of the "old-crop" year when growing conditions are highly important to the growing crop's production output. South America's main harvest month is March each year, with Brazil's harvest stretching from late January to April while Argentina's harvest runs from March to May most years.

Interestingly, traders often like to trade the July/November spread in soybeans to capture the difference in price resulting from different market fundamentals between the old- and new-crop years because U.S. summer heat (and prices) often spike in July and have the potential to create a big differential between the old- and new-crop prices.

FIRST-TRADE HOROSCOPE

The soybean futures first-trade horoscope chart has three striking oppositions among six planets. Striking because each pair of opposing planets is in exactly the same degree, just six zodiac signs apart. Usually, oppositions are not exact to the degree, and can be as much as 6-8 degrees apart and still qualify. Yet, this single chart has three exact oppositions, noted as 1, 2, and 3 in Figure 6.1.

Figure 6.1 Soybean Futures First-Trade Horoscope

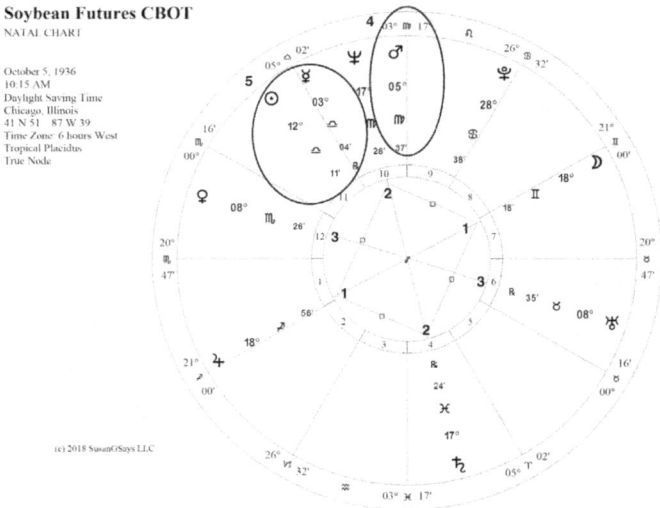

Each of these oppositions is strong because of their exactness, so these six points are prime candidates to watch as transiting planets hit any of these three oppositions. Remember, an opposition is like a tug-of-war between two planets. The goal is to find balance and compromise in the middle.

You've no doubt spotted that four of the six planets form a big square in the horoscope chart as well, which means that all four planets—Moon, Jupiter, Saturn, and Neptune—are activated whenever a transiting planet goes by one of them. This "grand square" is in the mutable signs, so gives the soybean market its ability to slip and slide easily. The Moon/Jupiter opposition (1), with Jupiter in its ruling sign of Sagittarius, is what can get the market overly emotional as news headlines and stories fly about. The Saturn/Neptune opposition (2) can help keep a lid on rumors getting out of hand.

The third opposition (3), between Venus and Uranus, also makes a formation with another planet—Mars. In this triangle (4), action-taker Mars is the mediator between Venus in Scorpio that wants to hide away and Uranus in Taurus that wants to initiate change based on solid ideas. Mars in Virgo blends the two into a compromise that takes a look at all the options and takes action only if it will be seen as staking out a leadership position for the soybean market. This is particularly the case because Mars is conjunct the chart's midheaven (MC), at 03 Virgo, and the "most elevated" planet in the chart, which gives it importance and prominence.

Finally, both the Sun and Mercury are in Libra (5). The Sun is always the most important planet in a horoscope chart, and Mercury rules trading. To have both in Libra indicates that fair-and-square is the way this market likes to roll.

HOROSCOPE PRICE CONVERSION

The soybean first-trade horoscope was the example used in Chapter 5 to show how to convert a market's natal horoscope chart into prices that can be used to gauge potential support and resistance. Remember to include each planet in the chart as well as the four "angles"—ascendant, descendant, MC and IC—in your conversion.

It's interesting to see that soybean prices seem to be attracted to the conversion levels from Venus and Saturn (Figure 6.2). The Venus price of 1298 was just 8 cents above the 1973 high of $12.90; another Venus level of 1658 was 5 cents shy of the July 2008 high at $16.63. The Saturn price of 1067 stopped the bull market in 2004 that peaked at $10.63; the all-time high in 2012 of $17.94 was just 7 cents beyond the Saturn level. Interestingly, Neptune prices marked the bottom and top of a bull run from October 1994-May 1997—to the penny!

Trading In Sync With Commodities

Table 6.1 Soybean Futures Price Conversion

Market	Soybean Futures									
1st Trade	October 5, 1936, 10:15 am, Chicago									
Source	CBOT Monthly Letter to Members									
Price unit	Cents per bushel									
Planet	Position	Conversion	360	720	1080	1440	1800	2160	2520	2880
Uranus	08 Taurus	38	398	758	1118	1478	1838	2198	2558	2918
Desc	20 Taurus	50	410	770	1130	1490	1850	2210	2570	2930
Moon	18 Gemini	78	438	798	1158	1518	1878	2238	2598	2958
Pluto	28 Cancer	118	478	838	1198	1558	1918	2278	2638	2998
MC	03 Virgo	153	513	873	1233	1593	1953	2313	2673	3033
Mars	05 Virgo	155	515	875	1235	1595	1955	2315	2675	3035
Neptune	17 Virgo	167	527	887	1247	.1607	1967	2327	2687	3047
Mercury rx	03 Libra	183	543	903	1263	1623	1983	2343	2703	3063
Sun	12 Libra	192	552	912	1272	1632	1992	2352	2712	3072
Venus	08 Scorpio	218	578	938	1298	1658	2018	2378	2738	3098
Asc	20 Scorpio	230	590	950	1310	1670	2030	2390	2750	3110
Jupiter	18 Sag	258	618	978	1338	1698	2058	2418	2778	3138
IC	03 Pisces	333	693	1053	1413	1773	2133	2493	2853	3213
Saturn rx	17 Pisces	347	707	1067	1427	1787	2147	2507	2867	3227

Figure 6.2 Soybeans Attracted to Venus and Saturn Prices

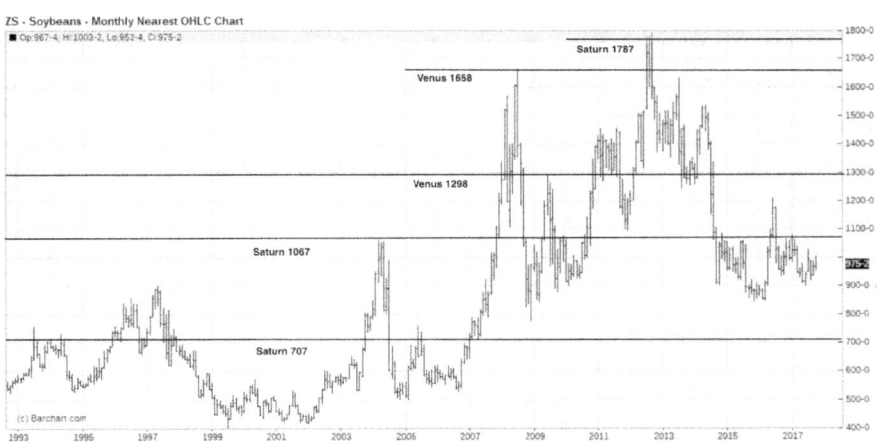

Source: Barchart.com

IMPORTANT SOYBEAN HIGHS

When you're looking at the important high prices in the soybean futures market, you have to start with the granddaddy of them all--$12.90 per bu., set on June 5, 1973—a price that stood as the all-time high for nearly 35 years.

83

On the heels of the 1972 Russian wheat sale that kicked off a new era of international interest and price volatility in the once-sleepy grain markets, the soybean market took the spotlight in 1973 as world protein demands outstripped supplies. Not only had the U.S. soybean crop been small, but the kicker was a warm-water El Nino that destroyed the anchovy crop harvested off the coast of Peru. Soybean futures hit $12.90 in early June, from a starting point near $3.50 the previous fall. Two weeks later, the U.S. government instituted an embargo on soybean exports. Fortunes were made on the floor of the Chicago Board of Trade during the run-up, and it put commodity trading on the financial map.

One of the biggest winners in this bullish soybean market was Gene Cashman, a former Chicago policeman who started with a $5,000 stake and was rumored to have made $100 million in the 1973 bean market.[25] Whatever the sum, it was enough money for Cashman to get into the Thoroughbred racing business. The next year, Cashman bought Elocutionist, who went on to win the Preakness Stakes in 1976.

The current all-time high in soybean futures is $17.94 ¾, set on September 4, 2012 because of poor U.S. crop prospects that year and unrelenting demand from China.

Astrologically, the 2012 high shows important planets being activated in the soybean first-trade chart from 1936. Figure 6.3 shows a "bi-wheel" of the first-trade chart as the inner wheel and the all-time high chart (cast for the traditional opening bell) as the outer wheel. This makes it easy to see the connections between the two charts.

1. Jupiter conjunct Moon
2. Mercury and Sun conjunct Mars; Mercury conjunct MC
3. Mars conjunct Venus

---

25   Leo Melamed with Bob Tamarkin, <u>Leo Melamed—Escape to the Futures</u> (New York: John Wiley & Sons, Inc., 1996) 441.

Trading In Sync With Commodities

Figure 6.3 All-Time Soybean High Triggers First-Trade Moon, Mars, Venus

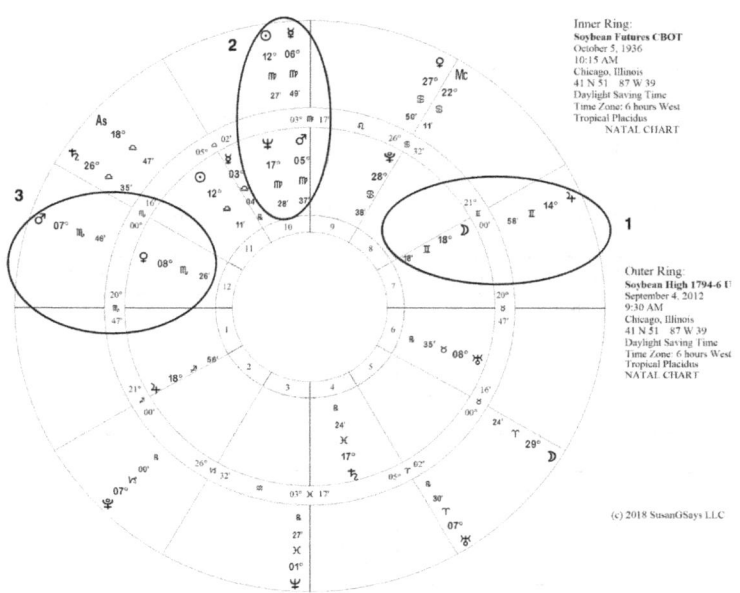

First, Jupiter conjunct the Moon indicated excessive emotion in the market, which is typically the case when a market peaks. Note that transiting Jupiter was opposite natal Jupiter, also a sign of peak expression.

Second, both the Sun and Mercury were conjunct the market's natal Mars at the top of the chart. These two fast-moving planets were triggers to the market's prominence, bringing attention to the market.

Finally, Mars was conjunct the market's natal Venus (money) and opposite natal Uranus (surprise). In any type of astrological application, Mars is seen as a primary trigger for making something happen—and particularly so when conjunct or opposite Uranus, as it was on this day in 2012.

Important to realize in this planetary set-up is that several different-length cycles were in play and converged simultaneously. Jupiter takes 12 years to go around the horoscope wheel, so the Jupiter/Moon conjunction present at the all-time high in soybeans is something that happens just once every 12 years. Mars has a two-year cycle, so is conjunct the soybean market's natal Venus only once every two years. However, both the Sun and Mercury will hit the market's natal Mars once a year, although not necessarily this close by sign and degree.

In Table 6.2, I have highlighted only the transiting aspects to the Sun and Moon in the soybean first-trade chart as they are the most important when looking for a high in soybeans. Be assured, though, that other planets and angles likely were being activated simultaneously, even though they are not mentioned here.

Table 6.2   Important Soybean Highs and Astrological Connections

Date	Price* and Planet	First-trade Sun	First-trade Moon
June 5, 1973	1290-0, Venus		Sun conjunct
Oct. 4, 1974	956-0, Ascendant	Venus, Pluto, Sun, Mars conjunct	
Apr. 22, 1977	1076-4	Pluto conjunct	Moon conjunct
Nov. 20, 1980	956-0, Ascendant		
Sept. 13, 1983	968-4, Jupiter		
June 23, 1988	1099-4	Moon conjunct	Venus, Mercury conjunct
July 17, 1993	755-0, Uranus	Jupiter conjunct	
Apr. 25, 1996	839-0, Pluto		Venus conjunct
July 12, 1996	856-0		Mars, Moon, Venus conjunct
May 7, 1997	903-4, Mercury		
Mar. 22, 2004	1062-0		
July 7, 2008	1663-0, Venus/Ascendant		
June 11, 2009	1291-2		Sun conjunct
Aug. 31, 2011	1456-0	Moon conjunct	
Sept. 4, 2012	1794-6		Jupiter conjunct
June 10, 2016	1208-4		Sun, Venus conjunct

* Prices are denoted in cents and eighths of a cent per bushel, the way you'd see the quote on a quote screen. Back when the grain markets began and prices were lower, prices had minimum ticks of one-eighth cent; now the grains trade in quarter-cent ticks, or two-eighths of a cent.

IMPORTANT SOYBEAN LOWS

Conjunctions between transiting planets and the first-trade horoscope for soybeans are clues to look for market lows, just as they are for pegging market highs. However, the planets involved are a bit different.

The first-trade Moon is not nearly as prominent at the time of price lows as it is during peaks, which are fueled by emotions. At lows, you're more likely to find complete disinterest and no emotional connection save disgust. However, the Sun remains important (both transiting and natal) and is involved in about 75% of the 21 lows I looked at from 1973-2017. Venus and Mercury also are more prominent in the astrological charts of the lows than of the highs.

In Figure 6.4, Venus and the Sun played important roles, with Mercury a two-way star. This was the October 1, 2014 low at $9.05 in the November 2014 contract that marked the bottom of a summer-long bear market that had started above $15 just five months earlier. (For those of you keeping score at home, a $6 move in beans equals $30,000 for a single contract.)

Mercury's role was that of both its price conversion level of 903 (just 2 cents away) and that transiting Venus was conjunct the first-trade chart's natal Mercury. Also interesting to note are two "trine" aspects of 120 degrees, which are generally supportive and help grease the skids in the underlying chart.

Figure 6.4 First-Trade Sun, Mercury, Mars Triggered at 2014 Soybean Low

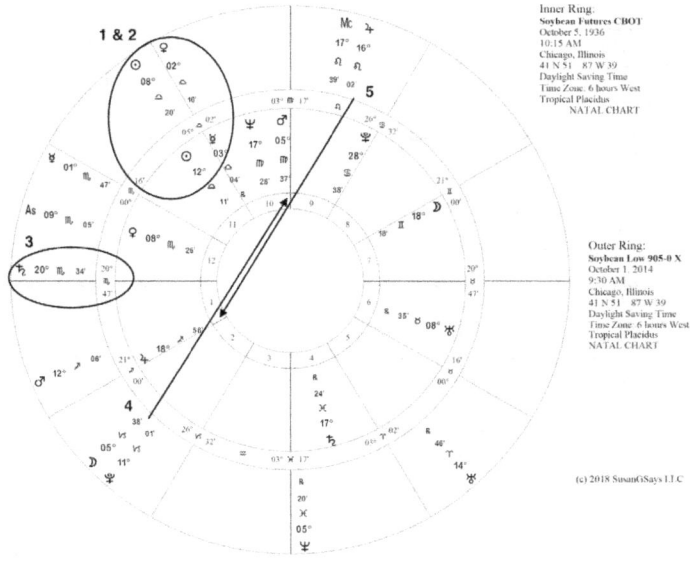

1. Transiting Venus conjunct first-trade Mercury
2. Transiting Sun conjunct first-trade Sun
3. Transiting Saturn conjunct first-trade ascendant
4. Transiting Moon trine first-trade Mars, within one arc minute of exact
5. Transiting Jupiter trine first-trade Jupiter

In Table 6.3, I have noted only the transits to the soybean first-trade Sun, Mercury and Venus as they appeared the most often over the years. If no transits are shown in the table for a particular low, it is because they were to planets other than these three.

Table 6.3   Important Soybean Lows and Astrological Connections

Date	Price* and Planet	First-trade Sun	First-trade Mercury	First-trade Venus
Dec. 15, 1975	439-4, Moon	Sun conjunct		Venus, Uranus conjunct
Aug. 16, 1977	497-0	Pluto conjunct		Uranus conjunct
Apr. 2, 1980	569-4, Venus	Sun opposite		Moon conjunct
Oct. 4, 1982	518-0, Mars	Sun conjunct	Venus, Mercury conjunct	
Sept. 2, 1986	467-2, Pluto			
Aug. 19, 1991	514-0, Mars/MC			
Oct. 10, 1994	531-0, Neptune	Sun conjunct		Mercury conjunct
Nov. 1, 1996	659-6		Venus, Saturn opposite	Sun, Mercury conjunct
July 9, 1999	401-4, Uranus			
April 2001 (4 days)	421-4		Venus opposite	
Jan. 2, 2002	415-4, Descendant			
Aug. 7, 2003	515-4, Mars			
Feb. 4 and 7, 2005	498-4, MC			
Nov. 8, 2005	544-2			Jupiter conjunct
Sept. 12, 2006	526-4, Neptune		Mars, Mercury conjunct	
Dec. 5, 2008	776-2, Descendant			
Oct. 5, 2009	878-6, Mars	Sun conjunct		
Dec. 12, 2011	1095-0			
Apr. 5, 2013	1355-4	Sun, Venus, Mars, Uranus opposite		Saturn conjunct
Oct. 1, 2014	905-0	Sun conjunct	Venus conjunct	

* Prices are denoted in cents and eighths of a cent per bushel, the way you'd see the quote on a quote screen. Back when the grain markets began and prices were lower, prices had minimum ticks of one-eighth cent; now the grains trade in quarter-cent ticks, or two-eighths of a cent.

TRANSITS TO WATCH IN SOYBEANS

The recurring themes at both extreme highs and lows in the soybean market say to me that the horoscope chart for when soybean futures first started trading in 1936 is sensitive to planetary transits—just like people!

HIGHS

Of the 16 extreme highs I examined from 1973 to 2017, a transiting planet was conjunct the first-trade Moon at 18 Gemini (similar degree in the same sign) half the time. Even more significant—at 88% of the time—was that the Moon itself (either transiting or natal) was conjunct another planet. The same was true for the natal or transiting Sun—conjunct another planet 88% of the time.

LOWS

At extreme lows in the soybean market, the Sun is more important than the Moon. In the 20 lows I examined from 1973 to 2017, the transiting or natal Sun was conjunct another planet in 16 instances, or 75%. The transiting or natal Moon was activated in these 20 charts just 40% of the time.

In contrast to the extreme high price horoscopes, both Venus and Mercury played an important role in identifying low prices. For each, the transiting or first-trade planet was conjunct another planet in 65% of the extreme lows. Also, planetary oppositions were more prevalent in the extreme low charts.

UPCOMING TRANSITS IN SOYBEANS

Keeping in mind the high-percentage involvement of the transiting and first-trade Sun and Moon connecting with the first-trade horoscope chart for soybean futures, I've found 12 dates from 2018 to 2020 that may be interesting to watch for future highs in the bean market.

Interestingly, a significant high in soybeans has never occurred in December, January, or February since 1973, so I ignored any of those potential dates. June had the most instances, at four, with July right behind with three. September had two highs and the other six months, one apiece.

In the 20 horoscope charts of important soybean price lows I examined from

1973-2016, the Sun, Mercury, and Venus were most prominent, either on the first-trade chart or in transit. As with the price highs, the conjunction (aligned with a first-trade planet by degree and sign) was dominant, but oppositions and trines were sometimes triggered as well.

So, in peering forward in time for similar-looking charts, I focused on finding clusters of times when the transiting Sun, Mercury, or Venus were conjunct or opposite the natal planets of the soybeans' first-trade chart. This led me to 16 dates through year-end 2020 to watch for potential lows in the soybean market. Note that I did include one potential low in March 2020, even though the previous lows I examined never occurred in March, May, or June.

I've set these dates up in a table where you (and I) can follow along and make notes about prices and market action around these dates. The dates in boldface are ones with particularly strong astrological transits vs. the soybean first-trade horoscope.

Table 6.4   2018 Potential Soybean Futures Highs or Lows

Date	High or Low	Actual Price (nearby contract)	Notes
May 9	High		
May 11	Low		
June 13	High		
July 25	Low		
August 31	High		
September 24	Low		
October 5	High		
October 15	Low		
December 10	Low		

Trading In Sync With Commodities

Table 6.5   2019 Potential Soybean Futures Highs or Lows

Date	High or Low	Actual Price (nearby contract)	Notes
February 26	Low		
April 2	Low		
April 29	High		
June 3	High		
August 30	High		
September 9	Low		
October 3	High		

Table 6.6   2020 Potential Soybean Futures Highs or Lows

Date	High or Low	Actual Price (nearby contract)	Notes
March 9	Low		
April 24	High		
April 28	Low		
May 22	Low		
June 8	High		
August 20	Low		
August 26	High		
September 8	Low		
October 7	High		
October 20	Low		
October 29	High		
November 27	Low		
December 9	Low		

OTHER CONFIRMED FIRST-TRADE DATA IN AG MARKETS

To get you started on your own research and exploration, feel free to use the following data on first-trade dates and times for other agricultural futures and options contracts. I'll be researching, writing, and publishing similar information about astrological connections with these markets in the future, so stay tuned!

I'm a stickler about getting correct first-trade data for commodity markets because it makes all the difference in seeing the transiting charts sync up at highs and lows. I'm confident that the data below is accurate, and have footnoted my sources. And, I'm constantly on the hunt to add more markets to the list. I welcome your suggestions and help at TeamCommodityTimes@yahoo.com.

Corn, wheat, oats futures	October 14, 1865, 11 a.m., Chicago[26]
Soybean options	October 31, 1984, 10:30 a.m., Chicago[27]
Soybean meal futures	August 29, 1951, 9:15 a.m., Chicago[28]
Soybean oil futures	July 17, 1950, 9:15 a.m., Chicago[29]

---

26   Chicago Board of Trade records: Series I – Organizational Records, Special Collections and University Archives, University of Illinois at Chicago, Rules, Regulations and By-Laws of the Board of Trade, Chicago, Ill., Adopted October 13th, 1865. pp. 9, 14, 15.

27   Chicago Board of Trade records: Series III – Secretary's Records, Special Collections and University Archives, University of Illinois at Chicago, Monthly Letter to Members, November 1, 1984, p. 4.

28   Chicago Board of Trade records: Series III – Secretary's Records, Special Collections and University Archives, University of Illinois at Chicago, Monthly Letter to Members, October 16, 1951, p. 4.

29   Chicago Board of Trade records: Series III – Secretary's Records, Special Collections and University Archives, University of Illinois at Chicago, Monthly Letter to Members, July 15, 1950, p. 7.

CHAPTER 7
Currencies

Euro FX Futures
May 19, 1998, 2:30 p.m., Chicago
Taurus Sun

Futures trading on the euro—the currency of the eurozone—began on May 19, 1998 for trade date May 20 on the Globex electronic trading system at the Chicago Mercantile Exchange.[30] At that time, the contract name was European Currency Unit (ECU) because the euro did not yet exist. It was an update to a dormant ECU futures contract the CME had listed in 1986, and was intended to convert its name to the Euro FX contract upon the euro's introduction on January 1, 1999. The euro replaced the ECU, which had been tracking a basket of European currencies since 1979, but was not an official currency.

The Euro FX futures contract listed by the CME Group evolved—as did the currency itself—out of the ECU futures contract launched with great fanfare (and competition) in January 1986, seven years after the ECU was first introduced as a currency rate and financial pricing mechanism among 10 member countries of the European Community. When the ECU converted to the euro at parity on January 1, 1999, the ECU futures contract listed the previous year changed its name to Euro FX.

The futures contract, which trades on the March, June, September, December quarterly cycle, typically is called "Euro FX" to distinguish it from the Eurodollar futures contract (launched in 1981) that is often referred to as simply the

---

30 "Special Executive Report S-3257." Chicago Mercantile Exchange. 15 May 15 1998, p. 2.

"Euro" contract. The Eurodollar contract is an interest rate contract that tracks the rate on U.S. dollars held in European banks.

EURO FX 101

Since 2001, the euro has been second only to the U.S dollar in trading volume as well as an international reserve currency, according to statistics from the Bank for International Settlements. In April 2016, when the most recent BIS survey was conducted, the euro traded an average of $1.6 trillion daily (on one side of 31 percent of all trades), compared with the U.S. dollar at $4.4 trillion (on one side of 88 percent of all trades).[31] The euro is the official currency of the eurozone, comprising 19 of the European Union's 28 countries.

As they say at the ballpark, get your pencils and scorecards ready for a brief genealogy of how European economic cooperation has evolved, and what a dizzying number of similar-sounding acronyms represent.

POST WW II PEACE

The post World War II goal of maintaining peace in Europe started with a 1951 treaty among the coal and steel industries in six European countries—Germany, France, Italy, the Netherlands, Belgium, and Luxembourg. The treaty put the industries in these countries under common management so that no one country could make weapons of war to be used against its neighbors.[32] These same six countries expanded their cooperation to other economic sectors to create the **European Economic Community (EEC)** with the Treaty of Rome in 1957 and the EEC's formal beginning on January 1, 1958; it formalized a Common Agricultural Policy in 1962. In 1968, customs duties among EEC members were removed, and the EEC also adopted a single custom duty on imports from all other countries, thus creating a single trading group.

The 1944 Bretton Woods agreement that tied currency values of the 44 WWII Allied nations to the price of gold and the U.S. dollar faltered in 1971 when

---

31 "BIS Triennial Central Bank Survey 2016." Bank for International Settlements. p. 13.

32 "A Peaceful Europe—the beginnings of cooperation." European Union. 11 July 2017.
<https://europa.eu/european-union/about-eu/history/1945-1959_en>

the United States went off the gold standard. The EEC subsequently created the **Exchange Rate Mechanism (ERM)** in 1972 that established narrow bands of fluctuations among member country currencies. A year later, in the EEC's first expansion, Denmark, Ireland, and the United Kingdom joined the coalition.

In 1979, the **European Currency Unit (ECU)** was adopted as part of the **European Monetary System (EMS)** in an attempt to stabilize exchange rate fluctuations. The ECU facilitated international pricing for financial instruments, but it was not a currency with coins or notes for cash transactions.[33]

MAASTRICHT TREATY STARTS EURO COUNTDOWN

The Maastricht Treaty, signed in February 1992 and effective November 1, 1993, officially renamed the European Community as the **European Union (EU)** and extended its joint efforts beyond commerce **(Economic and Monetary Union, or EMU)** into politics. The treaty provided a three-stage process to introducing the euro as a single currency for the European Union, starting in 1990 with easing the flow of capital, convergence of economic policies in 1994, and culminating with introduction of the euro and **European Central Bank (ECB)** on January 1, 1999.[34]

The euro replaced domestic currencies in 11 countries: Austria, Belgium, Finland, France, Germany, Ireland, Italy, Luxembourg, the Netherlands, Portugal, and Spain; Greece adopted the euro in 2001. Euro notes and coins became the legal currency in these 12 EU nations (the **eurozone**) on January 1, 2002, and by 2017 had expanded to 19 of 28 EU member countries. Notably, EU members Great Britain, Denmark, and Sweden did not convert their currencies to the euro. Also, the euro has been adopted by nearly a dozen EU-related microstates and territories as well as 22 countries outside the EU that peg their currency to the euro.[35]

---

33 "Glossary: European currency unit (ECU)." Eurostat. 11 July 2017. <http://ec.europa.eu/eurostat/statistics-explained/index.php/Glossary:European_currency_unit_(ECU)>

34 "Treaty of Maastricht on European Union." European Union. 11 July 2017. <http://eur-lex.europa.eu/legal-content/EN/TXT/?uri=URISERV:xy0026>

35 "Euro." Wikipedia. 11 July 2017. <https://en.wikipedia.org/wiki/Euro#Direct_usage>

Susan Abbott Gidel

FIRST-TRADE HOROSCOPE

The first-trade horoscope chart for the Euro FX futures contract is based on the Globex open for trade date May 20, 1998, which occurred at 2:30 pm on May 19, 1998 in Chicago (Figure 7.1). I settled on this date and time because: (1) the CME Special Executive Report said trading would start on May 19 with no special listing hours, i.e., the previous day's Globex session marked the start of trade-date trading; and (2) volume and open interest on May 20 were identical, at 2 contracts, which means two contracts were traded (created) and both remained open contracts at the May 20 trade date's close, i.e., there was no open interest for trade date May 19. (On May 21, there was volume of 1 and open interest of 1, which means one contract traded and it was to close a previous position.)

The Sun is in Taurus, the ruling sign of currencies, because it is ruled by the money planet, Venus. The Sun in Taurus, an Earth sign, indicates stability, which is always a good thing for a currency in my book. The Sun is conjunct Mars in Taurus (A), a sign in which Mars struggles to be as aggressive as it would like. However, the two together indicate power to move forward and steady-as-she-goes initiative.

The Moon in the first-trade Euro FX futures chart is in Pisces (B). Although the Moon likes watery Pisces, the sign brings the potential for confusion and deception among the public. The Moon is at a 90-degree angle to Pluto in Sagittarius, so has tension with international powers and is especially sensitive to them.

Virgo is the sign of the ascendant on the Euro FX first-trade chart (C), indicating a contract that is seen as data-driven and accountable. The rising sign is ruled by Mercury, which rules trading and data. Mercury also rules the sign on the chart's midheaven, Gemini (the twins), also fitting because the contract began life named ECU and later changed its name to Euro FX. The chart ruler, Mercury, is in the sign of Taurus in the 8th house, emphasizing the money aspect to the chart because Taurus rules currencies and the 8th house is the house of banking and foreign debts.

A final aspect worth noting on the Euro FX first-trade chart is that Jupiter is conjunct the descendant by less than 1 degree (D). Jupiter rules the sign it is in, Pisces, so is very strong and able to bring expansion to the contract. Indeed, Euro FX is among the top-traded currency contracts in the world.

Trading In Sync With Commodities

Figure 7.1 Euro FX First-Trade Horoscope Chart

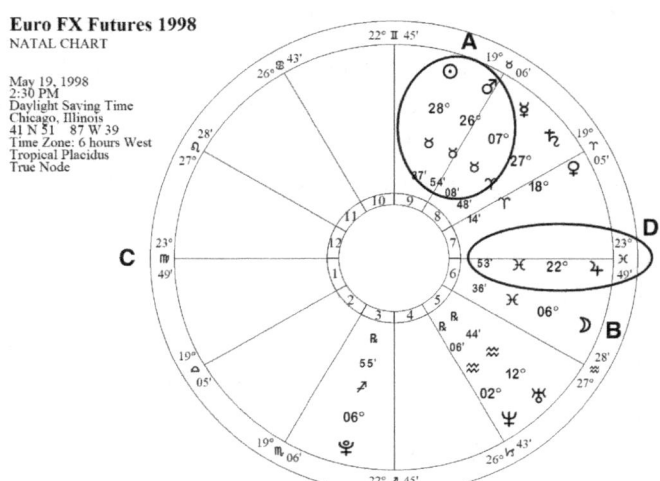

OTHER FIRST-TRADE POSSIBILITIES

You may be tempted (as I was) to consider other significant dates and times for the Euro FX futures first-trade horoscope chart. Here's why I didn't use any of the following:

1. Original launch of ECU futures at CME—January 15, 1986, 7:20 am, Chicago

The CME was about a week later than the FINEX division at the New York Cotton Exchange in listing futures on the ECU. In the end, neither contract survived, and it is clear that the CME's contract was revived from dormancy in 1998.

2. ECU futures listed on May 20, 1998 at 7:20 am, Chicago

This trade date shows initial volume in the contract that ultimately became the Euro FX futures contract traded today. The time is the start to Regular Trading Hours (RTH) at the CME, when open-outcry pit trading began. Based on the CME Special Executive Report and volume/open interest for May 20 noted earlier, I believe it is clear that trading opened during Globex hours on May 19, 1998.

97

Susan Abbott Gidel

3. Euro FX futures concurrent with official euro launch on January 4, 1999, 4:00 am, Frankfurt, Germany (9:00 pm on January 3 in Chicago)

Although the euro became the eurozone's official currency on Friday, January 1, 1999, the first business day to trade the currency was Monday, January 4. According to astrological researcher Nicholas Campion in *The Book of World Horscopes*, what I assume to be the official launch of cash trading in the euro began with a televised ceremony in Frankfurt at 4:00 am on January 4. The CME certainly could have coordinated the opening of a new Euro FX contract with that ceremony given that it had been trading currencies on Globex since 1992, but the contract was not new. It was the same contract that was listed in May 1998, just with a different name because of successful fruition of the European Monetary Union, with all open interest converting 1:1 to euro from ECU. So, business as usual for the ECU/Euro FX contract at the CME is the way I figure it, likely with a 6:00 pm Sunday opening that would have coordinated with the smattering of euro trades Campion reports were made in Australia and Tokyo before the Frankfurt kickoff.

THE IMPORTANCE OF VENUS

Interestingly, money planet—and ruler of currency markets—Venus is highlighted in the Euro FX futures first-trade chart by its connection to the natal horoscopes of both the European Union in 1993 and the euro's creation on January 1, 1999 (Figure 7.2). These connections confirm in my mind that the May 19, 1998 chart is the correct one to use for Euro FX futures.

When the European Union was formed (November 1, 1993 at 12:00 am in Brussels, Belgium), Venus was at 19 degrees of Libra. Natal Venus for the Euro FX futures contract is opposite that position, at 18 degrees Aries (A). Plus, note that action-taker Mars also was at 18 Libra (same as the EU natal chart) on January 1, 1999, when the euro came into existence. So, Mars—as it often does by transit—ignited the EU's natal Venus to create the currency. Later, both those points were activated by Venus in the first-trade chart of the Euro FX futures contract.

Thus, as we'll see later, this axis of 18-19 Libra/Aries is important to watch for planetary transits because it activates all three charts at once—the European

Union, the euro, and Euro FX futures trading. Note also on this tri-wheel chart that transiting Saturn at 27 Aries was opposite the EU's natal Jupiter at 27 Libra (B), adding weight to this 10-degree span of Aries/Libra when watching for news and fundamentals that affect the EU and the euro currency.

IMPORTANCE OF THE SUN AND MARS

From a trading perspective, another area to watch closely is 24-28 Taurus/Scorpio, which highlights an important connection in the natal chart for the European Union. In the EU formation chart, the Moon is at 24 Taurus, opposite three planets—Mercury at 19 Scorpio and Mars/Pluto at 24 Scorpio. This zodiacal opposition in the EU natal chart indicates that the public sentiment (Moon in the 10th) is in a constant balancing act (or tug-of-war if you prefer) with behind-the-scenes power and proclamations (Mercury, Mars, Pluto in the 4th).

The natal Sun and Mars in the Euro FX futures first-trade horoscope chart are at 26-28 Taurus, conjunct the EU's natal Moon and opposite the EU's natal Scorpio "stellium" of Mercury, Mars and Pluto (C).

Figure 7.2 Euro FX Futures Connects with EU and euro Horoscopes

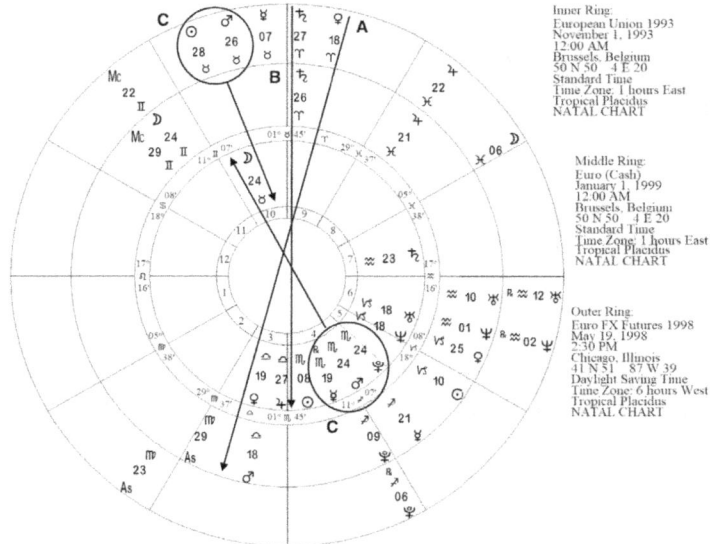

HOROSCOPE PRICE CONVERSION

The idea behind converting Euro FX futures natal planetary positions into prices is that each planet "vibrates" around that zodiac degree and so, too, might prices. Each planetary position is converted to a price starting with 0 Aries at zero and then moving around the zodiac its full 360 degrees. To get higher prices, simply add 360 to each preceding price.

For Euro FX Futures (Table 7.1), the MC, Uranus and Mars prices have been activated in six of the 15 significant highs and lows examined in the next section. As with any price level, please look at these planetary conversion prices as either support or resistance levels. Also note that these conversions extend only three decimal places rather than the five used in trading.

Table 7.1 Euro FX Horoscope Price Conversions

Market	Euro FX Globex									
Rulers	Taurus	Venus	Bill's book for "currency"							
1st Trade	May 19, 1998, 2:30 pm Chicago (Globex) for trade date May 20									
Source	CME Special Executive Report S-3257, May 15, 1988									
Price unit	USD cents per euro									
Planet	Position	Conversion	360	720	1080	1440	1800	2160	2520	2880
Venus	18 Aries	18	378	738	1098	1458	1818	2178	2538	2898
Saturn	27 Aries	27	387	747	1107	1467	1827	2187	2547	2907
Mercury	07 Taurus	37	397	757	1117	1477	1837	2197	2557	2917
Mars	26 Taurus	56	416	776	1136	1496	1856	2216	2576	2936
Sun	28 Taurus	58	418	778	1138	1498	1858	2218	2578	2938
MC	22 Gemini	82	442	802	1162	1522	1882	2242	2602	2962
Asc	23 Virgo	173	533	893	1253	1613	1973	2333	2693	3053
Pluto rx	06 Sag	246	606	966	1326	1686	2046	2406	2766	3126
IC	22 Sag	262	622	982	1342	1702	2062	2422	2782	3142
Neptune rx	02 Aq	302	662	1022	1382	1742	2102	2462	2822	3182
Uranus rx	12 Aq	312	672	1032	1392	1752	2112	2472	2832	3192
Moon	06 Pisces	336	696	1056	1416	1776	2136	2496	2856	3216
Jupiter	22 Pisces	352	712	1072	1432	1792	2152	2512	2872	3232
Desc	23 Pisces	353	713	1073	1433	1793	2153	2513	2873	3233

IMPORTANT EURO FX HIGHS

Since the euro was introduced in 1999, there have been eight significant highs in the Euro FX futures market. In all eight, the market's natal Moon or Mars were aspected by transiting planets by either conjunction or opposition. Transiting Venus made a conjunction or opposition to the Sun, Mercury, Venus, Mars, or the IC in five of the eight highs.

Figure 7.3 Euro FX Moon and Angles Show Important Price Levels

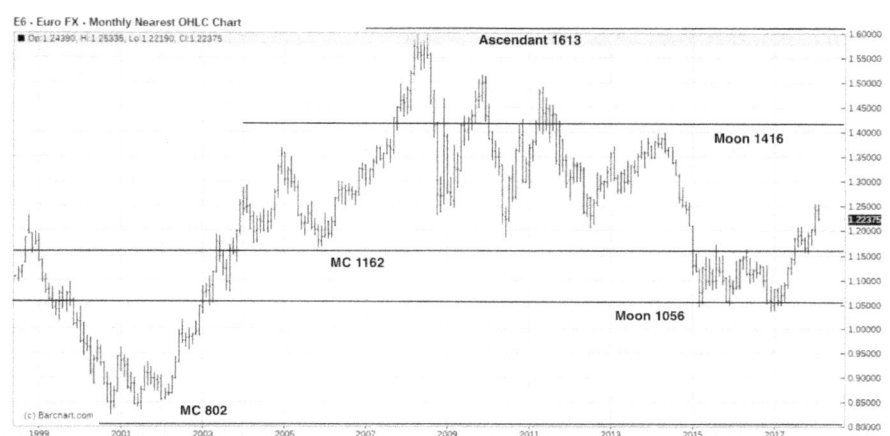

Source: Barchart.com

ALL-TIME EURO FX HIGH—1.59840 ON APRIL 22, 2008

The all-time high in Euro FX futures was 1.59840, set in the June contract on April 22, 2008 as the U.S. dollar was under pressure due to early concerns over what grew into the severe financial crisis of 2008. (The cash market hit its all-time high on July 15, 2008 at 1.6038, the day that September futures topped at 1.59550.)

Both important areas of the EU/euro/Euro FX tri-wheel were activated as the market marked its all-time high (Figure 7.4). First, the transiting Moon was opposite the futures contract's natal Mars/Sun conjunction (A), which ties in with the EU's Moon/Scorpio stellium opposition. Second, transiting Venus was conjunct the futures market's natal Venus (B), which also is connected to the EU's natal Venus and the euro's natal Mars.

In addition, transiting Mercury was conjunct the Euro FX futures natal Mercury (C), and transiting Uranus was conjunct the futures contract's natal Jupiter and descendant (D).

Figure 7.4 Euro FX Record High Transits Touch Five Natal Planets

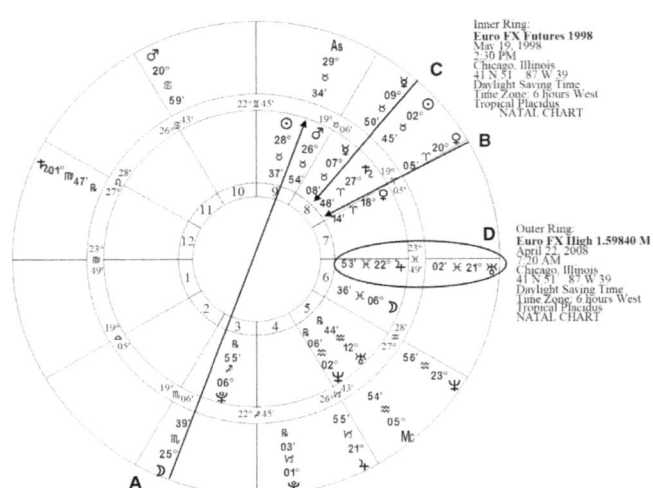

Table 7.2 Important Euro FX Highs and Astrological Connections

Date	Price	First-trade Moon	First-trade Mars	Transiting Venus
Dec. 30, 2004	1.36780	Uranus conjunct (wide)		Conjunct IC
Apr. 22, 2008	1.59840		Moon opposite	Conjunct Venus
July 15, 2008	1.59550	Mars, Saturn opposite		
Nov. 25, 2009	1.51400	Moon conjunct		Opposite Sun, Mars
May 4, 2011	1.49000, Mars price		Moon conjunct	Conjunct Venus
May 8, 2014	1.39460, Uranus price	Moon opposite	Sun conjunct (wide)	
Aug. 24, 2015	1.16030, MC price	Sun, Jupiter opposite		
May 3, 2016	1.16305, MC price		Mercury conjunct	Conjunct Mercury
Sept. 8, 2017	1.20975	Mars, Mercury opposite		Opposite Uranus

IMPORTANT EURO FX LOWS

Venus in the Euro FX futures natal horoscope is the planet to watch for identifying market lows, as it was activated in six out of seven significant lows since 2000. The Venus axis at 18-19 Aries/Libra connects the EU's natal Venus, the euro's natal Mars and the Euro FX contract's natal Venus (see Figure 7.2, A).

MARCH 13, 2015 LOW AT 1.04720

The horoscope biwheel for this low is overflowing with astrological connections with the Euro FX futures first-trade chart (Figure 7.5) as the eurozone was staggering amidst its own debt crisis (particularly Greece) and a massive quantitative easing program to support the economy.

The horoscope biwheel shows important connections in two areas: (1) the Venus axis of 18-19 Aries/Libra that connects the Euro FX futures contract with natal Venus of the EU and natal Mars of the euro's introduction; and (2) at 26-27 Aries/Libra, which includes the EU's natal Jupiter and the natal Saturn of both the euro and Euro FX futures. Transiting Mars and Uranus—a potent pair for triggering action—teamed up in conjunction with the Euro FX natal Venus (A). Transiting Venus was conjunct the Euro FX natal Saturn (B).

Three other important triggers stand out as well. First, the transiting Sun is in the same degree as the Euro FX natal Jupiter (C), something that happens just once a year and lights a fire under Jupiter's desire to be uplifting. Second, the transiting Moon was crossing the Euro FX IC at the bottom of the chart (D), an important "angle" in any chart that can signal a new beginning. Third, transiting Mercury was within just a few days of making a conjunction with the Euro FX natal Moon (E).

On a long-term basis, waiting for triggers from faster-moving planets were Jupiter opposite Euro FX natal Uranus (F) and Saturn conjunct Euro FX natal Pluto (G).

Figure 7.5 Transits Overflowing at Euro FX 2015 Low

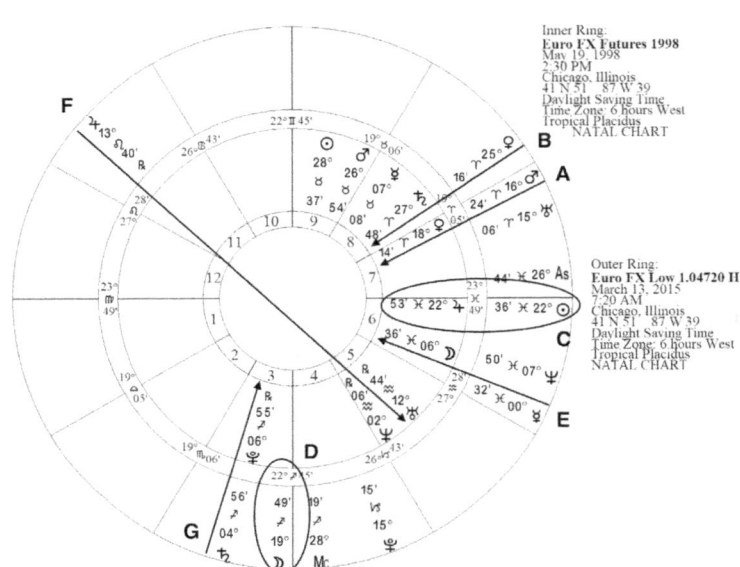

Table 7.3 Important Euro FX Lows and Astrological Connections

Date	Price	First-trade Venus	Transiting Venus
Oct. 26, 2000	0.82450	Moon opposite	Conjunct Pluto
Nov. 16, 2005	1.16650, MC price		
Oct. 27, 2008	1.23950	Moon, Mercury opposite	Conjunct Pluto
June 7, 2010	1.19300	Moon conjunct	
July 24, 2012	1.20710	Mars, Saturn opposite	Conjunct MC
Mar. 13, 2015	1.04720	Mars, Uranus conjunct	Conjunct Saturn
Dec. 15, 2016	1.03675, Uranus price	Jupiter opposite, Uranus conjunct	Conjunct Uranus

TRANSITS TO WATCH IN EURO FX

The main transits to watch in the Euro FX first-trade horoscope chart are primarily the two big axes that have connections across three natal horoscope charts—the European Union formation in 1991, the euro's introduction in 1999, and the Euro FX futures contract launch in 1998.

HIGHS

In previous highs in Euro FX, both the first-trade Moon and Mars have been activated in each instance. Watch the Moon at 06 Pisces and Mars at 26 Taurus for transits by conjunction or opposition, particularly by the transiting Sun, Moon, Mercury, Mars, and Venus.

Also watch transiting Venus for conjunctions/oppositions to natal Euro FX planets. At previous highs, transiting Venus was aligned with the Euro FX natal Venus twice, once with "inner planets" Mercury, Venus, and Mars, and once with the Euro FX natal IC.

LOWS

At significant lows in Euro FX futures prices, the money planet Venus has been activated in six of seven lows by conjunction or opposition as if to say "time to provide value and a good buying opportunity." In previous lows, the Moon has been involved three times, with Mars twice; Mercury, Jupiter, and Uranus had one connection each.

In the Euro FX first-trade chart, also watch conjunctions to the MC/IC axis as well as Pluto.

UPCOMING TRANSITS IN EURO FX

Based on the astrological transits present at previous highs and lows in the Euro FX market, I've looked into the future to see when similar patterns exist in 2018-2020.

I've set these dates up in the tables below where you (and I) can follow along and make notes about prices and market action around these dates. The dates in boldface are ones with particularly strong astrological transits vs. the Euro FX first-trade horoscope.

Table 7.4 2018 Potential Euro FX Futures Highs or Lows

Date	High or Low	Actual Price (nearby contract)	Notes
January 19	High	1.23150	High on January 25 at 1.25500
February 5	Low	1.23785	Kept moving lower
March 21	High		
May 3	Low		
May 15	High		
June 8	Low		
October 9	Low		
October 26	High		
November 5	Low		
December 17	Low		

Table 7.5 2019 Potential Euro FX Futures Highs or Lows

Date	High or Low	Actual Price (nearby contract)	Notes
January 4	High		
January 28	Low		
February 25	High		
March 27	High		
April 29	Low		
May 3	Low		
May 17	High		
June 7	High		
June 13	Low		
August 30	High		
October 29	High		
November 5	Low		
November 29	High		

Table 7.6   2020 Potential Euro FX Futures Highs or Lows

Date	High or Low	Actual Price (nearby contract)	Notes
February 23	High		
March 31	High		
April 21	Low		
June 15	Low		
July 30	Low		
August 25	High		
September 17	Low		
October 21	Low		
November 19	High		
November 27	Low		
November 29	High		
December 4	Low		
December 21	Low		

OTHER CONFIRMED FIRST-TRADE DATA IN CURRENCY MARKETS

The era of financial futures trading began when currency futures opened for trading on May 16, 1972 at the Chicago Mercantile Exchange. The previous year's collapse of the Bretton Woods agreement that had established fixed rates among the major currencies set the CME into motion and, with the help of Nobel laureate Milton Friedman, successfully attracted institutional interest in trading the new products.

According to a history of the CME, *The Merc*, by Bob Tamarkin, seven currency futures contracts began trading at 9 am on May 16, 1972 at two-minute intervals. Thus, each currency had its own mini-opening ceremony that included the display of the country's flag by a flag-bearer. I assume the currencies were introduced alphabetically, so I use the following times for their natal first-trade horoscope charts:

- British pound   May 16, 1972   9:00 am
- Canadian dollar   May 16, 1972   9:02 am

- Japanese yen   May 16, 1972   9:08 am
- Mexican peso   May 16, 1972   9:10 am
- Swiss franc   May 16, 1972   9:12 am

Note that the Deutsche mark and French franc (likely launched at 9:04 am and 9:06 am, respectively) are not on this list because those currencies ceased to exist as the euro became the official currency of the eurozone.

CHAPTER 8
Energy

Crude Oil Futures
March 30, 1983, 9:30 am, New York
Aries Sun

Crude oil futures are the cornerstone of the energy complex at the New York Mercantile Exchange (NYMEX) division of CME Group, but surprisingly trailed the first contract in the group—heating oil—by five years. Indeed, crude oil futures came on the scene two years after 10 years of energy price regulations were lifted by newly inaugurated President Ronald Reagan in January 1981.

Heating oil futures opened at NYMEX with a New York Harbor delivery specification in November 1978 as a re-tool of a failed Rotterdam-delivery contract from 1974. The struggling exchange, rocked by a potato futures scandal, had just two traders show up on opening day. But, within a year, money talked and a 20-cent-per-gallon difference between the futures price and cash prices (equal to $8,400 per one 42,000-gal. futures contract) gave wholesalers no choice but to buy futures and take delivery.[36] When crude oil futures launched—in stiff competition with the Chicago Board of Trade, which wanted a toehold in the newly unregulated price of oil and launched its contract on the same day—NYMEX was well on its way to being seen by the marketplace as the energy exchange.

The crude oil futures contract calls for delivery of West Texas Intermediate (WTI) crude oil (the U.S. benchmark, also called light sweet crude) in Cushing, Okla.

---

36   "An Industry Icon is Going Away: No. 2 Heating Oil Contract Will Breathe Its Last," The Barrel Blog, 29 July 29 2011. <http://blogs.platts.com/2011/07/29/an_industry_ico/>

From the start, NYMEX listed crude oil futures contracts for every month of the year. Today, trading volume and open interest tends to concentrate in the quarterly expirations of March, June, September, and December and the current front-month. Contracts are available up to nine years in the future to accommodate hedging of physical deals among cash-market participants.

CRUDE OIL 101

Exploration of crude oil uses—mainly to make kerosene to replace the increasingly expensive whale oil used for home lighting lamps—began in the mid-1840s. (Interestingly, crude oil's ruling planet Neptune was discovered on September 23, 1846.) But, the first oil strike did not occur until August 27, 1859 in Titusville, Penn., which then set off a rush to find more as oil became known as black gold and prices soared to $18 per barrel by January 1860—only to collapse to 10 cents by year-end 1861.[37]

The first big oil gusher—Spindletop, in Beaumont, Texas on January 10, 1901 at 10:30 am[38]—was a game-changer. It produced 50,000 barrels a day vs. total U.S. production at the time of 50 barrels a day. As a result, gasoline replaced ethanol as the cheap fuel that Henry Ford designed his automobiles to use, and the transportation industry became the primary outlet for crude oil and its products.

CRUDE OIL PRICING SCHEMES

In the midst of the Great Depression, another big Texas oil strike sent prices plummeting to 10 cents a barrel by mid-1931. As a result, the U.S. government tapped the Texas Railroad Commission (TRC) to control the spare capacity of East Texas crude oil production, effectively making it the global market's price arbiter from 1931 to 1971.

Meanwhile, the major international oil companies were exploring for oil overseas and cut 50/50 "concession" deals with countries like Saudi Arabia and Iran.

---

37 Downey, Morgan. Oil 101. (Wooden Table Press LLC, 2009) 3.

38 Howland, Ronald W. American Histrology. (Tempe, AZ: American Federation of Astrologers, Inc., 2014) 126.

This pricing system began to crack in the 1950s as the oil countries wanted a better deal, which led to not only nationalization of oil operations, but also to formation of the Organization of Petroleum Exporting Countries (OPEC) in 1960.

In 1970, however, U.S. oil production peaked and the TRC opened up the spigots. Now, OPEC nations were in control of crude oil's excess capacity. The major oil companies negotiated a deal with OPEC for the first time in February 1971, but it soon fell apart as the United States went off the gold standard later that year, which meant that the deal—priced in U.S. dollars—meant lower revenue for OPEC as the dollar weakened. The Arab oil embargo (in response to U.S. support of Israel in the Yom Kippur invasion 10 days earlier), which cut off supplies to the United States and the Netherlands (a European trading hub), was the death knell for the 1971 price agreement and soon all OPEC nations were selling oil at whatever price the market would bear.

Unfortunately, the United States also had imposed price and wage restrictions in 1971 that kept U.S. crude oil prices artificially below international market prices. These restrictions were not lifted entirely until President Reagan's first executive order in January 1981. Thus, fully free-floating prices created the volatility and risk that the crude oil futures contract stepped in to help producers and users manage in 1983.

FIRST-TRADE HOROSCOPE

The WTI crude oil futures contract began trading on NYMEX at 9:30 am on March 30, 1983.[39] The contract has the Sun in Aries, Moon in Scorpio and Gemini rising on the ascendant (Figure 8.1).

SUN IN ARIES

The Sun in Aries indicates the contract is a leader and unafraid to make waves. Indeed, it thumbed its nose at OPEC and the big oil companies who were in the habit of setting oil prices privately and with little transparency. Mercury is just 4 degrees away from the Sun, so is considered "combust," or obscured

---

39 "Bottom Line," Commodities Magazine, May 1983, p. 28.

by the light of the Sun (A). Mercury rules trading, so to be combust would seem to indicate less-than-stellar volume or activity, but this contract is the world's leading crude oil contract in volume. Mercury and the Sun are no doubt supported in their global ambitions by a trine (120-degree aspect) with Jupiter and Uranus in Sagittarius. Jupiter and Uranus in Sagittarius scream "huge upset internationally," which certainly was the case when this contract was introduced.

Figure 8.1   Crude Oil Futures First-Trade Horoscope

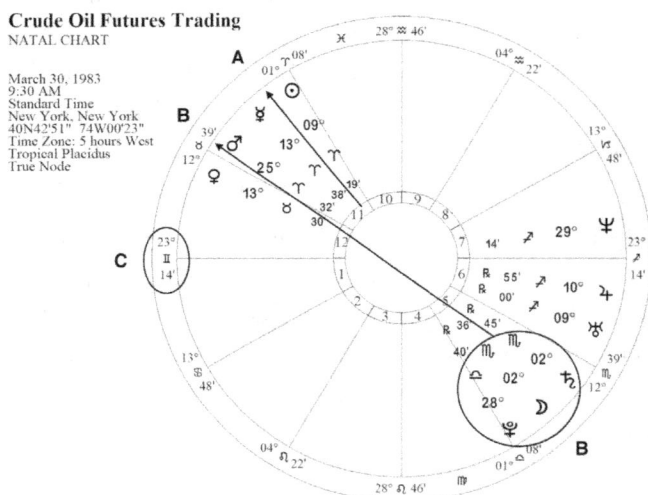

MOON IN SCORPIO

The Moon in Scorpio shows that intense research went into the contract's development, which was sensitive to the industry's deepest secrets. Indeed, with Saturn also at 2 degrees Scorpio, the contract's development also was sensitive to established industry norms and standard practices. Both the Moon and Saturn are conjunct Pluto, the planet of transformation, and opposite Mars in its ruling sign of Aries (B). The Mars/Pluto axis speaks to the contract's ability to create powerful change, and as shown later in this chapter is often activated at the time of important highs.

GEMINI ASCENDANT

The crude oil contract's ascendant is in the sign of Gemini, which makes Mercury the chart ruler, and appropriate that a futures trading contract is ruled by the planet that rules trading. Mercury also signifies speed, quickness, and changeability—all characteristics of a successful futures contract. Mercury has help in overcoming its combustness by being conjunct the fixed star Alpheratz, which symbolizes freedom of thinking and new ideas—and speed.

HOROSCOPE PRICE CONVERSION

Table 8.1 shows the conversion from planetary position to price for the WTI crude oil futures contract at NYMEX. (Refer to Chapter 5 for how to convert zodiacal positions into prices.) These prices can be used to gauge potential support and resistance.

Table 8.1 Crude Oil Futures Price Conversion Table

Market	WTI Crude Oil Futures									
Rulers	Pisces	Neptune								
1st Trade	March 30, 1983, 9:30 am, New York									
Source	May 1983 issue of Commodities Magazine, p. 28									
Price unit	Dollars and cents per barrel									

Planet	Position	Conversion	360	720	1080	1440	1800	2160	2520	2880
Sun	09 Aries	9	369	729	1089	1449	1809	2169	2529	2889
Mercury	13 Aries	13	373	733	1093	1453	1813	2173	2533	2893
Mars	25 Aries	25	385	745	1105	1465	1825	2185	2545	2905
Venus	13 Taurus	43	403	763	1123	1483	1843	2203	2563	2923
Asc	23 Gemini	83	443	803	1163	1523	1883	2243	2603	2963
IC	28 Leo	148	508	868	1228	1588	1948	2308	2668	3028
Pluto rx	28 Libra	208	568	928	1288	1648	2008	2368	2728	3088
Moon	02 Sco 36	212	572	932	1292	1652	2012	2372	2732	3092
Saturn rx	02 Sco 45	212	572	932	1292	1652	2012	2372	2732	3092
Uranus rx	09 Sag	249	609	969	1329	1689	2049	2409	2769	3129
Jupiter rx	10 Sag	250	610	970	1330	1690	2050	2410	2770	3130
Desc	23 Sag	263	623	983	1343	1703	2063	2423	2783	3143
Neptune	29 Sag	269	629	989	1349	1709	2069	2429	2789	3149
MC	28 Aq	328	688	1048	1408	1768	2128	2488	2848	3208

In the crude oil contract, put either one or two digits behind the decimal point, depending on price levels. For example, the Jupiter price of 970 could be $9.70, which was spitting distance from the all-time low at $9.75, or it could be $97.00. At the all-time high of $147.90, the IC price of 148 could have been read as $148.00 (10 cents higher than the actual high) while the Mars and Venus prices of 1465 and 1483 staked out the range of $146.50-$148.30 as resistance, with a midpoint of $147.40 (50 cents lower than the actual high).

Note in Figure 8.2 the prominence of Venus prices in marking major support and resistance levels.

Figure 8.2 Venus Prices Prominent in Crude Oil Support/Resistance

Source: Barchart.com

IMPORTANT CRUDE OIL HIGHS

I've identified 16 important highs on the monthly price chart since crude oil futures began trading in 1983. Each high had significant astrological transits to the first-trade chart for crude oil, mainly transits to the Mars/Pluto opposition or to the Sun/Mercury conjunction, which are outlined in Table 8.2.

ALL-TIME HIGH AT $147.90 ON JULY 11, 2008

Crude oil futures set an all-time high of $147.90 per barrel on July 11, 2008 as cracks in the financial crisis were beginning to widen. Although prices had been climbing in response to fundamental concerns about lack of supply (production caps and high-profile disruptions) and increasing global demand, crude oil futures speculators also were getting the evil eye as U.S. consumers paying more than $4 per gallon for gasoline looked for a scapegoat. (A June 2008 investigation by federal regulators into speculative activity showed no sign of price manipulation.[40])

---

40 "Interim Report on Crude Oil." Interagency Task Force on Commodity Markets. Washington, D.C., July 2008

Astrologically, the money planet Venus was in the spotlight. On July 11, 2008, transiting Venus was at 28 Cancer, forming a T-square to the crude oil first-trade opposition between Mars and Pluto, an axis that was activated in nearly half of the important highs outlined in Table 8.2.

Table 8.2 Important Crude Oil Highs and Astrological Connections

Date	Price (dollars per barrel)	Mars/Pluto	Sun/Mercury
Nov. 20, 1985	31.82		Mars opposite
July 16, 1987	22.76		Moon conjunct
Oct. 10, 1990	41.15		Mercury, Mars, Sun opposite Jupiter trine Moon square
Jan. 9, 1997	26.74, Neptune 269; IC 2668	Moon, Neptune, Jupiter square	
Sept. 20, 2000	37.80, Mercury 373	Venus conjunct Pluto	
Feb. 27, 2003	39.99	Moon, Venus square	Jupiter trine
Oct. 25, 2004	55.67		Moon conjunct Jupiter opposite
July 14, 2006	79.86		Saturn trine
July 11, 2008	147.90, Venus 1483	Venus square	
May 3, 2010	89.77		Mars trine
May 2, 2011	115.27	Jupiter/Mars conjunct Mars, opposite Pluto	Mercury, Venus conjunct
Mar. 1, 2012	110.96	Venus conjunct Mars	
Aug. 28, 2013	112.24, Venus 1123		Uranus conjunct Pluto, Jupiter square
June 20, 2014	107.73		Moon conjunct Mars opposite
May 13, 2015	62.75		Jupiter trine

More interestingly, transiting Venus filled in the empty sixth slot in a Grand Sextile, a rare formation of ease in which six planets/points are each separated by a 60-degree sextile (A and outline in Figure 8.3). In the crude oil first-trade chart, the five natal points include: Mars at 25 Aries, Ascendant at 23 Gemini, Pluto at 28 Libra, Neptune at 29 Sagittarius ,and the MC at 28 Aquarius. And, prices were near a Venus conversion price of 1483 ($148.30) from Table 8.1.

The fourth Venus connection was that transiting Jupiter was trine the market's natal Venus (B), a signal that things are as good as they get.

Two other connections also played into this day's significance. First, transiting Pluto was thisclose to the market's natal Neptune, which rules crude oil, as it was in the same degree as Neptune and just 2 minutes of astrological arc away from being exactly the same (C). (Pluto is the slowest-moving planet and was at 29 degrees Sagittarius from mid-June through end-July, so transformation in energy prices was something that was on the radar, but didn't really matter until the connection was almost exact.) Finally, the fast-moving Moon was the trigger—as it often is—when it hooked up with the crude oil market's natal Moon and Saturn (D).

Figure 8.3   Venus Prominent at Crude Oil All-Time High in 2008

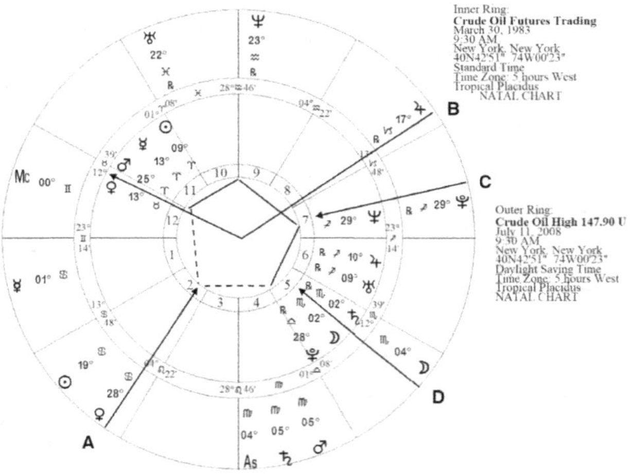

IMPORTANT CRUDE OIL LOWS

At important lows in the crude oil futures market, the natal Sun and natal Mars are important players as each was activated in 12 of the 17 lows since 1986 outlined in Table 8.3. For each of these two planets, focus in on transiting planets that are conjunct, opposite, or trine. Also, watch for any transiting planets that cross 22-29 Leo as they create a Grand Trine with Mars at 25 Aries and Neptune at 29 Sagittarius.

Table 8.3   Important Crude Oil Lows and Astrological Connections

Date	Price (dollars per barrel)	Sun	Mars	Grand Trine 22-29 Leo
Apr. 1, 1986	9.75 Jupiter 970	Sun conjunct, Moon square	Venus conjunct	
Oct. 5, 1988	12.13 IC 1228	Mars conjunct, Sun opposite, Moon trine	Mercury opposite	
Feb. 25, 1991	17.45	Venus conjunct	Moon square	
Dec. 20, 1993	13.75	Jupiter conjunct	Sun, Mars, Venus, Mercury trine	
Dec. 21, 1998	10.35	Mars opposite	Saturn conjunct	
Nov. 19, 2001	16.70			
Dec. 10, 2004	40.25	Jupiter opposite		
Dec. 13, 2004	40.25	Jupiter opposite		
Jan. 18, 2007	49.90, IC 508	Jupiter trine	Sun, Moon square	
Jan. 20, 2009	32.70, MC 328			
May 20, 2010	64.24			
Oct. 4, 2011	74.95, Mars 745	Sun, Mercury opposite		Mars trine
June 28, 2012	77.28, Venus 763	Venus opposite		
Nov. 7, 2012	84.05	Venus, Sun opposite		
Apr. 18, 2013	85.61	Mercury, Uranus conjunct		
Mar. 18, 2015	42.03			Jupiter trine
Feb. 11, 2016	26.05, Descendant 263, Ascendant 2603	Moon conjunct		

LOW OF OCTOBER 4, 2011 AT $74.95

The European debt crisis and potential Greece default had been weighing on crude oil prices since spring, as traders feared either could signal global recession and decreased demand for oil. Prices bottomed on this date in response to a surprisingly bullish U.S. crude oil inventories report, and easing of concerns in Europe.

Astrologically, the October 2011 low chart (Figure 8.4) reflects the two biggest indicators of a low based on analysis of previous lows since 1985 as outlined in Table

8.3: (1) Transiting Mars forming a Grand Trine with the first-trade chart's Sun/Mercury and Jupiter/Uranus conjunctions (A); and (2) Transiting Sun, Mercury, and Saturn were opposite the first-trade chart's Sun/Mercury conjunction (B). Other signals included transiting Venus opposite natal Mars (C) and transiting Moon trine natal Venus (D). Plus, the ruler of crude oil, Neptune, was aligned with the first-trade chart's midheaven (E) at the same zodiacal degree. (Neptune takes 165 years to go around the horoscope, and had been toying with the MC's 28 degrees Aquarius since April 2010, finally moving on in January 2012.)

Figure 8.4 Grand Trine and Sun Opposition Mark 2011 Crude Oil Low

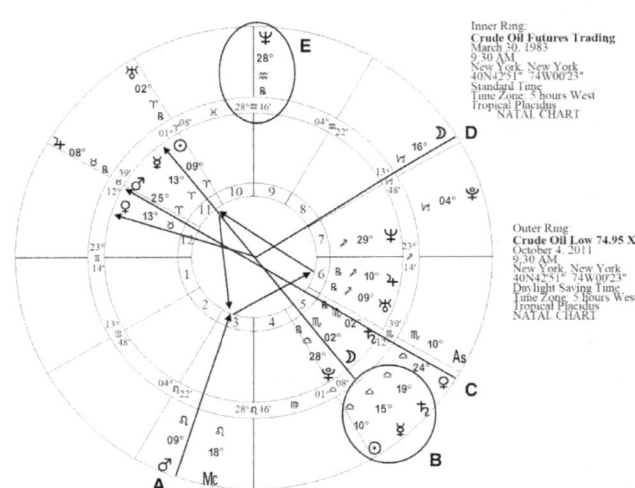

TRANSITS TO WATCH IN CRUDE OIL

Four primary transits pop out to focus on for potential highs and lows in the crude oil futures market—and one of them is the same for both highs and lows. That one is when transiting planets are conjunct, opposite or trine the first-trade chart's natal Sun. So, use your judgment for these transits to the Sun. Are prices rallying toward a top, or falling toward a bottom? Plus, the other signature transits will provide clues as well.

For highs, those clues are a Grand Trine with the Sun and Jupiter or a T-square to the Mars/Pluto axis. For lows, the clue is a Grand Trine with Mars and Neptune.

HIGHS

In five of the 16 highs noted in Table 8.2, the transiting planets completed either a Grand Trine (at least three planets making a large triangle with 120-degree angles) or a T-square (a transiting planet at right angles to two natal planets). And in one high (February 2003), both were present! These are two formations that jump out at astrologers as significant in any type of chart.

The Grand Trine is easy, breezy energy that greases the skids. In a price chart, it says "it's as good as it gets." In the crude oil first-trade chart, the Sun and Mercury in Aries are already trine to Jupiter and Uranus in Sagittarius. So, to complete the Grand Trine, a transiting planet would be anywhere from 9-13 degrees of Leo. Grand Trines occurred in:

- February 2003 with transiting Jupiter at 10 Leo
- July 2006 with transiting Saturn at 11 Leo
- May 2010 with transiting Mars at 13 Leo

A T-square is far more tense than a Grand Trine, yet signifies an important release of energy via the planet that makes the 90-degree angle to two planets that are opposite one another. In the crude oil first-trade chart, Mars and Pluto—cousins in the power department—are in opposition and are seeking compromise between the "do it" of Mars with the "transform it" of Pluto. So, when a planet squares this axis, the crude oil market sees it as a time for a change in direction. T-squares with Mars/Pluto occurred in the following high-price astrological charts:

- January 1997 with the Moon, Neptune and Jupiter at 25-27 Capricorn
- February 2003 with the Moon and Venus at 26-27 Capricorn
- July 2008 with Venus at 28 Cancer

LOWS

Interestingly, the Grand Trine is prominent in the astrological charts of price lows as well. But, this time it occurs when transiting planets are in the late degrees of Leo, making a trine to the first-trade Mars at 25 Aries and first-trade Neptune at 29 Sagittarius. Three of the lows in Table 8.3 occurred at the time of a Grand Trine:

- January 18, 2007 with transiting Saturn at 23 Leo
- May 20, 2010 with transiting Moon and Mars at 21-23 Leo
- November 7, 2012 with transiting Moon at 22 Leo and transiting Mars at 22 Sagittarius

A fourth low had three transiting planets trine to the first-trade natal Mars and conjunct natal Neptune—December 20, 1993 with transiting Mercury, Venus, and Sun at 20-28 Sagittarius.

Transiting aspects to the Sun are evenly spread across the conjunction, opposition, and trine. Pay particular attention, though, to two transits: (1) when the Sun is opposite the natal Sun, around the first week of October each year; and (2) when Jupiter is either opposite the natal Sun at 9 Libra, or trine the natal Sun at 9 Leo or 9 Sagittarius, any of which happen just once every 12 years because of the length of Jupiter's trip around the zodiac.

UPCOMING TRANSITS IN CRUDE OIL

Based on the astrological transits present at previous highs and lows in the crude oil futures market, I've looked into the future to see when similar patterns exist in 2018-2020.

I've set these dates up in the tables below where you (and I) can follow along and make notes about prices and market action around these dates. The dates in boldface are ones with particularly strong astrological transits vs. the crude oil first-trade horoscope.

Table 8.4 2018 Potential Crude Oil Futures Highs or Lows

Date	High or Low	Actual Price (nearby contract)	Notes
January 16	High	64.89 (G18)	Held for 5 trading days. Ultimate high on Jan. 25 @ 66.66 (H18)
March 12	Low		
June 8	High		
June 11	High		
July 6	Low		
August 14	High or Low		
November 7	Low		
November 29	Low		
December 3	High		
December 19	High or Low		
December 21	High or Low		

Table 8.5 2019 Potential Crude Oil Futures Highs or Lows

Date	High or Low	Actual Price (nearby contract)	Notes
January 14	High		
April 15	Low		
July 22	High		
August 1	High or Low		
August 6	High		
August 15	Low		
October 19	High or Low		
December 16	High		

Table 8.6 2020 Potential Crude Oil Futures Highs or Lows

Date	High or Low	Actual Price (nearby contract)	Notes
April 14	Low		
July 13	High		
July 14	High		
July 20	High		
September 14	High		
September 28	Low		
December 2	High		

OTHER CONFIRMED FIRST-TRADE DATA IN ENERGY MARKETS

I have not yet researched the other energy markets enough to provide confirmed first-trade data that includes both date and time of a market's launch. However, based on price data from Barchart.com, I'm comfortable that the first-trade dates are accurate for the following markets; I'm not sure of the opening bell times:

- Heating Oil (later ULSD)   November 14, 1978, New York
- Unleaded Gasoline (later RBOB)   December 3, 1984, New York
- Natural Gas   April 4, 1990, New York

If you have archives of any sort that note the first-trade time of these or any other energy contracts, please email them to me at TeamCommodityTimes@yahoo.com. Many thanks!

CHAPTER 9
Interest Rates

10-Year T-Note Futures
May 3, 1982, 10:00 am, Chicago
Taurus Sun

The 10-year Treasury note (T-note) futures contract showed its potential to be a leading interest rate contract from the get-go. It shattered the record for opening day trading volume with 33,502 contracts traded, a record for U.S. futures contracts that still stands.[41] The previous record had been set less than two weeks earlier, on April 21, 1982, when the Standard & Poor's 500 futures contract opened at the rival Chicago Mercantile Exchange with volume of 7,926 contracts.

The 10-year T-note contract had two big things going for it that led to its immediate acceptance in the marketplace. First, it was the follow-up offering from the Chicago Board of Trade to what had quickly become the most-traded futures contract in the world—U.S. Treasury bonds. The T-bond contract launched in 1977 and was in the right place at the right time when Federal Reserve policy made a dramatic shift in October 1979 to targeting money supply, not interest rates, in order to tame roaring double-digit inflation. On October 6, 1979, Fed Chair Paul Volcker's "Saturday Night Massacre" set interest rates free to find their own value, which immediately increased market volatility and the risk of owning bonds. The legend is that Salomon Brothers hedged a big underwriting in T-bond futures on October 8, the first trading day after Volck-

---

41 Sandor, Richard L. Good Derivatives—A Story of Financial and Enviromental Innovation. (New Jersey: John Wiley & Sons, Inc., 2012) 159.

er's announcement.⁴² As a result, other users quickly began to offset interest rate risk by hedging with futures. By 1981, T-bond futures were the world's leading contract, and interest rate players globally were comfortable with hedging their exposure at the CBOT, which lead to instant acceptance of the new 10-year T-note futures. Second, the exchange was strategic in selecting the day to launch the contract—just two days prior to a $4 billion Treasury sale of 10-year notes.⁴³

What made both the T-bond and T-note futures contracts immensely popular was the innovation of a conversion system so that collateralized vault receipts of instruments with varying terms and coupons could be delivered against the standardized contract specification. Richard Sandor, who designed the CBOT's first interest rate contract in GNMAs and chaired exchange committees overseeing design of T-bonds and T-notes, describes the deliverable instrument as a "fictional… bond with an 8 percent coupon."⁴⁴ In 2000, the exchange changed the deliverable coupon rate to 6 percent to reflect the overall decline in interest rates since the 1970s and early 1980s and to be more in line with the terms of new issues.

Today, the 10-year T-note futures contract is a world benchmark and the most-traded U.S. interest rate contract because it is in the sweet spot of maturity for U.S. and international investors as well as governments and corporations that borrow money.

10-YEAR T-NOTE 101

The 10-year T-note has been in the Treasury's arsenal of raising money for more than 200 years. Indeed, in 1790, the newly formed U.S. Treasury began issuing 10-year notes with a 6 percent coupon in order to pay debts accumulated during the Revolutionary War.⁴⁵ The deal was that the federal government assumed $21.5 million in debt from the states and, in return, provided the states

---

42   Ibid., p. 156.

43   Cohen, Laurie. "First-day volume record for Treasury note futures." Chicago Tribune. 4 May 1982, p. B6.

44   Sandor, Richard L. Good Derivatives—A Story of Financial and Enviromental Innovation. (New Jersey: John Wiley & Sons, Inc., 2012) 158.

45   "Funding Act of 1790," Wikipedia. 4 August 2017. <https://en.wikipedia.org/wiki/Funding_Act_of_1790>

U.S. Treasury securities, "backed by the full faith and credit" of the United States along with 6 percent interest.

Ever since, U.S. Treasury securities have been considered the equivalent of a risk-free rate of return because of that initial wording that pledged the "full faith and credit" of the United States that stood behind every T-note, T-bond, or T-bill. When the rating agencies began evaluating creditworthiness, the United States earned the highest ranking of AAA from Moody's in 1917. Nearly 100 years later, however, Standard & Poor's dropped the U.S. ranking to AA+ in 2011, the first downgrading in U.S. history.[46]

In the 1970s, two oil shocks (read more about those in Chapter 8 on Crude Oil) had spurred inflation, three recessions, and a level of government debt that had doubled since 1974 to more than $1 trillion by year-end 1981. Interest rates were on the rise, and with an inverted yield curve, there was big demand for shorter-term issues, which meant plenty of liquidity to support a futures contract.

For example, when the 10-year T-note futures contract was listed in May 1982, the constant maturity rate (how the Treasury tracks rates) was 13.62 percent, just coming off the all-time high of 15.32 percent set the previous September, according to data from the St. Louis Fed. Meanwhile, the comparable rate for the 30-year T-bond in May 1982 was 13.24 percent vs. its all-time high of 14.68 percent in October 1981. By the early 2000s, the 10-year T-note had become the dominant instrument to the point that the government didn't even issue 30-year T-bonds from February 18, 2002 to February 9, 2006.

FIRST-TRADE HOROSCOPE

The 10-year T-note futures contract opened for trading on May 3, 1982 at 10:00 am.[47] The contract's Sun is in Taurus, ruled by Venus. Taurus is a great Sun sign for an interest rate contract because its reputation will be one of stability and following through on what is promised. Plus, Taurus is ruled by Venus, the planet

---

[46] "History of the United States public debt," Wikipedia. 4 August 2017. <https://en.wikipedia.org/wiki/History_of_the_United_States_public_debt>

[47] Chicago Board of Trade records: Series III – Secretary's Records, Special Collections and University Archives, University of Illinois at Chicago, Monthly Letter to Members, May 3, 1982, p.1.

that rules money! The contract's Moon is in Virgo, which says no matter how crazy trading might get, there is always an undercurrent of staying focused on the details and serving the public. The Moon has additional import in this natal horoscope because it is the ruler of the chart given that the sign of Cancer is on the ascendant, which indicates the contract is seen as providing protection.

The most interesting aspect of the 10-year T-note first-trade chart is a formation called the "mystic rectangle," formed by four planets—Mercury, Uranus, Venus, and Mars—that are all connected to one another (Figure 9.1). Mercury opposite Uranus (A) and Venus opposite Mars (B) form the two main axes of the rectangle. That makes each planet one of the corners of the rectangle, and each planet connected to two other planets by either sextile (60 degrees) or trine (120 degrees). As we'll see later on in this chapter, these four planets often are activated by transiting planets at significant market turns.

Venus gets special mention for a couple of other reasons as well. First, it is the sign of Pisces, its absolute favorite sign, and less than one degree away from the highest point in the chart, the midheaven. Both give Venus an oomph in strength. Second, Venus also is opposite the natal Moon, which is the chart ruler, and a tag-a-long participant in the mystic rectangle—wide in its opposition to Venus and its conjunction with Mars, but still close enough to play along.

Figure 9.1   Mystic Rectangle Marks 10-yr. T-note Natal Horoscope

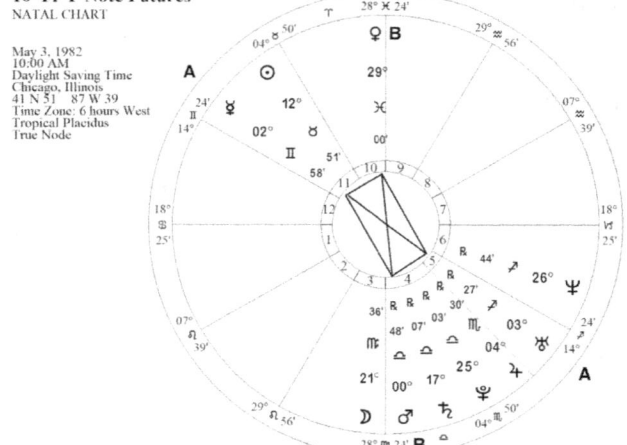

HOROSCOPE PRICE CONVERSION

Table 9.1 shows the conversion from planetary position to price for the 10-year T-note futures contract at CBOT. (Refer to Chapter 5 for how to convert zodiacal positions into prices.) These prices can be used to gauge potential support and resistance (Figure 9.2).

10-year T-note futures are priced in full points and halves of 1/32 of a point, and Table 9.1 prices can be used with the hyphen that separates the two either one or two places in from the right. For example, the ascendant price of 828 was a close match for the November 23, 1984 high of 82-28. Nine years later, the ascendant price of 1188 was near the price high of 117-18 on September 7, 1993. Other planetary price conversions include:

- The Sun price line of 1122 was important resistance in 2001 (112-26) and then support in 2008 (111-25) and 2009 (112-51)

- The Neptune price conversion of 986 was near the 1994 low of 99-04. In 2016, the price conversion one column over at 1346 provided resistance to the summer highs at 134-07 and 134-075

- The Jupiter price conversion of 934 was spot on with the January 2000 low at 93-43

- The Pluto price conversion of 925 was equally spot on with the May 1990 low 92-52

Table 9.1   10-yr. T-note Price Conversions

Market	10-Year T-note Futures									
Rulers	Scorpio	Pluto								
1st Trade	May 3, 1982, 10:00 am									
Source	CBOT Monthly Letter to Members May 3, 1982									
Price unit	Points. Points and 32nds.									
Planet	Position	Conversion	360	720	1080	1440	1800	2160	2520	2880
Sun	12 Taurus	42	402	762	1122	1482	1842	2202	2562	2922
Mercury	02 Gemini	62	422	782	1142	1502	1862	2222	2582	2942
Asc	18 Cancer	108	468	828	1188	1548	1908	2268	2628	2988
Moon	21 Virgo	171	531	891	1251	1611	1971	2331	2691	3051
IC	28 Virgo	178	538	898	1258	1618	1978	2338	2698	3058
Mars rx	00 Libra	180	540	900	1260	1620	1980	2340	2700	3060
Saturn rx	17 Libra	197	557	917	1277	1637	1997	2357	2717	3077
Pluto rx	25 Libra	205	565	925	1285	1645	2005	2365	2725	3085
Jupiter rx	04 Scorpio	214	574	934	1294	1654	2014	2374	2734	3094
Uranus rx	03 Sag	243	603	963	1323	1683	2043	2403	2763	3123
Neptune rx	26 Sag	266	626	986	1346	1706	2066	2426	2786	3146
Desc	18 Cap	288	648	1008	1368	1728	2088	2448	2808	3168
MC	28 Pisces	357	717	1077	1437	1797	2157	2517	2877	3237
Venus	28 Pisces	358	718	1078	1438	1798	2158	2518	2878	3238

Figure 9.2 10-yr. T-note Planetary Price Support/Resistance

Source: Barchart.com

IMPORTANT 10-YEAR T-NOTE HIGHS

At the 14 important highs in the 10-year T-note contract since 1982 examined in Table 9.2, no individual planet is in play for more than half of them. However, the contract's natal Sun tops the list at 50 percent, most of which were activated by the transiting Sun, Moon, Mars, or Jupiter.

The corners of the mystic rectangle (Mercury/Uranus, Mars/Venus) are activated by transit in roughly 40 percent of these highs. The big planetary nasties—Saturn and Pluto—put the hammer down when transiting planets activated them in six of the 14 highs.

NOVEMBER 1, 2001 HIGH AT 112-26

This high illustrates how astrological judgment and current market conditions must come into play when deciding whether transits could produce a low or a high price. On November 1, 2001, a signature for a market low occurred with transiting Mars trine to the 10-year T-note's natal Mercury and Mars (Figure 9.3, A). However, Saturn was the deciding factor in making this the day for a high, with Mercury and Venus conjunct (B) and Jupiter square (C) to the planet that instills limits. (Mercury and Venus also were conjunct Pluto.) And, the

Trading In Sync With Commodities

cherry on top was that the Sun's price conversion of 1122 was dead-on with the first four numerals in the high price.

Figure 9.3   Saturn Stars at 2001 High in 10-yr. T-note

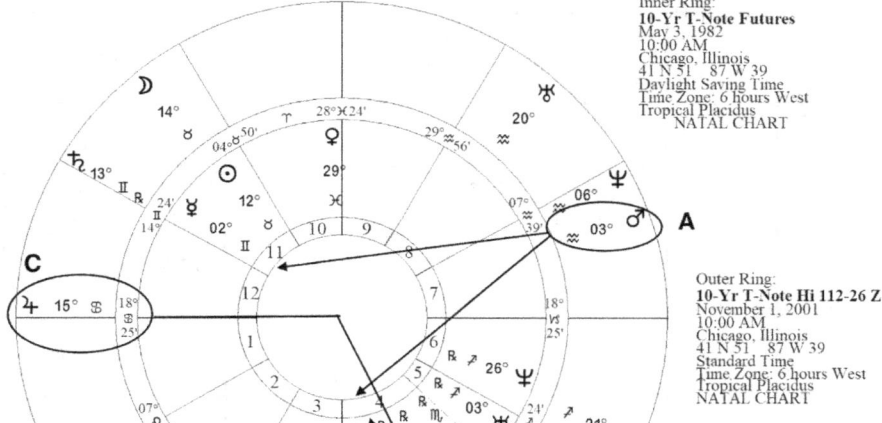

Table 9.2   Important Highs in 10-Year T-Notes

Date	Price*	Natal Sun	Natal Mercury	Natal Venus	Natal Mars	Natal Saturn	Natal Pluto
May 5, 1983	87-18	Sun conjunct					
Nov. 23, 1984	82-28		Sun, Moon opposite				
Apr. 16, 1986	105-16			Mercury conjunct	Mercury opposite	Moon square	

129

Aug. 1, 1989	102-16	Sun, Moon square		Jupiter, Uranus square	Jupiter, Uranus square		
Sept. 7, 1993	117-18	Sun trine				Mars, Jupiter conjunct	
Feb. 13, 1996	115-28	Jupiter opposite (wide)	Moon opposite	Venus conjunct	Venus opposite		Mercury, Neptune square
Oct. 9, 1998	117-06		Moon conjunct			Sun conjunct	Mercury conjunct
Nov. 1, 2001	112-26	Sun opposite, Moon conjunct	Mars trine		Mars trine	Mercury, Venus conjunct; Jupiter square	Mercury, Venus conjunct
June 16, 2003	121-06		Mercury, Venus conjunct				Mars, Sun trine
Mar. 17, 2008	121-52			Sun conjunct	Sun opposite		
Dec. 17, 2008	130-51	Saturn conjunct Moon; Sun conjunct Neptune					
June 1, 2012	135-58					Sun, Mercury, Venus trine	Saturn conjunct
June 24, 2016	134-07			Sun, Venus square	Sun, Venus square		
July 6, 2016	134-075	Moon square				Sun, Mercury square	Venus square
Sept. 8, 2017	128-035	Sun, Pluto trine	Mercury, Mars square			Moon opposite	Jupiter conjunct

*Contract deliverable changed to 6% coupon from 8% coupon in 2000

IMPORTANT 10-YEAR T-NOTE LOWS

At important lows in the 10-year T-note futures contract, the Sun is the primary planet to watch. In 13 of 14 significant lows since 1982, the Sun has been involved in the transit of the day—either with the contract's natal Sun being activated or by the transiting Sun activating a natal planet.

Other natal planets that crop up in more than one-third of these lows include transits to the contract's natal Mercury, Mars, and Pluto (ruler of debt). Also interesting is that Mercury and Mars were activated simultaneously three times when transiting planets were at 00-03 Aquarius, forming a Grand Trine.

JUNE 11, 2009 LOW AT 112-51

After 10-year T-note prices had marked an all-time high in December 2008 on the heels of the financial crisis, prices set back substantially. The June 2009 reaction low ultimately supported a rally that lasted until prices peaked three years later at the current all-time high of 134-075.

The transiting Moon making a Grand Trine with Mercury and Mars shown in Figure 9.4 (A) set the stage for a potential low. (Be aware that the Moon hits this spot in early Aquarius once a month.) But the kicker was that the contract's natal Sun was being activated by three other planets. Venus and Mars were conjunct the Sun (B), and Saturn was making a 120-degree trine (C). Plus, prices were in the neighborhood of the Sun's conversion price of 1122.

Table 9.3 outlines the 14 significant lows in 10-year T-notes from May 1982 to December 2017 and the transits that activated the contract's natal horoscope.

Figure 9.4 Grand Trine and Sun in Play at 2009 10-yr. T-note Low

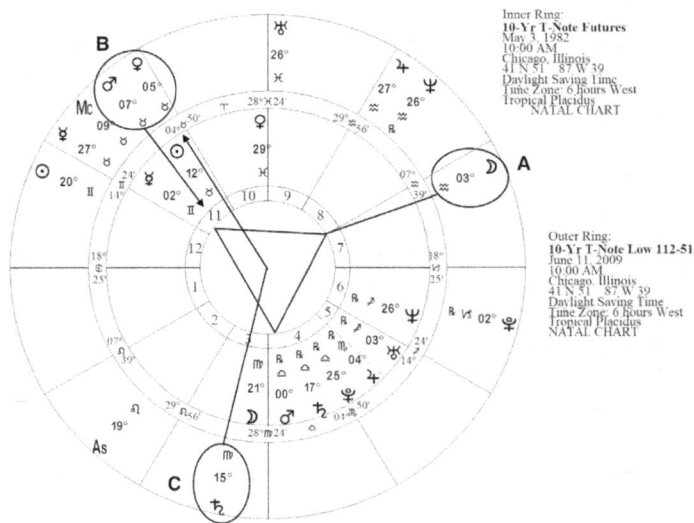

Table 9.3 Important Lows in 10-Year T-Notes

Astrological transits to significant natal planets						
Date	Price*	Sun	Grand Trine 00-03 Aq	Mercury	Mars	Pluto
June 23, 1982	68-02	(only Uranus trine Moon)				
May 30, 1984	70-34	Mercury conjunct		Venus, Sun, Moon conjunct		
Mar. 7, 1985	77-22		Jupiter	Grand Trine	Grand Trine, Mercury opposite	Venus, Mars opposite
Oct. 19, 1987	86-34	Mercury, Venus, Pluto opposite				Sun conjunct
May 2, 1990	92-52; Pluto price 925	Sun, Mercury conjunct			Venus opposite	
Nov. 7, 1994	99-04; Neptune price 986	Sun, Venus opposite; Moon trine				Mercury conjunct
Apr. 11, 1997	105-04	Mercury conjunct				Sun, Venus opposite
Jan. 21, 2000	93-43; Jupiter price 934		Sun, Neptune, Mercury	Grand Trine	Grand Trine	
Mar. 15, 2002	101-46	Mars conjunct			Sun opposite	
June 28, 2006	104-02	Saturn, Moon, Mars square; Jupiter opposite		Venus conjunct		
Oct. 16, 2008	111-25; Sun price 1122	Moon conjunct, Jupiter trine				Sun conjunct
June 11, 2009	112-51; Sun price 1122	Venus, Mars conjunct; Saturn trine	Moon	Grand Trine	Grand Trine	
Dec. 31, 2013	122-49	Sun, Mercury, Pluto trine				Moon conjunct
Dec. 20, 2016	122-290	Mercury, Pluto trine				

*Contract deliverable changed to 6% coupon from 8% coupon in 2000

TRANSITS TO WATCH IN 10-YEAR T-NOTES

The Sun is the most important planet to watch when looking for a high or low price in 10-year T-note futures. The contract's natal Sun at 12 Taurus was activated by a major transit (conjunction, opposition, square, trine) in more than half of the important highs and lows since trading in 10-year T-notes began in 1982. And, if the natal Sun wasn't involved, the transiting Sun likely was activating one of the contract's natal planets. Between the two, the Sun was involved more than 90 percent of the time. So, if the Sun isn't in play, the other transits might not mean much.

Next up in both highs and lows were the four corners of the mystic rectangle. I focused on Mercury and Mars, understanding that a conjunction to either one meant an opposition, trine, or sextile to the others (Venus and Uranus). Interestingly, when transiting planets hit 00-03 Aquarius, forming a Grand Trine with the contract's natal Mercury and Mars, it signaled three lows in the 28 total I had identified since 1982, but zero highs.

Two other natal planets to watch are Saturn and Pluto. Transits to Saturn were more often seen at times of important high prices (six highs to three lows), while transits to Pluto appeared equally, at six highs and six lows.

UPCOMING TRANSITS IN 10-YEAR T-NOTES

Based on the astrological transits present at previous highs and lows in the 10-year T-note futures market, I've looked into the future to see when similar patterns exist in 2018-2020.

I've set these dates up in the tables below where you (and I) can follow along and make notes about prices and market action around these dates. The dates in boldface are ones with particularly strong astrological transits vs. the 10-year T-note first-trade horoscope.

Table 9.4   2018 Potential 10-Year T-Note Futures Highs or Lows

Date	High or Low	Actual Price	Notes
April 9	High		
May 21	Low		
August 7	Low		
September 20	Low		
October 18	Low		

Table 9.5   2019 Potential 10-Year T-Note Futures Highs or Lows

Date	High or Low	Actual Price	Notes
January 2	High		
January 11	Low		
January 24	High		
February 5	High		
April 19	Low		
May 10	Low		
May 22	High		
June 10	High		
September 5	High		
September 13	High		
October 7	High		
October 18	Low		
November 26	High		
December 5	Low		
December 20	High		

Table 9.6   2020 Potential 10-Year T-Note Futures Highs or Lows

Date	High or Low	Actual Price	Notes
January 24	Low		
April 9	High		
May 1	Low		
September 23	High		
October 28	High		
December 21	Low		
December 28	Low		

OTHER CONFIRMED FIRST-TRADE DATA IN INTEREST RATE MARKETS

Many interest rate futures contracts have come and gone as market trends and demands have shifted. I have not listed them or researched them much, choosing to focus on currently active contracts.

Note that the list below covers only U.S.-listed futures contracts, even though there are many active contracts internationally that represent the other main borrowing costs in other countries, e.g., Britain's long gilt or the Japanese government bond. As I move my research more into the international arena (or as I happen to come across the data), those contracts will be added. If you have written documentation that supports the first day and time of listing on a non-U.S. exchange, I am all ears at TeamCommodityTimes@yahoo.com.

FUTURES

Eurodollars   December 9, 1981, 9:55 am, Chicago[48]

OPTIONS ON FUTURES

10-Year T-Notes   May 1, 1985, 10 a.m., Chicago[49]

---

48   "CFTC approves new Merc contract." Chicago Tribune. Business Ticker, 9 December 1981, p. C1.

49   Chicago Board of Trade records: Series III – Secretary's Records, Special Collections and University Archives, University of Illinois at Chicago, Monthly Letter to Members, April 1, 1985, p. 2.

CHAPTER 10
Metals

Gold Futures
December 31, 1974, 9:45 am, New York
Capricorn Sun

The beginning of the gold futures market is directly tied to legislation that lifted a 41-year ban on U.S. citizens owning gold that began during the Great Depression. The legislation allowed President Gerald Ford to authorize private ownership of gold through year-end 1974, with authorization automatic on January 1, 1975.

The New York Times reported that four futures exchanges were preparing to list gold futures contracts due to the new legislation—the Commodity Exchange (COMEX), the New York Mercantile Exchange (NYMEX), the Chicago Board of Trade (CBOT), and the Chicago Mercantile Exchange (CME).[50] Because of its strength in other metals futures markets and established connections with the gold dealers in London, COMEX's 100-oz. contract ultimately became the primary gold futures market in the United States. However, the CME gold contract, sized at 1 kilogram (35.3 oz.), gave it a run for its money for several years. Volume shifted definitively to New York in 1979-1980 as gold had its historic run-up to all-time highs above $800.

The COMEX gold futures contract opened on December 31, 1974 at 9:45 a.m. in New York. In promotional techniques now long gone, the exchange ran a display ad in *The New York Times* on opening day that announced the start of

---

50   Maidenberg, H.J. "Wall St. Firms Getting Set for Bullion," The New York Times. 2 September 1974.

trading. It also encouraged a request for more information about the contract and futures trading by clipping out a coupon and mailing it in.

Today, COMEX is owned by CME Group and offers two other gold futures contracts in different contract sizes, in addition to the 100-oz. benchmark size. The more popular of the two is the E-micro gold contract, sized at 10 troy oz., or 1/10 the standard contract, with the same 10-cent tick size. The second alternative is the E-mini gold contract, sized at 50 troy oz. and carrying a 25-cent tick. Gold futures trade for delivery in February, April, June, August, October, and December.

GOLD 101

Throughout history, gold has been the most precious of the precious metals, signifying wealth and prosperity, be it in a king's crown or a queen's jewelry. Because gold is malleable, rare, durable, and portable, it was a favored choice (along with silver) to be turned into coins as a means of monetary exchange some 2,500 years ago. According to the World Gold Council, gold was first made into coins by King Croesus of Lydia (now part of Turkey) around 550 BCE.

Gold was integral to worldwide monetary systems for more than 250 years, beginning in 1717 when Britain first effectively adopted a gold standard.[51] In the next century, Britain formalized its gold specie standard based on a new gold sovereign coin in 1821, and formally adopted a gold standard in 1844 when Bank of England paper notes were fully backed by gold.

In the United States, the Mint and Coinage Act of 1792 defined the U.S. dollar, associated it with the value of the widely used Spanish silver dollar, and established a fixed ratio of gold at 15 times the price the silver (later increased to 16:1),[52] a ratio that still is used as a benchmark for traders today. Silver was used for U.S. coins of $1 or less, while gold was used for coins of $2.50, $5, and $10.

Both the U.S. Civil War and World War I put a serious crimp in the ability to tie monetary policies and currencies to the price of gold. A year into the Civil War, the United States created a paper "greenback" that was deemed legal ten-

---

51 "Gold Standard," Wikipedia. 14 August 2017. <https://en.wikipedia.org/wiki/Gold_standard>.

52 "Coinage Act of 1792," Wikipedia. 10 September 2017. <https://en.wikipedia.org/wiki/Coinage_Act_of_1792>.

der, but had no connection to gold or silver, in order to pay its bills. Seventeen years later, in 1879, the United States made these paper greenbacks convertible into gold, thus tying the lighter paper money to the heavier metal money. Both Germany and Britain abandoned the gold standard during WWI as it became untenable because of war expenses. Britain returned to the gold standard in 1925, linking notes to the price of gold bullion rather than for exchange into gold coins. The return was short-lived, however, as the Great Depression's run on banks forced Britain off the gold standard in 1931.[53]

In the United States, the Federal Reserve—created in 1913 to be the country's central bank—was required to have enough gold to back 40 percent of its paper Federal Reserve notes (paper money). During the Depression, both U.S. banks and European central banks began cashing in their notes for U.S. gold, which then limited the amount of currency the Fed could have in circulation and tied its hands in stimulating the economy.

This is when newly elected President Franklin D. Roosevelt stepped in with Executive Order 6102 of April 5, 1933 that prohibited hoarding of gold or gold certificates by U.S. citizens. The penalty for ignoring the Order was $10,000 and/or up to 10 years in prison. Although small amounts of gold or gold coins could be retained, the rest was to be turned in to the Fed at the prevailing rate of $20.67 per oz. by May 1, 1933.

Nine months later, the official price of gold was raised to $35 per oz. by virtue of the Gold Reserve Act of 1934. The price remained there until President Nixon closed the gold window on August 15, 1971, no longer allowing conversion of U.S. dollars into gold. This is when the gold standard came to an end, as the U.S dollar had become the world's primary reserve currency after the Bretton Woods agreement of 1944 in which major currencies were linked to the dollar at fixed rates.

Nixon's decision thus created a free-floating and risky environment for both gold and currencies, which led to the creation of futures markets for those products in 1974 and 1972, respectively. Interestingly, a gold bullion futures contract similar to the one trading in London had been discussed in 1933, but the

---

53   "Gold Standard," Wikipedia. 14 August 2017. <https://en.wikipedia.org/wiki/Gold_standard>.

U.S. Treasury "…has not asked the Commodity Exchange, which recently absorbed the National Metal Exchange, to draw up plans for such a market…"[54]

FIRST-TRADE HOROSCOPE

Gold futures began trading at COMEX in New York on December 31, 1974 at 9:45 am.[55]

SUN IN CAPRICORN

Gold's first-trade/natal Sun is in the Earth sign of Capricorn, fitting for a precious metal that comes from deep within the earth. With the Sun in Capricorn, this market is stable and has longevity. Two other planets—Mercury (trading) and Venus (money)—also are in Capricorn, forming a three-planet "stellium" that adds extra oomph to the gold market's Capricorn tendencies.

MOON IN LEO

The Moon in gold's first-trade chart is in Leo, the sign ruled by the Sun, which is the planet that rules the gold market. That makes the two luminaries connected in a significant way. It also gives the market some emotional pizzazz that easily can bring it center stage.

ASCENDANT IN AQUARIUS

With Aquarius rising, the gold market is seen as being a maverick that marches to its own drummer, reacting to this rumor and that rumor with abandon. However, those reactions often fall under the umbrella of "flight to safety," which is exactly what you could expect when both the market's Sun and Ascendant are ruled by Saturn, the planet that provides grounding and stability.

OTHER IMPORTANT HOROSCOPE FEATURES

The most dominant feature of the gold market's first-trade horoscope chart (Figure 10.1) is the collection of three planets in Capricorn—Sun, Mercury,

---

54 "Gold Suits Loom For The Treasury." The New York Times. May 28, 1933.
55 "Gold Futures" display ad. The New York Times. December 31, 1974.

and Venus—directly opposite Saturn, the ruler of Capricorn (A). The Capricorn stellium provides more gravitas to the market's Sun-sign Capricorn characteristics of being a long-lasting, stable contract because all three planets are stronger when working together.

At first glance, Saturn opposite the Sun, Mercury, and Venus might seem to put a damper on the market's identity (Sun), trading (Mercury), and monetary value (Venus) because Saturn is a restrictive force that establishes boundaries. In opposition, it can be seen as in a tug-of-war with what the stellium wants to accomplish. However, Saturn is the ruler of Capricorn, so brings a more positive, helpful energy to the stellium, even in opposition. Thus, Saturn can help the Sun, Mercury, and Venus be deliberate and measured and not let trading volume or prices get wildly out of control. Saturn insists on providing value over the long haul.

Gold's first-trade contract also has three other connections that point toward three interesting points to watch for potential market movement as those points are activated by planets as they move through the sky. The first is a "yod" (B), formed by Mercury (trading), Jupiter (exaggeration), and the Moon (emotion). A yod is also known as the Finger of God, because fated events can happen when the yod's apex (the Moon, in this case) or the point opposite the yod apex is activated by a planetary transit. Therefore, watch closely when planets hit 13 degrees of either Leo or Aquarius; in other words, conjunct or opposite the first-trade Moon. For example, Venus was opposite the gold's first-trade Moon at the 2014 high of $1392 and the 2016 low at $1123.

The other two connections are based on two planets that are in trine (120 degrees apart) and form a Grand Trine when a transiting planet fills in the empty spot in the triangle. With a Grand Trine, things simply fall into place easily, with little or no effort. The first pair or planets in trine are the economic-oriented planets Jupiter and Saturn; a Grand Trine in Water signs forms when a transiting planet is going over 13-15 degrees of Scorpio, the same as the 9th house cusp (C). The second pair of planets in trine is the Moon in Leo and Mars in Sagittarius, forming a Grand Trine in Fire when a planet transits 13-14 degrees of Aries (D).

Figure 10.1   Gold Futures First-Trade Horoscope

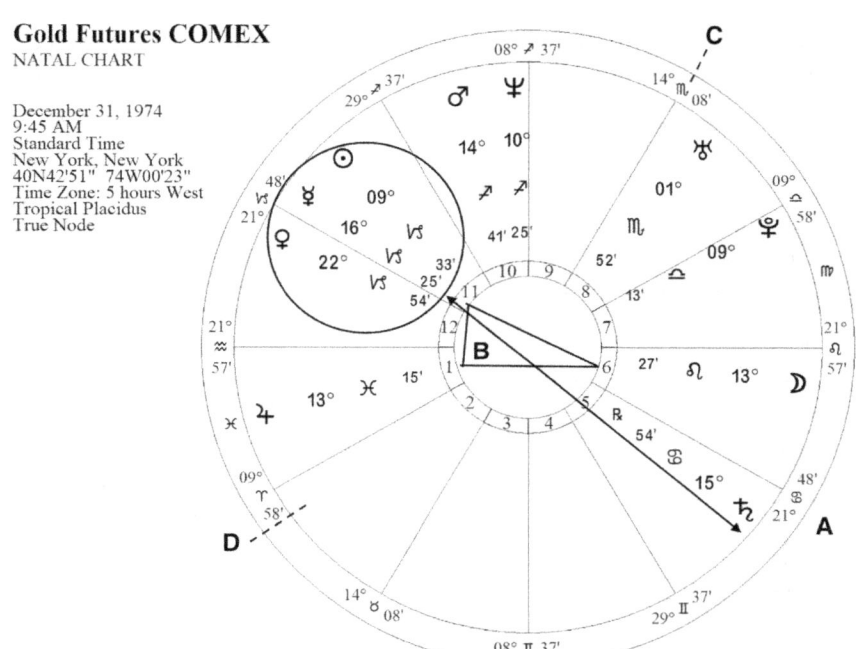

HOROSCOPE PRICE CONVERSION

The price conversion table that changes planetary positions into prices has worked especially well in the gold market, particularly the ascendant/descendant axis. In 1980, the blow-off top high of $875 went just $14 past the descendant price of $861; that high remained the record for 28 years. The 2011 high of $1920 was just $13 shy of the Moon's price of $1933.

In the other significant highs and lows discussed next in this chapter, prices converted from the first-trade chart's "angles," often appeared—mostly on the ascendant/descendant axis. Of the 20 highs reviewed since 1978, the price of 13 of those highs was within $14 of a price conversion point (Descendant—4; Ascendant—3; Saturn—3; MC—1; Venus—1; and Moon—1).

For significant gold market lows, getting within $10 of a price conversion point occurred in 75% of the 18 lows examined since 1978; more than 50% of the lows were within $5 of a price conversion point. The ascendant was involved the most, with 5 out of 18 connections. Then, nearly every other planet got into the act, with price lows associated with price conversion points for the Sun, Venus, Mars, Jupiter, Saturn, Neptune, Uranus, and Pluto. Only the Moon and Mercury prices did not translate into a gold market low.

Table 10.1 Gold Horoscope Price Conversions

Market	Gold Futures									
Rulers	Sun	Leo								
1st Trade	December 31, 1974, 9:45 am, New York									
Source	COMEX ad in NYT on 12/31/74 with date and time									
Price unit	Dollars per oz.									
Planet	Position	Conversion	360	720	1080	1440	1800	2160	2520	2880
IC	08 Gemini	68	428	788	1148	1508	1868	2228	2588	2948
Saturn rx	15 Cancer	105	465	825	1185	1545	1905	2265	2625	2985
Moon	13 Leo	133	493	853	1213	1573	1933	2293	2653	3013
Desc	21 Leo	141	501	861	1221	1581	1941	2301	2661	3021
Pluto	09 Libra	189	549	909	1269	1629	1989	2349	2709	3069
Uranus	01 Scorpio	211	571	931	1291	1651	2011	2371	2731	3091
MC	08 Sag	248	608	968	1328	1688	2048	2408	2768	3128
Neptune	10 Sag	250	610	970	1330	1690	2050	2410	2770	3130
Mars	14 Sag	254	614	974	1334	1694	2054	2414	2774	3134
Sun	09 Cap	279	639	999	1359	1719	2079	2439	2799	3159
Mercury	16 Cap	286	646	1006	1366	1726	2086	2446	2806	3166
Venus	22 Cap	292	652	1012	1372	1732	2092	2452	2812	3172
Asc	21 Aq	321	681	1041	1401	1761	2121	2481	2841	3201
Jupiter	13 Pisces	343	703	1063	1423	1783	2143	2503	2863	3223

Figure 10.2 Gold Planetary Prices Mark Support and Resistance

Source: Barchart.com

IMPORTANT GOLD HIGHS

Three factors rise to the top when analyzing what astrological factors played a role in important gold market highs since futures trading began in 1974:

1. Major transits (conjunct, opposite, square, trine, sextile) to gold's first-trade conjunction between Mercury and Venus at 16-22 Capricorn. In 18 of 20 highs examined, this pair of planets was activated by transit at the time of a market high. Mercury had 16 of 20 hits, while Venus had 14 of 20 hits.
2. Planetary ingresses, i.e., when a planet changes zodiac sign. Nine of 20 highs occurred on days of a sign change. Three highs were on days when the Sun changed signs (Aquarius, Libra, Virgo). Another three belonged to the day Mercury changed signs (two Scorpio, one Aquarius). Venus had two sign changes (Virgo and Cancer), with Saturn at one (Libra).
3. Price levels that align with planetary prices, determined by converting the gold first-trade chart planetary zodiac positions into prices. Half of the highs were connected to these planetary prices, mostly on the first-trade charts "angles," the ascendant (3), descendant (3), or MC (1).

SEPTEMBER 6, 2011 HIGH AT $1920.80

Gold futures topped at $1920.80 in the October 2011 contract on the first trading day after the Labor Day holiday, following a summer of concern about the European debt crisis and fears of a global economic slowdown that climaxed over the U.S. holiday weekend, when German voters expressed displeasure with the leadership's plan to help bail out Greece.

Here's how the planets played a role in that all-time record high, as shown in Figure 10.3:

- A   Activating the money planet, transiting Mars, at 22 Cancer, was exactly opposite the gold contract's first-trade Venus at 22 Capricorn; it also was opposite the first-trade Mercury.
- B   Indicating prices were in a good-as-it-gets area, transiting Sun, at 13 Virgo, was exactly opposite the gold contract's first-trade Jupiter at 13 Pisces; transiting Venus also was opposite natal Jupiter.

- C Transiting Sun and Venus promoted ease of trading as they were trine the gold market's natal Mercury.

- D In an easy, positive transit that occurs just twice every 12 years, transiting Jupiter, at 10 Taurus, was just one degree beyond an exact trine with the gold market's natal Sun, at 9 Capricorn.

- E Emotional intensity came from the transiting Moon, which was approaching the gold market's natal Sun as the market opened, and hit it exactly at 3:30 pm that day. Indeed, trading volume peaked that day at 447,296 contracts as futures traded in a $78 range, the highest volume of the month.

- F Putting a damper on prices was transiting Saturn at a 90-degree angle to both the gold market's natal Mercury and natal Saturn.

Figure 10.3 Gold Transits at 2011 High Connect to Natal Horoscope

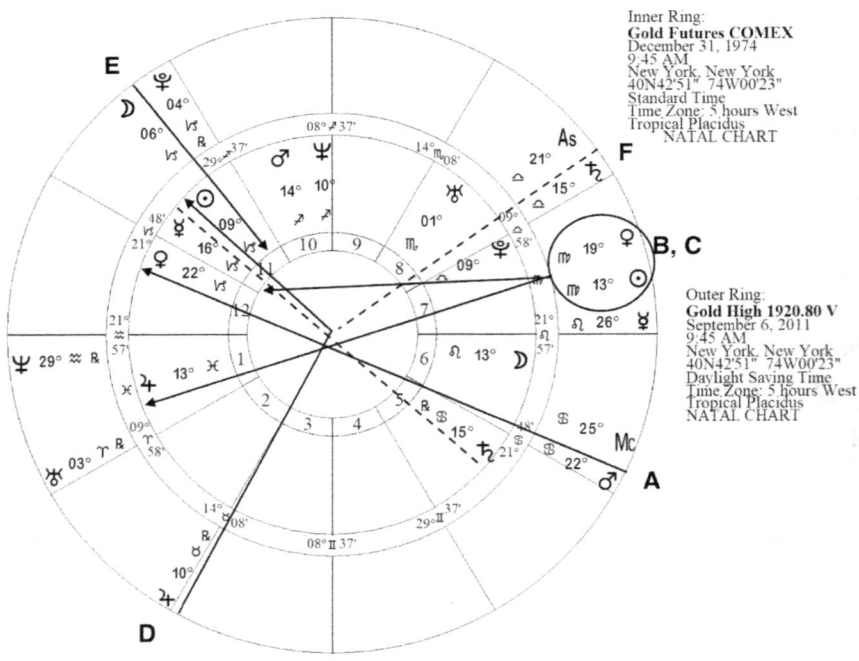

Trading In Sync With Commodities

Table 10.2 Important Highs in Gold

	Astrological transits to Mercury/Venus conjunction + Sign ingresses						
Date	Price	Conjunct	Opposite	Trine	Square	Sextile	Ingress
Oct. 30, 1978	247.00					Venus, Uranus, Mercury, Mars	
Jan. 21, 1980	875.00			Mars			Sun, Mercury @ 00 Aquarius
Sep. 23, 1980	729.00			Jupiter			Sun, Saturn @ 00 Libra
Sep. 8, 1982	501.00			Grand Trine–Sun, Moon			Venus @ 00 Virgo
Jan. 31, 1983	511.00	Mercury		Moon			
Feb. 16, 1983	514.00					Venus, Mars	
Dec. 14, 1987	502.30	Venus				Mars	
Aug. 2, 1993	409.00	Uranus, Neptune	Mercury	Mars			Venus @ 00 Cancer
Feb. 2, 1996	417.50	Mercury				Venus, Saturn	
Sep. 28, 1999	321.00			Moon, Saturn			
Oct. 5, 1999	327.50			Saturn			Mercury @ 00 Scorpio
Feb. 5, 2003	388.90	Mercury					
May 12, 2006	732.00		Mars	Sun, Mercury		Moon, Jupiter	
Mar. 17, 2008	1014.60	Jupiter					
Dec. 3, 2009	1227.00	No connections to Mercury/Venus. Mars conjunct and Sun trine to the Moon; Sun conjunct and Mars trine to Mars.					
Aug. 23, 2011	1912.80		Mars		Saturn		Sun @ 00 Virgo
Sep. 6, 2011	1920.80		Mars	Sun, Venus	Saturn		
Oct. 5, 2012	1796.40				Sun		Mercury @ 00 Scorpio
Mar. 17, 2014	1392.60	No Mercury/Venus connections. Jupiter opposite and Moon square to first-trade Sun. Venus opposite first-trade Moon.					
July 6, 2016	1180.20	Pluto	Sun, Mercury, Venus		Uranus	Mars	

145

IMPORTANT GOLD LOWS

The Venus/Mercury conjunction at 16-22 Capricorn is significant in both highs and lows in the gold market. However, Venus takes the lead on days of lows while Mercury is more dominant on days of highs. Watch for the Sun, Venus, Mars, and Jupiter to be conjunct, square, or trine Venus on the day of a low. Interestingly, Mercury was only conjunct or opposite Venus during a low. Venus was activated in 13 out of 18 lows examined since 1974.

Another similarity between days of gold market lows and highs is that of planets changing signs. For lows, pay close attention to when Jupiter moves into a new sign, as it was at 00 degrees of a sign in three of the lows shown here; the lows seem especially important when Jupiter is joined by another planet also moving into a new sign.

The gold market's first-trade Sun is a planet to watch when looking for a low. It was activated in half of the lows in Table 10.3 mostly by conjunctions or trines from the transiting Sun, Moon, Mercury, Mars, Jupiter, or Saturn. Note that Venus transits to the Sun were not present in these lows. However, Venus was either conjunct or opposite the gold market's first-trade Moon in four of these 18 lows.

Once again, the planetary price conversions are impressive at the time of important lows in the gold market. Of the 18 examined below, 11 lows were within $5 of a planetary price and 13 lows were within $10.

DECEMBER 29, 2011 LOW AT $1525.00

Less than four months after reaching an all-time high, gold prices dropped nearly $400 per oz. ($40,000 per single 100 oz. futures contract) in the front-month serial January 2012 contract on December 29, 2011. Although no planetary price was involved, several other astrological connections played a role, as shown in Figure 10.4:

- A   The Sun was within two days of a "solar return" with the first-trade gold horoscope, and was especially powerful as Pluto was at the identical degree of 07 Capricorn, just two degrees away from the gold market's natal Sun at 09 Capricorn.

Solar return is the name astrologers use for birthdays, both of which celebrate the return of the Sun to where it was at the time of birth and start a new cycle. Pluto's orbit of the Sun takes 248 years, so this conjunction was rare. Indeed, the Sun and Pluto were (or will be) conjunct at the same degree of Capricorn just 15 times between December 22, 2008 and January 20, 2029, and then not again for another 248 years.

Two years later, on December 31, 2012, the transiting Sun and Pluto were conjunct at 09 Capricorn, the same the as the gold market's first-trade Sun. That day (a Monday) marked a short-term high in the market at $1681, basis the February 2013 contract. By week's end, the market had dropped as low as $1626, a loss of $55 per oz.

- B   Action-taker Mars was activating both Venus and Mercury in an easy trine.

- C   Money planet Venus was approaching an exact opposition with the gold market's natal Moon.

- D   Trading boss Mercury was conjunct the gold market's natal Mars, stimulating the need to take trading action.

- E   Both Jupiter and Uranus had just changed signs, and were at 00 of Taurus and Aries, respectively.

Figure 10.4   Gold Natal Planets Activated at 2011 Low

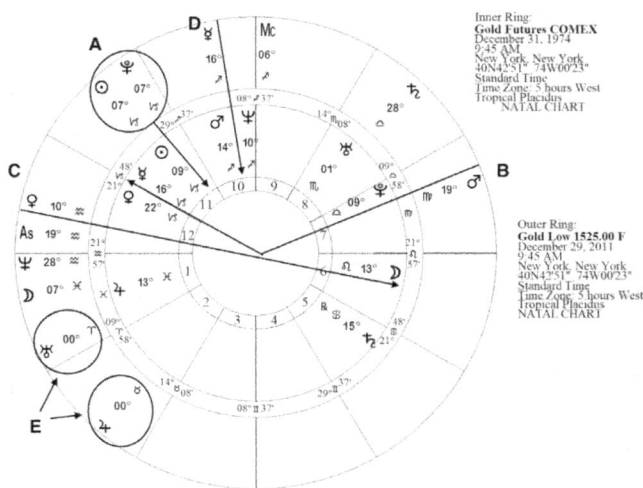

Table 10.3 Important Lows in Gold

Astrological transits to Venus and the Sun + Sign ingresses						
Date	Price	Planetary Price	Aspect to Venus	Mercury to Venus	Aspect to Sun	Ingress
Nov. 16, 1978	194.20	Pluto 189			Saturn trine	
Mar. 27, 1980	453.00		Grand Trine Saturn, Venus			
June 21, 1982	294.70	Venus 292	Venus trine			Jupiter @ 00 Scorpio
Feb. 25, 1985	281.00	Sun 279				
Mar. 10, 1993	326.00	Asc 321	Moon, Venus square		Mars opposite	
Sep. 13, 1993	341.40	Jupiter 343	Mars, Jupiter square			
Aug. 25, 1998	252.50	Neptune 250; Mars 254				
Apr. 2, 2001	255.00	Mars 254	Moon opposite			
Apr. 7, 2003	319.30	Asc 321	Mars conjunct; Sun square			
Oct. 6, 2006	560.50	Pluto 549; Uranus 571				
Oct. 24, 2008	680.80	Asc 681	Jupiter conjunct; Saturn trine		Jupiter conjunct; Moon trine	
Feb. 2, 2010	1044.30	Asc 1041		Conjunct		
Dec. 28, 2011	1525.00		Mars trine		Sun, Pluto conjunct	Jupiter @ 00 Taurus; Uranus @ 00 Aries
May 16, 2012	1526.70		Sun, Jupiter trine		Grand Trine, Pluto, Mars, Mercury	
June 28, 2013	1183.20	Saturn 1185		Opposite	Sun opposite	Jupiter @ 00 Cancer; Venus @ 01 Leo
Dec. 31, 2013	1182.00	Saturn 1185	Venus conjunct		Sun, Pluto, Mercury conjunct	
Nov. 27, 2015	1051.10	Asc 1041; Jupiter 1063	Jupiter trine; Venus square			
Dec. 15, 2016	1123.90				Mercury conjunct	

TRANSITS TO WATCH IN GOLD

Based on previous important highs and lows in the gold futures market, I recommend paying attention to transits that are activating the market's Capricorn planets in the first-trade horoscope chart. They include the Sun (09 degrees), Mercury (16 degrees), and Venus (22 degrees). Mercury (almost exactly in the middle of this trio) seems more attuned to market highs, while the Sun and Venus seem more attuned to market lows.

Also, as dates for interesting transits approach, pay attention to the planetary price conversion shown in Table 10.1, which have been within $10 of a high or low more than 50 percent of the time in the 38 charts examined in this chapter. In particular, the market seems attracted to the planetary prices of the Ascendant, Descendant, and MC (midheaven), especially for highs.

UPCOMING TRANSITS IN GOLD

Based on the astrological transits present at previous highs and lows in the gold futures market, I've looked into the future to see when similar patterns exist in 2018-2020.

The three big planets to watch for activating transits that could mark a high or low in the gold futures market are the Sun, Mercury, and Venus—all in the sign of Capricorn and all close enough together often to be stimulated by the same transit. The dates shown in in the following three tables focus on transits to those three planets, along with another interesting market seen in previous high/low charts—a planet moving into a new zodiac sign.

In the past, it seems as if the Sun and Venus are activated more at lows, while Mercury is more closely activated at a high. But, certainly there are examples of the reverse. Plus, when I've examined the individual horoscope charts associated with the dates below, there are usually other astrological factors in play that sway me toward marking the date as one for a potential high or low, even though there is not room to expound on those factors here. And, of course, market action as we approach each of these dates will be invaluable in helping discern if the market is heading toward a low or a high. But, at any rate, the dates below are worthy of putting in your calendar to pay attention to happenings in the gold futures market. The most interesting astrological chart connections, to me, are the dates in bold.

I've set these dates up in the tables below where you (and I) can follow along and make notes about prices and market action around these dates. The dates in boldface are ones with particularly strong astrological transits vs. the gold first-trade horoscope.

Table 10.4   2018 Potential Gold Futures Highs or Lows

Date	High or Low	Actual Price (nearby contract)	Notes
January 5	High	1324.70 (G18)	Jan. 4 high at 1327.30. Ultimately rallied to 1365.40 on Jan. 25 (G18)
February 21	High		
March 21	High		
April 27	High or Low		
May 25	Low		
September 11	Low		
September 14	High		
October 10	High		
December 21	High		
December 26	Low		

Table 10.5   2019 Potential Gold Futures Highs or Lows

Date	High or Low	Actual Price (nearby contract)	Notes
January 11	Low		
March 15	High		
April 9	High		
May 9	High or Low		
May 16	High		
June 11	High		
June 19	High or Low		
September 3	Low		
September 6	High or Low		
October 24	High		
December 10	High		

Trading In Sync With Commodities

Table 10.6   2020 Potential Gold Futures Highs or Lows

Date	High or Low	Actual Price (nearby contract)	Notes
January 13	Low		
February 27	Low		
March 20	High or Low		
March 26	Low		
May 5	High		
October 15	Low		
November 11	High or Low		
December 28	Low		

OTHER CONFIRMED FIRST-TRADE DATA IN METAL MARKETS

Important to note in the following first-trade data below is that the dates for the copper and silver markets at COMEX do not match those distributed by the Commodity Futures Trading Commission. Although the CFTC might be technically accurate that the first silver trade at COMEX occurred on July 5, 1933, when the newly merged and newly named exchange opened in its new building, the astrological charts of the two dates tell me that the June 1931 opening at the National Metal Exchange is the one to use.

For the two LME contracts, it will be interesting to see which time—when it first opened for trading, or when the first trade occurred—produces the more valuable first-trade horoscope chart. I'll be examining that plus other metals markets in Trading In Sync Supplements. If you have solid information on first-trade dates and times for other metal markets, please email them to TeamCommodityTimes@yahoo.com.

Copper   May 15, 1929, 10:00 am, New York[56]
Silver   June 15, 1931, 10:00 am, New York[57,58]

---

56   "Tin Trading Is Light." The New York Times. May 15, 1929.
57   "Rules Formulated For Silver Trading." The New York Times. May 14, 1931.
58   "Market Opens Here For Silver Futures." The New York Times. June 16, 1931.

LME Gold Futures[59]   July 10, 2017, London
                       1:00 am, open for trading
                       7:48:03 am, first trade
LME Silver Futures[60] July 10, 2017, London
                       1:00 am, open for trading
                       9:48:05 am, first trade

---

59   Email from LME official to Susan Gidel, September 26, 2017.
60   Email from LME official to Susan Gidel, September 26, 2017.

CHAPTER 11
Stock Indexes

Standard & Poor's 500 Index

March 4, 1957, 10:00 am, New York

Pisces Sun

In a departure from all the other chapters in this book that examine the connections between astrology and the first-trade charts of a futures contract, this chapter has not only two possible futures contract connections, but also the start date of the underlying cash market to consider. As you'll see later, all three horoscope charts provide valuable insights at times of significant market highs and lows, but the "mother" chart, in my opinion, is that of the founding of the S&P 500 index itself in 1957.

Standard & Poor's was formed in 1941 as two financial statistics companies joined forces. Poor's Publishing Co. had roots to 1860 in providing information about railroad companies,[61] the tech stocks of their day at the beginning of the Industrial Revolution. Standard Statistics Co. was founded in 1906 to cover non-railroad companies, and introduced its first stock index of 233 stocks in 1923.[62]

The Standard & Poor's 500 Index was introduced on March 4, 1957 as a way to track a broad cross-section of the stock market as opposed to just the 30 stocks that made up the well-known Dow Jones Industrial Average. It replaced the

---

61   "Our History." S&P Global. 3 October 2017. <https://www.spglobal.com/who-we-are/our-company/our-history>.

62   Valetkevitch, Caroline. "Timeline—Key Dates and Milestones in the S&P 500's History." Reuters. 28 March 2013.

S&P 90 index, originally introduced by Standard Statistics in 1926.[63,64]

The 1970s bear market, battered by inflation resulting from the changing crude oil market landscape globally, brought about two developments that put the S&P 500 into what would become the driver's seat among indexes by the mid-1980s. First, pension fund managers and other institutional investors began to use the S&P 500 as the benchmark to beat for their own portfolio performance.[65] Second, the first mutual fund tied to the index—what is now the Vanguard 500 Index Fund—was created in 1976 so that individuals could invest in the outcome of the stock market as a whole.[66]

By 1978 (five years after the Chicago Board Options Exchange opened to list options on stocks), U.S. futures exchanges were beginning to think about listing futures contracts on stock indexes, and were working to resolve both regulatory and logistical hurdles. By 1980, the Chicago Mercantile Exchange had cut its first licensing deal with Standard & Poor's to list a futures contract on the S&P 500, based on analysis that portfolio managers would be a big source of trading volume as natural hedgers.[67] The CME agreed to pay Standard & Poor's an annual licensing fee of $200,000[68] plus 10 cents per trade up to a certain capped amount for exclusive rights to a futures contract on the index.[69] It was a wise decision, indeed, to be better safe than sorry in going the licensing route from the start. It took 15 years of court battles over public domain/private licensing rights before Dow Jones & Company agreed to a license with the Chicago Board of Trade to list a futures contract on the Dow Jones Industrial Average.

---

63   "What Happened on March 4, 1957." OnThisDay.com. 3 October 2017. <http://www.onthisday.com/date/1957/march/4>.

64   Valetkevitch, Caroline. "Timeline—Key Dates and Milestones in the S&P 500's History." Reuters. 28 March 2013.

65   Sandor, Richard L. Good Derivatives. (Hoboken, N.J.: John Wiley & Sons, Inc., 2012) 61.

66   Valetkevitch, Caroline. "Timeline—Key Dates and Milestones in the S&P 500's History." Reuters. 28 March 2013.

67   Melamed, Leo and Bob Tamarkin. Leo Melamed—Escape to the Futures. (New York: John Wiley & Sons, Inc., 1996) 294.

68   Gidel, Susan Abbott. Stock Index Futures & Options. (New York: John Wiley & Sons, Inc., 2000) 48.

69   Melamed, Leo and Bob Tamarkin. Leo Melamed—Escape to the Futures. (New York: John Wiley & Sons, Inc., 1996) 295.

S&P 500 INDEX INTRODUCTION

I use the time of the New York Stock Exchange opening bell in 1957, 10:00 am, as the launch time of the S&P 500 index. The horoscope chart that time creates has great synergy with the natal horoscopes of the United States as well as the prevailing stock index at the time, the Dow Jones Industrial Average, so I think it's a good time.

SUN IN PISCES

The S&P 500 index natal Sun is in Pisces, the last sign of the zodiac. Pisces is the sign that belongs to visionaries and those on a transformational path. As time later proved, development of this index ultimately transformed the way investors interacted with the U.S. stock market, be it by benchmarking, investing in a mutual fund, or trading derivatives. At 13 degrees Pisces, the S&P 500 is trine to the natal sun of the United States, which was at 13 degrees Cancer on July 4, 1776. This connection indicates that the index has the green flag from the country on representing its identity.

MOON IN ARIES

With its natal Moon in Aries, the S&P 500 index is not shy about letting the public know what is what. Whether we want to hear it or not, the S&P 500 will tell us the truth about what is going on.

ASCENDANT IN GEMINI

Gemini—the sign that rules stock indexes—is fittingly on the S&P 500 ascendant. Because the ascendant represents the "personality" of the index, Gemini rising says this index is all about data, distribution, and trading. Interestingly, at 04 Gemini, the S&P 500 index ascendant is opposite the natal Moon of the Dow Jones Industrial Average, at 04 Sagittarius, and trine the natal Mars of the United States at 04 Leo—which means all three entities are tied together in an astrologically significant way.

OTHER IMPORTANT HOROSCOPE FEATURES

The biggest standout on the S&P 500 index natal horoscope chart (Figure 11.1) is the three-planet stellium in Pisces that includes the Sun, Mercury, and Venus (A). As we'll see later in this chapter, those three planets often play key roles at the time of significant market turns. Directly opposite part of this stellium is Pluto, at 28 degrees of Leo (B). Because Pluto moves so slowly, I consider it opposite just Mercury, at 00 Pisces, where it is 2 degrees apart. The 5 degrees to get to Venus is wide in my book.

Figure 11.1 S&P 500 Index Natal Horoscope

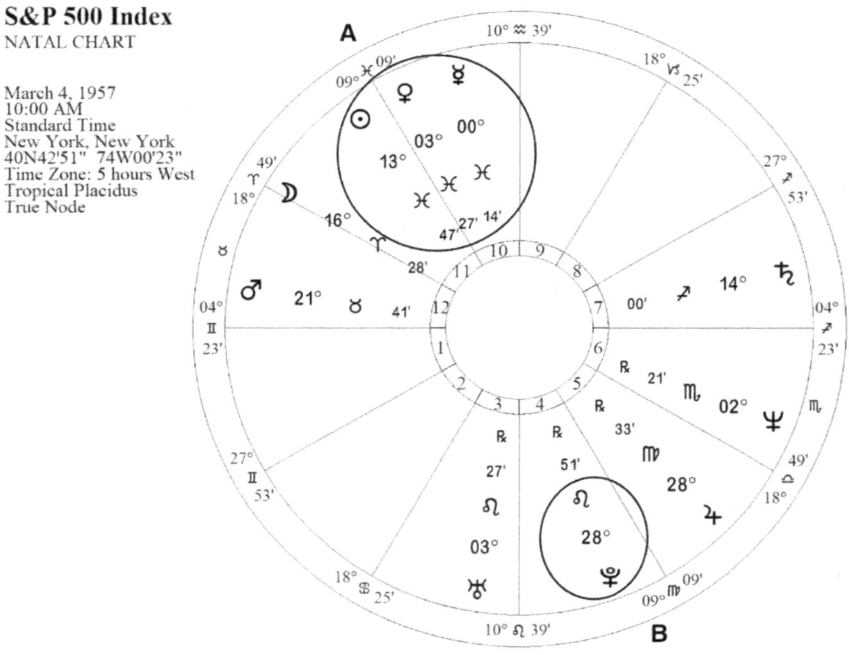

FUTURES FIRST-TRADE HOROSCOPES

Two futures contracts on the S&P 500—the original S&P 500 (ticker symbol SP) from 1982 and the electronic-only E-mini S&P 500 (ticker symbol ES) from 1997, both trade at CME Group in Chicago. It took little more than three years for volume in the electronically traded E-mini S&P 500 to overtake that of the larger, open-outcry contract, and now the E-mini S&P 500 is one of the most traded futures contracts in the world.

The E-mini S&P 500 is valued at $50 per point in the underlying index, so if the S&P 500 is at 2000, the E-mini contract value equals $100,000. The S&P 500 contract tick value is $250 per index point, so at the same index level represents $500,000 in contract value. Both contracts trade on the quarterly March, June, September, December expiration cycle.

Both futures contracts are available for trading nearly around the clock, opening each afternoon, Sunday-Thursday, at 5:00 pm (Chicago) and closing on the trade date the next day at 4:00 pm, after a trading halt from 3:15 to 3:30 pm. The original S&P 500 contract trades open-outcry from 8:30 am to 3:15 pm, then switches to electronic for the overnight hours.

S&P 500 FUTURES
April 21, 1982, 9:00 am, Chicago

The S&P 500 futures contract was not the first of its kind to open for trading, but it quickly became the leader. Having received regulatory approval the day before, the Chicago Mercantile Exchange began trading its signature stock index futures contract in Chicago when the opening bell at the New York Stock Exchange rang in New York. First-day trading volume was an industry-record 7,926 contracts—one that fell within weeks after the 10-year T-note opened across town at the Chicago Board of Trade. The S&P 500 was the right index with the right futures contract, introduced at the right time, just four months before the 1980s bull market began—and lifted annual CME trading volume by 40 percent in its first year.[70]

The S&P 500 futures first-trade Sun is in Taurus, which gives the contract its stability and longevity. Its first-trade Moon is in Aries, just like that of the S&P 500 index, and likewise brings a tell-it-like-it-is-whether-you-want-to-know-or-not energy to daily trading. The futures contract's Cancer ascendant shows how the contract is seen by hedgers as a protection tool against stock portfolio losses.

The biggest and most important connection between the S&P 500 futures first-trade horoscope and the S&P 500 index horoscope (Figure 11.2) is that the futures contract's Venus and midheaven (MC)—both at 15 Pisces—are con-

---

70   Tamarkin, Bob. The Merc. (New York: HarperBusiness, 1993) 279.

junct the Sun of the 1957 index start date, at 13 Pisces (A). Venus—the money planet—is at its absolute best in Pisces, and is extremely strong at the top of the S&P 500 futures chart. That the futures contract Venus is conjunct the underlying index Sun emphasizes the ability to make money with the derivative contract based on the identity of the original index.

Also striking is that the S&P 500 futures contract's first-trade Uranus, is within 1 degree of the S&P 500 Index descendant, at 04 Sagittarius (B), thus increasing the possibility of quick changes as planets cross that important angle. Another angle, the future contract's ascendant, at 08 Cancer, easily connects hedging with the underlying index by a trine aspect as it splits the difference between the index Venus and Sun (C). All in Water signs, the markets and money move fluidly between the index and the futures contract.

Figure 11.2   S&P 500 Futures Connects Strongly with S&P 500 Index

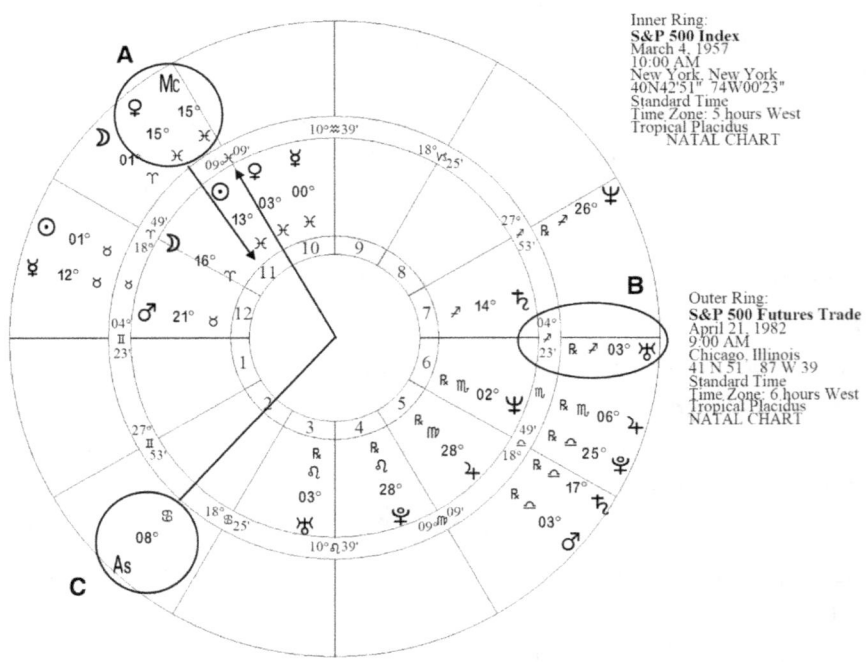

E-MINI S&P 500 FUTURES
September 9, 1997, 10:30 am, Chicago

Launching the E-mini S&P 500 futures contract was a daring move by the Chicago Mercantile Exchange as it was the industry's first electronically traded contract that was open during regular open-outcry trading hours.[71] But, the heat was on to address not only the newfound online stock trading of the dot-com era, but also the potential appeal to retail traders of the new DJIA futures contract at its rival, the Chicago Board of Trade. So, the CME bit the bullet, made its flagship contract into a retail-friendly contract size, put it on an electronic platform—and beat the CBOT to the punch by listing the E-mini S&P a month before DJIA futures opened.

Based on (1) coverage of opening day by *The Wall Street Journal* that said the day's volume was about 8,000 contracts (7,494 to be exact) in the four-hour and 45-minute session[72] and (2) that the big S&P closed at 3:15 pm, I am using 10:30 am for the E-mini S&P 500 first-trade chart. Once again, given the synergies between the E-mini S&P 500 and other related horoscope charts, it works for me.

Figure 11.3 shows how the horoscope charts of the original S&P 500 index, the big S&P 500 futures contract, and the E-mini S&P 500 futures contract interact, even though they are separated by as much as 40 years:

- A   The E-mini S&P 500 has its Sun at 16 Virgo, opposite the S&P 500 index Sun at 13 Pisces and the S&P 500 futures Venus/MC at 15 Pisces, making this axis extremely strong.

- B   Similarly, the E-mini S&P 500 first-trade Mercury, at 02 Virgo, is opposite the S&P 500 Index natal Mercury/Venus combination, emphasizing the trading aspect of the index and the futures contract.

- C   The E-mini S&P 500 also has a planet aligned with that strong 04 Sagittarius descendant of the underlying index that includes

---

71 Gidel, Susan Abbott. <u>Stock Index Futures & Options.</u> (New York: John Wiley & Sons, Inc., 2000) 52.

72 Lucchetti, Aaron. "'Mini' Contract Based on S&P 500 Opens Big on CME." <u>The Wall Street Journal.</u> September 10, 1997, p. C30.

the big contract's natal Uranus. This is yet another reason to pay attention to transits at 03-04 Sagittarius, because they affect the underlying S&P 500 index and both futures contracts.

- D   The E-mini S&P 500 ascendant, at 04 Scorpio, is aligned with the big contract's first-trade Jupiter at 06 Scorpio and the S&P 500 Index natal Neptune at 02 Scorpio. Throw in the S&P 500's natal Sun across the wheel at 01 Taurus, and the 01-06 axis of Taurus/Scorpio is another to watch closely as transiting planets cross it.

Figure 11.3   Strong Connections Between S&P 500 Index and Two Futures Contracts

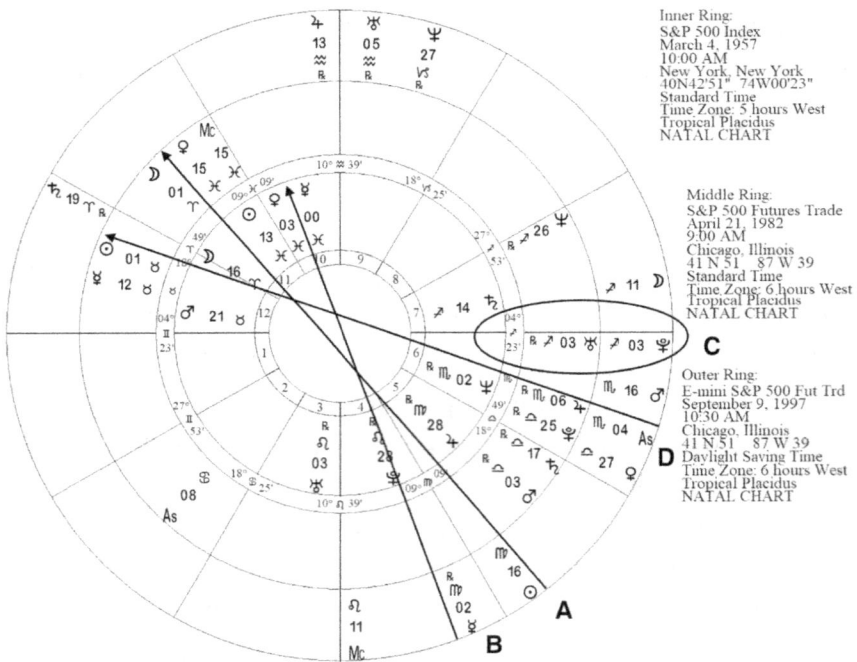

SYNERGIES WITH THE S&P 500 INDEX

The astrological synergies with the S&P 500 index from 1957 don't stop with the two futures contracts that bear its name. The S&P 500 index horoscope chart also shows some pretty amazing connections with three others: (1) the

Dow Jones Industrial Average, first published in 1896; (2) the founding of the United States in 1776; and (3) the first-ever exchange-traded fund, Standard & Poor's Depository Receipts (SPDR), launched in 1993.

All of the synergies are listed in Table 11.1. Read them going across from the S&P 500 index natal planet in the left column for how that planet connects to the planet or point from the other charts in the top row. For example, "Conjunct Venus, MC" in the first box under S&P 500 Futures means that the S&P 500 index Sun is conjunct the S&P 500 futures Venus and midheaven.

To me, two synergies stand out in particular. First—and almost amazingly—the natal Moon of the S&P 500 Index from 1957 has a connection with every one of these other natal horoscope charts. (The E-mini connection is that the S&P index Moon is the apex of a "yod" that forms by making 150-degree aspects to the E-mini's first-trade Sun and Mars.) These connections mean that a transit to the S&P index natal Moon at 16 Aries also activates planets in all the other charts—all at once!

Second, I'm stunned by the gravitation toward 04 Sagittarius—the important descendant angle in the S&P 500 Index horoscope—by all these charts, except for the SPDR. There are 360 degrees in the zodiac wheel and just 10 planets in each chart. To have the horoscope charts of two stock indexes, two futures contracts, and the United States all have a planet or angle hone in on one of those degrees astounds me in its astrological beauty. But, wait, there's more. Although not shown in this table, the futures contract for the Dow Jones Industrial Average first-trade horoscope has three planets in that area as well—Pluto, Mars, and the Moon. There is simply no denying the importance of transits in the 03-05 Sagittarius area to the U.S. stock market because of these synergies.

Table 11.1 S&P 500 Index Natal Horoscope Connections

S&P 500 Index	S&P 500 Futures	E-mini S&P 500 Futures	SPDR ETF	DJIA	USA (Sibley)
Sun	Conjunct Venus, MC	Opposite Sun			Trine Sun
Moon	Opposite Saturn	Yod apex (Sun, Mars)	Opposite Jupiter	Conjunct Descendant	Opposite Saturn
Mercury		Opposite Mercury			Conjunct Moon; Trine Venus/Jupiter
Venus		Opposite Mercury			Conjunct Moon; Trine Venus/Jupiter
Jupiter					Conjunct MC
Saturn					Conjunct Ascendant
Uranus			Opposite Sun, Moon, Mercury	Conjunct Jupiter	
Neptune					Trine Venus
Pluto					Opposite Moon
Descendant	Conjunct Uranus	Conjunct Pluto		Conjunct Moon, Opposite Sun	Opposite Uranus

HOROSCOPE PRICE CONVERSION

Again, in a departure from the previous chapters, you'll find four horoscope price conversion tables to peruse—one for the cash index, two for the futures contracts, and one that combines the common zodiac degrees across all three.

S&P 500 INDEX

Like the horoscope chart itself, the S&P 500 index price conversion table that converts zodiac planetary positions into prices has more hits for highs and lows than those of the two futures contracts (Table 11.2). Of the significant highs and lows examined since 1982, prices on the S&P index conversion table were in play for 17 highs and 14 lows. The midheaven (MC) and Uranus price conversions were tied with three highs and one low each. Interestingly, all the Jupiter hits were associated with market lows.

Trading In Sync With Commodities

Table 11.2   S&P 500 Index Planetary Price Conversions

Market	S&P 500 Cash Index									
Rulers	Gemini	Mercury	Jupiter alternate							
1st Trade	March 4, 1957; 10 am									
Source	Standard & Poor's; used 10 am NYSE open									
Price unit	1 point									
Planet	Position	Conversion	360	720	1080	1440	1800	2160	2520	2880
Moon	16 Aries	16	376	736	1096	1456	1816	2176	2536	2896
Mars	21 Taurus	51	411	771	1131	1491	1851	2211	2571	2931
Asc	04 Gemini	64	424	784	1144	1504	1864	2224	2584	2944
Uranus rx	03 Leo	123	483	843	1203	1563	1923	2283	2643	3003
IC	10 Leo	130	490	850	1210	1570	1930	2290	2650	3010
Pluto rx	29 Leo	158	518	878	1238	1598	1958	2318	2678	3038
Jupiter rx	28 Virgo	178	538	898	1258	1618	1978	2338	2698	3058
Neptune rx	02 Scorpio	212	572	932	1292	1652	2012	2372	2732	3092
Desc	04 Sag	244	604	964	1324	1684	2044	2404	2764	3124
Saturn	14 Sag	254	614	974	1334	1694	2054	2414	2774	3134
MC	10 Aq	310	670	1030	1390	1750	2110	2470	2830	3190
Mercury	00 Pisces	330	690	1050	1410	1770	2130	2490	2850	3210
Venus	03 Pisces	333	693	1053	1413	1773	2133	2493	2853	3213
Sun	13 Pisces	343	703	1063	1423	1783	2143	2503	2863	3223

S&P 500 FUTURES

In the S&P 500 futures market, price conversions were evenly split, with nine highs and 10 lows (Table 11.3). Interestingly, the Sun price was associated with three lows, but zero highs.

Table 11.3   S&P 500 Futures Planetary Price Conversions

Market	S&P 500 Futures									
Rulers	Gemini	Mercury	Jupiter alternate							
1st Trade	April 21, 1982, 9:00 am, Chicago (matched 10 am NYSE open)									
Source	CFTC for date; NYSE opening time									
Price unit	1 point									
Planet	Position	Conversion	360	720	1080	1440	1800	2160	2520	2880
Moon	01 Aries	1	361	721	1081	1441	1801	2161	2521	2881
Sun	01 Taurus	31	391	751	1111	1471	1831	2191	2551	2911
Mercury	12 Taurus	42	402	762	1122	1482	1842	2202	2562	2922
Asc	08 Cancer	98	458	818	1178	1538	1898	2258	2618	2978
IC	15 Virgo	165	525	885	1245	1605	1965	2325	2685	3045
Mars rx	03 Libra	183	543	903	1263	1623	1983	2343	2703	3063
Saturn rx	17 Libra	197	557	917	1277	1637	1997	2357	2717	3077
Pluto rx	25 Libra	205	565	925	1285	1645	2005	2365	2725	3085
Jupiter rx	06 Scorpio	216	576	936	1296	1656	2016	2376	2736	3096
Uranus rx	03 Sag	243	603	963	1323	1683	2043	2403	2763	3123
Neptune rx	26 Sag	266	626	986	1346	1706	2066	2426	2786	3146
Desc	08 Cap	278	638	998	1358	1718	2078	2438	2798	3158
MC	15 Pisces	345	705	1065	1425	1785	2145	2505	2865	3225
Venus	15 Pisces	345	705	1065	1425	1785	2145	2505	2865	3225

E-MINI S&P 500 FUTURES

The price conversion table for the E-mini S&P 500 futures contract has been associated with five highs and five lows since trading began in 1997 (Table 11.4). So far, the midheaven (MC) is the only point that has two connections, both highs.

163

Table 11.4 E-mini S&P 500 Futures Planetary Price Conversions

Market	E-mini S&P 500 Futures									
Rulers	Gemini	Mercury	Jupiter alternate							
1st Trade	September 9, 1997, 10:30 am, Chicago									
Source	CFTC for date; my research with WSJ article for time									
Price unit	1 point									
Planet	Position	Conversion	360	720	1080	1440	1800	2160	2520	2880
Saturn rx	19 Aries	19	379	739	1099	1459	1819	2179	2539	2899
Desc	04 Taurus	34	394	754	1114	1474	1834	2194	2554	2914
MC	11 Leo	131	491	851	1211	1571	1931	2291	2651	3011
Mercury rx	02 Virgo	152	512	872	1232	1592	1952	2312	2672	3032
Sun	16 Virgo	166	526	886	1246	1606	1966	2326	2686	3046
Venus	27 Libra	207	567	927	1287	1647	2007	2367	2727	3087
Asc	04 Scorpio	214	574	934	1294	1654	2014	2374	2734	3094
Mars	16 Scorpio	226	586	946	1306	1666	2026	2386	2746	3106
Pluto	03 Sag	243	603	963	1323	1683	2043	2403	2763	3123
Moon	11 Sag	251	611	971	1331	1691	2051	2411	2771	3131
Neptune rx	27 Cap	297	657	1017	1377	1737	2097	2457	2817	3177
Uranus rx	05 Aq	305	665	1025	1385	1745	2105	2465	2825	3185
IC	11 Aq	311	671	1031	1391	1751	2111	2471	2831	3191
Jupiter rx	13 Aq	313	673	1033	1393	1753	2113	2473	2833	3193

COMMON DEGREES

The beauty of having three unique horoscopes associated with a single market is that the synergies among them are easily seen with the price conversion table. In Table 11.5, the planets from all three horoscopes that are within 5 degrees of each other are sorted by zodiac position, and then their individual prices converted. What results are clumps of prices that can be used as heftier areas of support or resistance than just a single price on its own. Note that each of the three horoscopes is represented in two degree areas—02-06 Scorpio and 03-04 Sagittarius—granting all-around importance to those prices.

Most interesting is that the end of the price cycle—at 13-15 Pisces—seems significant in marking major market turning points (Figure 11.4). For example, the August 1987 top was 342 in the S&P 500 futures contract vs. the 343-345 prices that converted from the S&P index Sun and the futures contract's Venus and MC. This area also marked the highs in 1999 and 2015 as well as the lows in 2015 and 2016.

Table 11.5 Planetary Price Conversions Cluster at Common Degrees

Converting Horoscope into Prices										
Market	S&P 500 Cash Index, S&P 500 Futures, E-mini S&P 500 Futures common degrees									
Market	S&P 500 Cash Index (SPC), S&P 500 Futures (SP), E-mini S&P 500 Futures (ES) common degrees									
Rulers	Gemini	Mercury	Jupiter alternate							
Price unit	1 point									
Planet	Position	Conversion	360	720	1080	1440	1800	2160	2520	2880
Moon SPC	16 Aries	16	376	736	1096	1456	1816	2176	2536	2896
Saturn ES	19 Aries	19	379	739	1099	1459	1819	2179	2539	2899
Sun SP	01 Taurus	31	391	751	1111	1471	1831	2191	2551	2911
Desc ES	04 Taurus	34	394	754	1114	1474	1834	2194	2554	2914
IC SPC	10 Leo	130	490	850	1210	1570	1930	2290	2650	3010
MC ES	11 Leo	131	491	851	1211	1571	1931	2291	2651	3011
Jupiter SPC	28 Virgo	178	538	898	1258	1618	1978	2338	2698	3058
Mars SP	03 Libra	183	543	903	1263	1623	1983	2343	2703	3063
Pluto SP	25 Libra	205	565	925	1285	1645	2005	2365	2725	3085
Venus ES	27 Libra	207	567	927	1287	1647	2007	2367	2727	3087
Neptune SPC	02 Scorpio	212	572	932	1292	1652	2012	2372	2732	3092
Asc ES	04 Scorpio	214	574	934	1294	1654	2014	2374	2734	3094
Jupiter SP	06 Scorpio	216	576	936	1296	1656	2016	2376	2736	3096
Uranus SP	03 Sag	243	603	963	1323	1683	2043	2403	2763	3123
Pluto ES	03 Sag	243	603	963	1323	1683	2043	2403	2763	3123
Desc SPC	04 Sag	244	604	964	1324	1684	2044	2404	2764	3124
Moon ES	11 Sag	251	611	971	1331	1691	2051	2411	2771	3131
Saturn SPC	14 Sag	254	614	974	1334	1694	2054	2414	2774	3134
MC SPC	10 Aq	310	670	1030	1390	1750	2110	2470	2830	3190
IC ES	11 Aq	311	671	1031	1391	1751	2111	2471	2831	3191
Jupiter ES	13 Aq	313	673	1033	1393	1753	2113	2473	2833	3193
Sun SPC	13 Pisces	343	703	1063	1423	1783	2143	2503	2863	3223
MC SP	15 Pisces	345	705	1065	1425	1785	2145	2505	2865	3225
Venus SP	15 Pisces	345	705	1065	1425	1785	2145	2505	2865	3225

Figure 11.4 Planetary Prices and S&P 500 Support/Resistance

Source: Barchart.com

IMPORTANT S&P 500 HIGHS

Transits to the three planets in Pisces in the S&P 500 Index natal horoscope—Sun, Mercury, and Venus—are the most important to watch as indicators of a potential high in the market. Of the 23 highs I examined since S&P 500 futures opened in 1982, half (11) involved transits to the S&P Index natal Sun, with those to Mercury (8), Venus (9), and the Descendant (9) not far behind. Transits to the S&P 500 Index natal Moon came in at seven out of 23, including the pre-financial crisis high in October 2007.

1. S&P 500 INDEX SUN

As noted in the previous section and Table 11.1, paying attention to the S&P 500 Index natal Sun (13 Pisces) also means you're automatically paying attention to significant planets in other significant charts: (1) S&P 500 futures Venus and midheaven; (2) E-mini S&P 500 Sun; and (3) USA Sun. In the 23 highs examined, transiting planets were opposite or conjunct the S&P 500 Index Sun eight times, evenly split.

2. S&P 500 INDEX MERCURY/VENUS

The S&P 500 natal Mercury (00 Pisces) and Venus (03 Pisces), when activated by transiting planets, also mean the E-mini S&P 500 natal Mercury is highlighted. In addition, the S&P 500's Mercury/Venus combination is tied in with the 1776 horoscope of the United States in two significant ways. First, the pair is conjunct with the USA's natal Moon, representing the public. Second, they are trine the USA's natal Venus and Jupiter, representing abundance and prosperity.

3. FUTURES CONTRACTS PLANETS TO WATCH

In addition to transits to planets in the S&P 500 Index horoscope, there are a couple more from the first-trade charts of the two futures contracts to keep on the radar. First, watch for conjunctions or oppositions to the S&P 500 futures contract natal Mars, at 03 Libra. Transits to this planet were present in five of the 23 highs examined. Second, watch for conjunctions to the E-mini S&P 500 futures contract midheaven, at 11 Leo. In the 12 highs examined since the contract opened, two involved planets conjunct the E-mini's MC, the highest point in the chart and one of the four important angles.

OCTOBER 11, 2007 HIGH—1576.09

The first cracks of the 2008 financial crisis were beginning to appear in mid-2007 as investing and lending tension over subprime housing loans began to stretch and then snap. In the headlines that summer was news that a hedge fund from Bear Stearns heavily invested in the subprime derivatives was taking a serious hit. (Bear Stearns went under in March 2008 as a result.) Then, even the banks were getting so nervous that they quit lending to each other in the overnight market, creating a liquidity crisis that was highlighted when BNP Paribas refused withdrawals from hedge fund clients.

On October 11, 2007, when the S&P 500 made a record high at 1576.09 (1586.75 in the E-mini S&P 500 futures contract) that would not be surpassed for another six years, the market was breathing a sigh of relief that the Fed would likely cut interest rates again by the end of the year. Two days earlier, release of the Fed's minutes from its September 18 meeting—when it cut rates for the first time in four years—had made it clear that was the intention.

In this case, the market did its job of anticipating the future, topping two months before economic recession officially began in December 2007 (but not identified as "official" until a year after the fact). Here's how the planets called the top (Figure 11.5):

- A   The New Moon in Libra was opposite the natal Moon of the S&P 500 index, which also is connected to significant points in a host of related charts as discussed previously. A transiting opposition is akin to mid-summer—the peak of expression—which in this case, turned out to be the peak in the market.
- B   Venus and Mercury in the S&P 500 index chart were activated from two directions. First, by opposition from Venus (money) and Saturn (restriction). Second, by trine from Mars (action), which greased the skids for trading activity.
- C   The Sun in the S&P 500 index horoscope chart also was activated from two directions. First, transiting Mercury was coming up

on an exact trine with the S&P's Sun, and working well with transiting Mars, too, in support of action-oriented trading activity. Second, transiting Uranus was beyond the S&P 500 by two degrees, but still close enough to be considered conjunct and influencing some energy in terms of delivering a change of trend.

- D   Finally, transiting Jupiter remained conjunct the S&P 500 index natal Saturn, having been exactly aligned just two weeks earlier. Jupiter exaggerates what it touches, and in this case, it was touching reality-check Saturn. Once again, the message was that the party was over.

Figure 11.5   S&P 500 Peaks at New Moon in October 2007

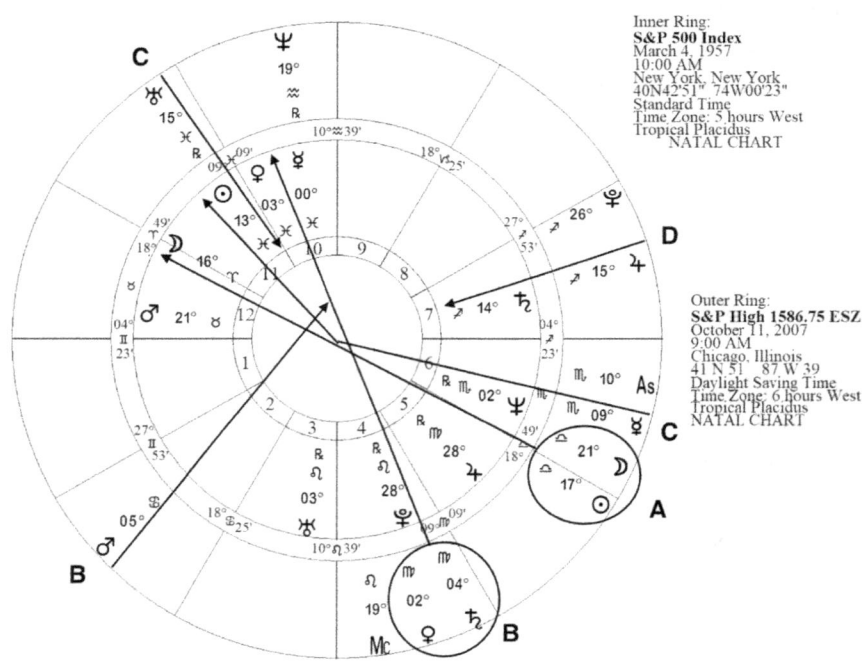

Trading In Sync With Commodities

Table 11.6   Important Highs in S&P 500 Futures

Astrological connections to the S&P 500 Index Sun, Mercury, Venus, Mars						
Date	Price	Planetary Price*	S&P Sun	S&P Mercury	S&P Venus	S&P Mars
Sep. 4, 1986	256.40	SPC Saturn 254	Mercury, Sun, Moon opposite			
Mar, 26, 1987	305.70	SPC MC 310				Mars conjunct
Aug. 25, 1987	339.45	SPC Sun 343; SP Venus, MC 345	Moon opposite	Mars, Sun, Venus opposite	Venus opposite	
Jan. 3, 1990	364.80	SP Moon 361	Sun, Neptune sextile			
Jan. 15, 1992	422.85	SP Asc 424	Jupiter opposite; Uranus, Neptune sextile		Jupiter opposite; Mars, Mercury sextile	Pluto opposite
Jan. 31, 1994	483.10	SPC Uranus 483	Sun conjunct; Jupiter trine	Mercury conjunct	Jupiter trine	
Sep. 29, 1995	592.60					Mars opposite
Feb. 13, 1996	667.10	SPC MC 670		Sun, Mars conjunct		
May 23, 1996	683.20					Mercury conjunct
Feb. 19, 1997	820.40	SP Asc 818			Sun conjunct	
Oct. 7, 1997	992.25	SP Neptune 986, SP Desc 998				
July 20, 1998	1199.40	SPC Uranus 1203				
July 19, 1999	1431.20	SP MC/Venus 1425		Venus opposite	Venus opposite	
Mar. 24, 2000	1574.00	SPC IC 1570; ES MC 1571	Venus conjunct		Mercury conjunct	
May 22, 2001	1319.00	SP Uranus & ES Pluto 1323; SPC Desc 1324				
Mar. 19, 2002	1177.50	SP Asc 1178	Mercury conjunct			

169

Oct. 11, 2007	1586.75	SPC Pluto 1588	Uranus conjunct	Venus, Saturn opposite	Venus, Saturn opposite	
May 19, 2008	1441.00	SP Moon 1441		Saturn opposite	Saturn opposite	Moon opposite, Venus conjunct
Apr. 26, 2010	1216.75	SPC IC 1210, ES MC 1211				
May 2, 2011	1373.50	ES Neptune 1377		Neptune conjunct		
May 19, 2015	2133.70	SPC Sun 2143				
Nov. 3, 2015	2110.00	SPC MC 2110; ES IC 2111; ES Jupiter 2113	Jupiter opposite			
Aug. 23, 2016	2191.50			Sun opposite		

*SPC = Cash; SP = Futures; ES = E-mini futures

IMPORTANT S&P 500 LOWS

In keeping your eyes open for a low in the S&P 500, several planets in the 1957 index horoscope chart are often activated. The Sun and Moon have the most tallies, at 10 out of 19 lows examined since 1982. Jupiter, Venus and Uranus are tied at 8, with Mercury close behind at 7.

SUN, MOON, URANUS

In whittling down transits that seem especially significant at market lows, I've chosen to focus on those to the S&P 500 index natal Sun, Moon, and Uranus. In market lows, it was the supportive, easy trine aspect to the S&P 500 Sun that dominated, in six out of 10 instances. For market highs, the Sun was most often aspected by conjunction or opposition, either of which can tend to mark the end of a movement.

The S&P 500 Moon was activated at a market low in 10 of 19 instances, mostly by conjunction or opposition from the Sun (8) or Venus (5). The Sun is opposite the S&P 500 Moon in October every year, which may be part of the reason why eight of the 19 lows since 1982 have occurred in that month.

The S&P 500 natal Uranus, at 03 Leo, is connected to the United States horoscope at the country's IC, or 4th house cusp. This is considered a point where change is made and new ideas spring forth—both of which apply to the character of Uranus. Although not part of that stunning collection of points at 03-04 Sagittarius, the S&P 500 natal Uranus is 120 degrees away from it in trine aspect. So, as with trines to the S&P 500 Sun, activation of the S&P 500 index Uranus makes a trine with everything associated with the S&P 500 natal descendant at 04 Sagittarius (see Table 11.1).

JULY 6, 2010 LOW—1003.10

In the summer of 2010, the stock market was under pressure as it adjusted to the reality of new regulations spawned from the financial crisis of 2008 (Dodd-Frank would be signed into law on July 21, 2010), continued concerns over the European debt crisis, and the "Flash Crash" of May 6 that pinned high-frequency traders for sending the S&P 500 down about 65 points and back within 36 minutes.

The S&P 500 bottomed on the first day back from the long July 4 holiday weekend, holding the important barrier of 1000 on the chart. Astrologically, the S&P 500 index natal Sun and Uranus were both in play as they can be at an important low. In addition, natal Jupiter was part of the action, too. Here's how it looked astrologically (Figure 11.6):

- A   Transiting Sun at 14 Cancer was making a trine to the S&P 500 natal Sun at 13 Pisces.
- B   The S&P 500 index natal Sun also was activated by transiting Mars, across the chart in opposition at 16 Virgo.
- C   Slow-moving Saturn was at the same degree as the S&P 500 natal Jupiter, a connection that occurs every 29 years.
- D   Across the chart from the S&P 500 natal Jupiter were transiting Jupiter and Uranus.
- E   Transiting Jupiter and Uranus also were trine to the S&P 500 index natal Uranus, providing a big boost of energy.

Susan Abbott Gidel

Figure 11.6 Transits to Sun, Jupiter, Uranus Mark 2010 Low in S&P 500

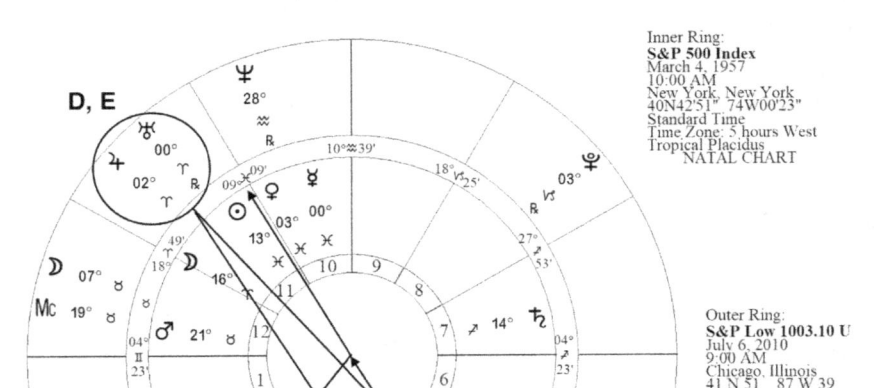

Table 11.7 Important Lows in S&P 500 Futures

Astrological transits to the S&P 500 Index Sun, Moon, and Uranus						
Date	Price	Planetary Price*	Sun	Moon	Uranus
Sep. 12, 1986	226.65		Sun opposite, Jupiter conjunct		
Oct. 20, 1987	181.00	SPC Jupiter 178; SP Mars 183	Mercury, Venus, Pluto trine		
Aug. 23, 1990	305.20	SPC MC 310			Jupiter conjunct
Oct. 11, 1990	295.60			Mercury, Venus, Sun opposite	

Trading In Sync With Commodities

Oct. 5, 1992	390.00	SP Sun 391	Grand Trine with Venus, Mars	Sun opposite	Moon opposite
Apr. 4, 1994	434.75		Jupiter trine	Sun conjunct	Moon opposite
July 16, 1996	610.25	SPC Saturn 614			Uranus opposite; Moon, Mercury conjunct
Oct. 8, 1998	929.00	SP Pluto 925; ES Venus 927; SPC Neptune 932		Sun, Venus opposite	
Oct. 18, 1999	1241.60	SP IC 1245; ES Sun 1246	Venus opposite	Sun opposite	
Mar. 22, 2001	1088.50	SP Moon 1081		Venus conjunct	
Sep. 21, 2001	939.00	SP Jupiter 936; ES Asc 934	Jupiter trine		
July 24, 2002	771.30	SPC Mars 771	Venus opposite		Moon opposite; Jupiter, Sun, Mercury, Mars conjunct
Oct. 10, 2002	767.50	SP Mercury 762; SP Mars 771	Neptune trine	Sun opposite	
Mar. 17, 2008	1253.10	SPC Jupiter 1258			Moon conjunct
Mar. 6, 2009	663.30	ES Uranus 665	Sun conjunct	Venus conjunct; Moon trine	
July 6, 2010	1003.10		Sun trine, Mars opposite		Jupiter, Uranus trine
Oct. 5, 2011	1106.80	SP Sun 1111		Sun, Mercury, Saturn opposite	
Oct. 15, 2014	1813.50	SPC Moon 1816; ES Saturn 1819		Venus, Sun opposite; Uranus conjunct	
Aug. 24, 2015	1831.00	SP Sun 1831; ES Desc 1834	Sun, Jupiter conjunct Pluto and opposite Mercury, Venus. Mercury conjunct Jupiter		
Feb. 11, 2016	1803.50	SP Moon 1801			Moon trine

*SPC = Cash; SP = Futures; ES = E-mini futures

TRANSITS TO WATCH IN S&P 500

Because of the many planetary overlaps with the S&P 500 index horoscope with the two futures contracts based on the S&P 500 index, I consider the natal chart of when the cash index was created in 1957 to be the main one to use when looking at transits that could portend a potential high or low in the stock market.

Keep your eyes on five planets—Sun, Moon, Mercury, Venus, and Uranus—when watching for a change of trend in the S&P 500 market.

1. Sun—tends toward conjunctions or oppositions at market highs; trines at market lows.
2. Moon—favors conjunctions or oppositions from the Sun at lows; from other planets at highs.
3. Mercury—conjunctions or oppositions at highs, particularly when a planet matches it at 00 Pisces; the same at lows, but not as frequent as at highs.
4. Venus—sees conjunctions or oppositions at both highs and lows as well as occasional trine.
5. Uranus—particularly sensitive to conjunctions and oppositions from the Moon at lows, but also watch for transits from the Sun, Mercury, Mars, and Jupiter.

UPCOMING TRANSITS IN S&P 500

Based on the astrological transits present at previous highs and lows in the S&P 500 futures market, I've looked into the future to see when similar patterns exist in 2018-2020.

I've set these dates up in the tables below where you (and I) can follow along and make notes about prices and market action around these dates. The dates in boldface are ones with particularly strong astrological transits vs. the S&P 500 Index natal horoscope of 1957.

My scan of transits to the S&P 500 index from 2018 through 2020 produced nearly double the number of potential highs vs. potential lows, I think largely because the variables I focus on for identifying a low occur less frequently than those that occur for a high. Interestingly, one date in each year has the transit potential to be either a low or a high—August 23, 2018; April 5, 2019; and February 21, 2020. We'll just have to wait and see where the market is trending going into those periods to figure out whether a top or bottom ultimately is favored.

In the following tables, three dates warrant particular attention:

- **August 23, 2018**—This is one of the days that could be a high or a low, although the September 6, 2018 chart two weeks later favors a low. Both have natal Uranus in a Grand Trine with transiting Saturn and Uranus. Whatever takes place, will take place easily, suddenly and with authority.
- **August 30, 2019**—This date harkens back to October 19, 1987 and the Crash of 1987 because it, too, has five planets in Virgo, all opposite the S&P 500 natal Sun, Venus, and Mercury.
- **November 10, 2020**—On this day, the S&P 500 natal Sun and Moon—always a horoscope's most important planets—are each activated by two planets. Because the transiting Sun is trine the S&P 500's natal Sun, the nod goes toward this being a market low.

Table 11.8   2018 Potential S&P 500 Futures Highs or Lows

Date	High or Low	Actual Price	Notes
February 18	High		
May 22	High		
July 23	High		
August 23	High or Low		
September 6	Low		
November 8	High		
November 27	Low		

Table 11.9   2019 Potential S&P 500 Futures Highs or Lows

Date	High or Low	Actual Price	Notes
February 19	High		
April 5	High or Low		
August 23	High		
August 30	High		
September 6	High		
October 10	Low		
November 6	High		

Table 11.10 2020 Potential S&P 500 Futures Highs or Lows

Date	High or Low	Actual Price	Notes
February 21	High or Low		
March 3	High		
April 3	Low		
May 13	High		
July 27	Low		
August 26	High		
October 9	Low		
November 10	Low		
November 25	High		
December 4	High		

OTHER CONFIRMED FIRST-TRADE DATA IN STOCK INDEXES

DJIA Cash	May 26, 1896, 3:00 pm, New York*
S&P 500 Options on Futures	January 28, 1983, 9:00 am, Chicago[73]
SPDR ETF	January 22, 1993, 9:30 am, New York[74]

*Although not confirmed from other sources, I use the NYSE close of that year, 3:00 pm, as the "birth time" of the Dow Jones Industrial Average on the theory that whoever was doing the calculating had nothing more than a pencil, a piece of paper and maybe an adding machine available. To calculate a new stock average once a day, based on the day's closing prices just seems to make sense to me. Plus, it creates a horoscope chart that has the natal Moon at 04 Sagittarius—opposite the natal Sun and completing a Grand Trine in Fire with Mars and Jupiter. It also is a degree area that connects with horoscope charts for the S&P 500 cash index, S&P 500 futures and E-mini S&P 500 futures as well.

---

[73] "Open Outcry" newsletter. Chicago Mercantile Exchange. January 1983, p. 1.

[74] Prestbo, John A. "Legacy of the 1987 Crash: The ETF." The Wall Street Journal. 9 October 2017.

CHAPTER 12
Outlook 2018-2020

Now that we've examined each of six major market sectors—ag, energy, metals, currencies, interest rates, and stock indexes—it's time to see how they jibe in the future. This is exciting because being able to get a big-picture outlook into the future was a major reason I wrote this book.

I've always been fascinated about what makes markets move, and always have enjoyed the well-rounded view of the world I've gotten for more than 40 years by observing the commodity futures markets. I truly believe that markets can digest world news and tell you what it means faster than any reporter, pundit, or tweeter. That's because words are just words, but money talks. So, when traders use money to take a position based on world news and events, it is best to listen.

Clearly, I do not have a crystal ball that can see into the future. No one does. But what I do have is an astrological ephemeris that gives me dates when big planetary shifts will occur in the future as well as when they occurred in the past. And, now that I've researched the astrological signatures for market turns in six markets representing major economic sectors, I've got dates for potential changes in market trends. Put the two together, and there are some interesting time periods to watch. You can put them on your calendar way ahead of time and then see how your other trading signal tools may or may not begin to align with them.

For now, I'll stick to the three years leading up to the next U.S. presidential election year of 2020—a period that could contain a stock market high that is followed by a substantial bear market.

WATCHING FOR A TOP IN STOCKS

Although this book focuses on the Standard & Poor's 500 index because of its trading dominance in the stock index futures category, I've also done research on how long-term astrological cycles play into market highs and lows based on the Dow Jones Industrial Average, which has data back to when it was first published in 1896.

Interestingly, the DJIA was introduced just seven months before the start of the longest astrological cycle that has economic significance, the 45-year cycle of Saturn and Uranus. Thus, it's easy to compare how the stock market moved with this cycle. We currently are in the tail end of the third Saturn/Uranus cycle since the DJIA began, and the similarities of stock price movement with certain periods of the cycle are striking.

In all three cycles to date (1897-1942, 1942-1988, and 1988-2032), here's how the DJIA behaved:

1. Made a significant low in the six months previous to the initial Saturn/Uranus conjunction (the start of each astrological cycle)
2. Made an all-time high near the Saturn/Uranus opposition (the halfway point of each astrological cycle)
3. Suffered a severe correction from those all-time highs (47 percent in Cycle I, 36 percent in Cycle II, 54 percent in Cycle III)
4. Recovered from the correction after the all-time high at the opposition, surpassing that high five to six years later.
5. Set the ultimate high of the 45-year Saturn/Uranus cycle in the last 13 years of the cycle—year 32 (1989) in Cycle I and year 45 (1987) in Cycle II.

Based on the first two Saturn/Uranus cycles since the DJIA began, the years 2017-2020 are prime ones to watch for a potential ultimate high of Cycle III, the Saturn/Uranus cycle that began in 1988 and ends in 2032.

Granted, there are only two other cycles with which to compare. But, the consistency of stock market behavior with astrological cycle aspects through the first half of the current cycle and a few years beyond makes a compelling argument to be on alert as Saturn and Uranus make their final, "waning" trine and final, "waning" square of Cycle III, from 2017-2021.

In Cycle I (1897-1942), the ultimate high in the stock market was the 1929 high near 380 on the Dow (Figure 12.1). That occurred six months before the final Saturn/Uranus square of the cycle. Then, the Dow dropped 89% to its Great Depression low in 1932. The similar period in the current cycle would be in the last half of 2020, before the waning Saturn/Uranus square begins in February 2021.

Figure 12.1 Dow Peaks in 1929 Before Saturn/Uranus Waning Square

In Cycle II (1942-1988), the ultimate high in the stock market was very near the cycle's end, at the August 1987 high of 2722 (Figure 12.2). However, the Dow did make a significant high during the waning trine (120-degree aspect) between Saturn and Uranus, at 1051 in 1973, and then dropped by 47 percent into 1974. After pressure from the Saturn/Uranus square in 1975-1977, the Dow ultimately rose to its cycle high in 1987.

Susan Abbott Gidel

Figure 12.2 Dow Peaks in 1987 Near End of Saturn/Uranus Cycle

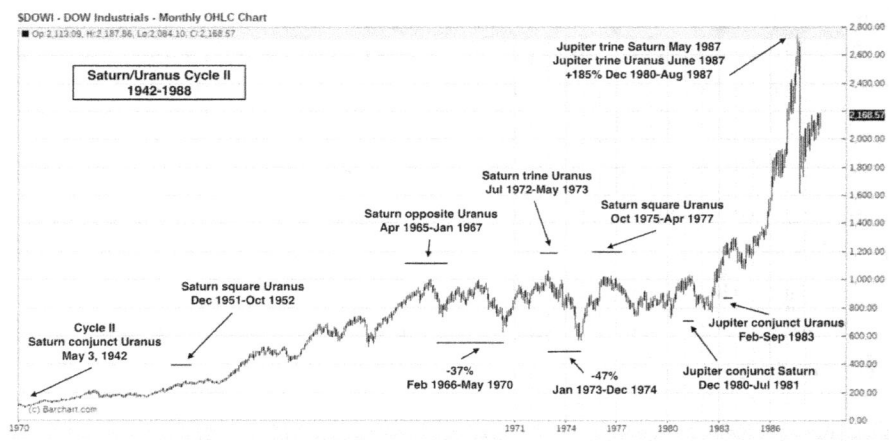

The waning trine in the current cycle occurred from December 2016 to November 2017—a period that saw new record highs in the Dow nearly every month (Figure 12.3). If Cycle III follows the pattern of Cycle II, look for a severe correction from the high that occurs in the waning trine/waning square period of 2017-2020, with the ultimate high for this 45-year period sometime in the late 2020s.

Figure 12.3 Dow Seeking Ultimate High in Saturn/Uranus Cycle Ending 2032

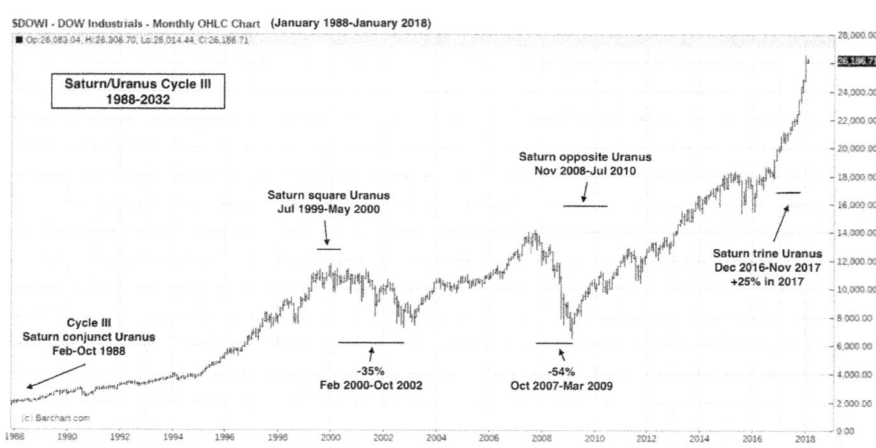

In conclusion, what the two previous Saturn/Uranus cycles reveal is that there is potential for a significant high in the DJIA—and a subsequent decline of 47 percent to 89 percent—as the planets are in the last third to last quarter of the 45-year cycle, from December 2016 to December 2021.

What the two previous cycles also reveal is that the last push to the ultimate cycle high was fueled both times by the first third of the Jupiter/Uranus cycle, from conjunction through waxing trine. In Cycle III, this occurs from April 2024 through October 2028. Thus, there is potential for the ultimate high in Cycle III to follow more the pattern of Cycle II, with the waning trine/waning square high of 2017-2020 later surpassed. I will be examining this more in later supplements to this book, so stay tuned!

MY BOOMER PERSPECTIVE

As a card-carrying, middle-of-the-pack Baby Boomer, I have been driven to focus on how the stock market behaves during the Saturn/Uranus cycle for a very selfish reason. I need to take my investments earmarked to fund retirement off the table before the stock market does its next deep dive because I'm running out of time to recover from that. I can't afford to take a hit like many of us did in 2000 or 2008 and the years it takes for the market to get back to even, let alone continue to climb.

Here are the facts about recovery times—and they are measured in years, if not decades. The ultimate high in Cycle I—380 in the Dow in 1929—was not surpassed for 25 years, until 1954. The ultimate high in Cycle II (2746 in the Dow in 1987, that occurred very late in the cycle) was surpassed two years later to the day; however, the penultimate high in Cycle II (at the Saturn/Uranus trine) in January 1973 at 1067 on the Dow, was not surpassed until November 1982, nearly 10 years later.

Whether the stock market high that I see as possible in the 2017-2020 period is the final one of this Saturn/Uranus cycle (like Cycle I) or the penultimate one (like Cycle II), I'll be well into my retirement years when the next Saturn/Uranus cycle starts in 2032. So, I'm pretty sure I won't be here for the all-time stock market high of Cycle IV—when Saturn is opposite Uranus in 2056-57—unless I beat my family's genes and live to 100.

BUSINESS CYCLE SHIFTS

A second reason for awareness about the potential for a stock market peak by 2020 is that the current U.S. economic cycle that began in June 2009, as measured by the National Bureau of Economic Research, is long in the tooth. If the expansion continues to July 2019, it will set a new record of 121 months. As I've learned from Ph.D. economist Robert F. Dieli of RDLB, Inc. in his monthly reports, understanding when conditions are ripe for a turn in the business cycle is helpful not only for business planning, but also for being positioned well for the stock market top that typically arrives pre-recession (although NBER identifying when recession begins could come months, if not years, after the fact). That's because the end of economic expansion and entrance into recession signifies not just a stock market correction, but a true bear market, such as occurred in 2000 and 2008. As I discuss later in this chapter, 2019 has some astrological potential for an end to the current expansion.

A third indicator that we are in a period of economic highs comes from a cycle discovered after the Great Depression by economist Louise McWhirter. The McWhirter Cycle shows that the U.S. business cycle peaks with the Moon's North Node in the sign of Leo and is at its bottom when the North Node is in sign 180-degrees opposite, Aquarius. The North Node entered Leo in May 2017 and stays there until November 2018.

Thus, the stock market high that is established in 2017-2021 could be in place as the all-time high for several years—six to 16 years if it follows the pattern of Cycle II, or up to 25 years if it follows the pattern of Cycle I. The McWhirter cycle indicates the next period of peak U.S. economic activity will be when the North Node is once again in Leo, from December 2035 to May 2037, just three years into the new Saturn/Uranus cycle.

2018—REFLECTION AND REVIEW

Overall, 2018 is a year of reflection and review because of the preponderance of planets in retrograde motion, which means they are not working at their highest potential. On vacation. Slacking off on their duties. A time when it's hard to make forward progress.

The first two months of 2018 are pretty good. With the exception of New Year's Day, all the planets are direct in motion for January and February. Then, the slacking off begins and doesn't end until near Labor Day. We get a month of breathing room until Venus (the planet ruling money) turns retrograde on October 5. Venus doesn't turn direct until mid-November, when Mercury takes the retrograde baton through early December.

MARCH 2018

Jupiter turns retrograde on March 14—which can be hard on the stock market—and a week later, the transits point toward a potential high in the gold and Euro FX markets.

APRIL 2018

Saturn and Pluto turn retrograde within four days of each other, on April 18 and April 22, respectively. Both in Capricorn, they insist on providing needed structure to changes in business and government.

MAY 2018

Uranus, the disrupter, moves into the Earth sign of Taurus on May 15, and the results literally could be earth-shaking. Be on alert if you are in an earthquake-prone area. (In 2011, the last time Uranus changed zodiac signs, the 9.0 magnitude earthquake that rocked Japan and its nuclear plants at Fukishima occurred two days before Uranus entered the sign of Aries.)

Over a two-week period from May 11 to 25, five of the six markets covered in this book could be making significant trend changes. Look for potential highs in soybeans, Euro FX, and the S&P 500, and potential lows in gold and 10-year T-notes.

On May 25, Jupiter (retrograde) makes the second of three trine aspects to Neptune. The first was on December 2, 2017 and the third occurs on August 19, 2018. This relationship can be both visionary as well as crisis-oriented. The entire 10-month period also might make it easy for inflation to expand.

JUNE 2018

Two markets show the potential for a change in trend on June 8—a high in crude oil and a low in Euro FX. Ten days later, Neptune joins Jupiter, Saturn, and Pluto by turning retrograde on June 18. On June 26, Mars piles on the retrograde train for a total of five planets retrograde out of a possible eight. At the Mars retrograde and into the first half of August, watch for news about Chinese debt issues.[75]

JULY 2018

July 2018 marks 32 months before the first Saturn/Uranus waning square, when the DJIA topped in Cycle II in 1973 at 1051, then dropped 47% over next 21 months.

The first astrological signature in July is that Venus hits the degree of the 2017 Great American Eclipse on July 8, which could bring a spurt of news about U.S./North Korea tensions—or perhaps some conciliatory gestures given that Venus is the planet of both love and money.

A bit of retrograde pressure eases on July 10, when Jupiter turns direct in motion. However, Mercury starts its second retrograde period of the year on July 26.

The partial solar eclipse on July 13 portends endings and separations in personal relationships. That theme is echoed at the total lunar eclipse on July 27, the day after Mercury retrograde begins. So, that would be a good time to review current relationships or renew previous ones.

AUGUST-SEPTEMBER 2018

From August 7 to 18, every planet but Venus and Jupiter are in retrograde motion as Uranus joins the backward-movement party on the 7th. Then, Mercury turns direct on August 19, with Mars following suit on August 27.

On August 19, Jupiter makes its final trine to Neptune, so the issues that appeared in December 2017 and/or May 2018 should have some closure. Four days later, on August 23, the astrological transits hitting the S&P 500 index

---

75 Schoeppel, Marie. "The Hangover: In 1997, It Was Bangkok—In 2019, It's Beijing," GlobalTrendCycles.com. 3 November 2017. <https://www.globaltrendscycles.com/finance/2017/6/27/china-financial-collapse-2019>.

natal chart activate planets that have been stirred up in previous highs and lows in the market, so either is a possibility. Look to news about U.S./North Korea nuclear tensions to be a trigger during this period as the Sun transits the degree of the Great American Eclipse on August 21.

However, on September 6, the third trading day after Labor Day, the transiting planets are in a position associated with a low in the S&P 500 market. Perhaps not coincidentally, that is also the day that Saturn turns direct in motion, lifting its foot off the brake that has been there since it turned retrograde in mid-April. On September 5, Mercury crosses the degree of the Great American Eclipse of 2017, adding to the fire power.

OCTOBER 2018

Pluto turns direct in motion on October 1. But the money planet, Venus, goes retrograde on October 5, putting a potential damper on the stock market until it turns direct on November 16.

NOVEMBER 2018—MID-TERM ELECTION HUBBUB

The astrological universe is rockin' and rollin' on November 5-9, a period that includes the U.S. mid-term elections on November 6 when voters will decide who occupies all 435 seats in Congress and 33 out of 100 seats in the Senate for the 116th Congress that begins in January 2019. In addition, gubernatorial elections will be held in 36 of 50 states as well as three U.S. territories.

On Election Day, three significant astrological events occur:

1. Uranus, which is retrograde, moves back into the sign of Aries, where it stays until early March 2019. Coming from staid Taurus, this jolt into Aries could be explosive and stay that way for four months.
2. It is the 28th day of the 7th lunar month, one associated with stock market bearishness.
3. The Moon's North Node moves into the sign of Cancer through May 5, 2020, a period that economist Louise McWhirter associated with a top in the U.S. real estate market. What's more, Jupiter in Scorpio is trine the North Node in Cancer on November 7-8, further supporting the idea of a peak in real estate, according to McWhirter.

In addition, three markets show indications of a trend change during that trading week—a high in the S&P 500 and lows in Euro FX and crude oil.

On Friday, November 9, Jupiter moves into its ruling sign of Sagittarius, where it will stay until December 2019. This carries an optimistic flavor as well as one in which justice seeks its highest good. A week later, Venus turns direct on November 16 and could lift its downer-effect on the markets. The next day, however, Mercury turns retrograde until December 6, so trading could go haywire. Neptune turns direct on the Sunday after Thanksgiving.

DECEMBER 2018

After the hubbub of November, December is pretty quiet from an astrological perspective. Mercury turns direct in motion on December 6, lifting worries about travel delays over the year-end holidays.

The day before the winter solstice of December 22, astrological transits point toward a low in the crude oil market and a high in gold.

2019—LOOKING TOPPY

Interesting astrological forces converge in 2019—particularly at mid-year—that point toward a potentially significant top in the stock market:

1. The peak effect from the August 21, 2017 total solar eclipse that crossed the United States (the Great American Eclipse) is from March to October.

2. On August 23, the planetary lineup mirrors a signature that occurred at the 1987 high. On October 19, 1987, the Dow Jones Industrial Average dropped a record 22.6 percent.

3. Three potential ends to the June 2009 economic expansion, based on astrological signatures, are in play in January, June, and September.

JANUARY 2019

January is one of the three months in 2019 that shows astrological potential for an end to the U.S. economic expansion that began in June 2009. Of the three, this is the second strongest, with Jupiter square Neptune (exact on January 13) and Jupiter opposite the USA natal Uranus placement from 1776.

On January 6, Uranus turns direct in motion on the same day as a partial solar eclipse that is about involvement with unusual groups, something that Uranus represents. Go figure. The connected total lunar eclipse is on January 15.

In between the two eclipses, watch for lows in the gold and 10-year T-note markets on January 11.

MARCH 2019

March is the first of eight consecutive months identified by astrologer Ben Dykes as the "shared peak" for expression of the energy from the total solar eclipse that crossed the United States on August 21, 2017. Dykes uses an ancient astrological technique to calculate the start and length of eclipse effect based on the horoscope house in which the eclipse falls, in this case, for Washington, D.C. Where the three timelines overlap is the period of potential peak effect, which is from March to October 2019.

Mercury spends most of March in retrograde motion, turning backward on March 5 and forward on March 28.

Uranus moves back into the sign of Taurus on March 6, and will stay in that sign until July 2025. This positioning can be seen as bringing change down to earth, grounding it, and making it solid.

Watch for highs in gold on March 15 and in Euro FX on March 27, based on previous astrological transits against their first-trade horoscope charts.

APRIL 2019

April is a big month for big planets to turn retrograde and start putting the brakes on expansion (Jupiter on April 10), transformation (Pluto on April 24) and restriction (Saturn on April 30). Saturn and Pluto are within 3 degrees of each other in Capricorn, and are starting to insist that the transformation of business and government get serious.

Before any of these planets turn retrograde, watch for a potential high in the S&P 500 market on April 5. Although indicated by previous astrological transits to the S&P 500 natal chart, perhaps the index is getting a whiff of the upcoming retrogrades.

JUNE 2019

June is the strongest month of three this year for a potential end to the June 2009 economic expansion. As in January, Jupiter remains square to Neptune (exact on June 16). But now, the Sun is conjunct the country's natal Uranus, which is a strong aspect. If the economic expansion continues to June 2019, it will tie the record of 120 months set from March 1991 to March 2001.

Neptune turns retrograde on June 21, the day before the summer solstice, for the next five months.

JULY 2019

This summer's total solar eclipse occurs on July 2, and is visible in Chile and Argentina. Its matching lunar eclipse is on July 16. Interestingly, the solar eclipse is within 3 degrees of the natal Sun of the United States. The eclipse's delineation is that there is worry or obsession regarding young people or transforming situations that can be turned into a positive. This eclipse may indicate that leaders of the U.S. government take positive action regarding transformation and youth.

Astrologer Marie Schoeppel cast the eclipse chart for Beijing, China and notes that it is on the house cusp that rules currency and financial systems, thus could provide market chaos.[76] Indeed, she warns that China is in a similar astrological setup in late 2019 through the first half of 2020 as was seen in Asian debt crisis of 1997-98.

After the holiday, Mercury turns retrograde on July7 and doesn't reverse course until August 1.

AUGUST 2019

August is my candidate for the month of peak effect from the total solar eclipse across the United States on August 21, 2017 because four planets activate the degree of the eclipse by transit from August 16 to 28.

---

76   Schoeppel, Marie. "The Hangover: In 1997, It Was Bangkok—In 2019, It's Beijing," GlobalTrendsCycles.com. 3 November 2017. <https://www.globaltrendscycles.com/finance/2017/6/27/china-financial-collapse-2019>

Pay particular attention on August 16, when Mars hits the 2017 eclipse degree of 28 Leo 53, for news about nuclear weapons and tension between the United States and North Korea. That was a new topic at the time of the 2017 eclipse and was stamped as the signature of the Great American Eclipse two weeks later when North Korea tested its first H-bomb just 11 hours before transiting Mars—the planet of war and aggression—activated the eclipse degree exactly.

By August's end, the Sun, Moon, Mercury, Venus and Mars are all in the sign of Virgo together, for the first time since the high preceding the Crash of 1987. (It is only the second time since 1987 that five planets are in Virgo simultaneously; that was in September 2011, with the Sun, Moon, Mercury, Venus and Saturn.) What's more, astrological transits indicate the potential for a high in the S&P 500 market on August 23 and August 30. Also look for potential highs in the Euro FX and soybean markets on August 30.

Jupiter turns direct in motion on August 11, which supports an expansive effect of whatever occurs later in the month. One day later, Uranus starts its retrograde path in Taurus, which brings some reflection to potential sudden events, that lasts into the new year.

SEPTEMBER 2019

September is the least likely of this year's three astrologically based options for a potential end to the June 2009 economic expansion. Like January, Jupiter is square to Neptune in the sky (exact on September 21) and opposite the natal Uranus of the United States.

In the 10 days that span September 3-13, astrological transits project the potential for highs or lows in four markets. These include highs in the S&P 500 and 10-year T-note, a low in soybeans and two possibilities in gold—a low plus either a high or a low.

Saturn gets back down to business when it turns direct in motion on September 18.

OCTOBER-NOVEMBER 2019

The lunar calendar signifiers of bearish potential in the stock market coincide with the astrological transits that point to potential for highs in the gold, crude oil, and 10-year T-note markets.

October 24-25 mark days 27 and 28 of the 7th lunar month, which can have bearish potential for the stock market, according to author Christopher Carolan. This is especially the case when October's full moon falls between October 3 and October 19 as it does this year (on October 13). The dates for highs in the commodity markets span October 18-24.

Astrological transits are activating the first-trade horoscope chart of Euro FX futures in ways that point toward potential highs on October 29 and November 20, with a low in between on November 5.

Pluto kicks up the power for transformation of business and government as it turns direct in motion on October 3. On Halloween, Mercury turns retrograde and doesn't reverse to direct until November 20.

When Neptune turns direct in motion on November 27, the day before Thanksgiving, all the planets but Uranus are moving forward.

DECEMBER 2019

After 13 months of optimism and freedom to explore new ideas while Jupiter was traveling through its own sign of Sagittarius, the jolt will be rough when it shifts into the sign of Capricorn on December 2. All sign changes deliver a shift in energy, but this one could be brutal because Jupiter moves from its favorite sign to one of its least favorite. Freedom-loving Jupiter simply does not care for the shackles that Capricorn wants it to wear.

Economically, though, Jupiter in Capricorn supports grounded, solid development as it makes a trine to Uranus in Taurus on December 15. The Jupiter/Uranus cycle is a 13.8-year economic cycle that supports enthusiasm for new ideas. This is the final, waning trine of the cycle that began in 2011; they next are conjunct and begin a new cycle in April 2024.

On either side of the Jupiter/Uranus trine, there is potential for highs in two markets—gold on December 10 and crude oil on December 16.

The day after Christmas, a solar eclipse may bring traumatic transformation and sudden endings in relationships. Its matching lunar eclipse occurs on January 10, 2020.

2020—STARTS ROUGH, GETS WORSE

There's just no bones about it—the U.S. presidential election year is going to be a rough one, based on what astrology can tell us. Right away, planet heavyweights converge on January 12 to deliver some tough messages. In May, three astrological shifts at mid-month suggest it might be good to "sell in May and go away." Another, bigger round of tough messages occurs around Election Day. As the year ends, there is a paradigm shift in economic values that will last for the next 200 years. Whew! What a year!

JANUARY 2020

Mark your calendars now for January 10-13, 2020, and be on alert for some difficult news and difficult markets. This four-day period could be pivotal for the United States.

A full moon/lunar eclipse kicks things off on January 10. The eclipse is important because the Moon in Cancer is directly opposite a nearly exact conjunction of Saturn and Pluto in Capricorn. Any full moon sheds light on what was begun two weeks earlier at the new moon, which in this case concerned traumatic transformation and sudden endings in relationships. This full moon is in the Moon's ruling sign of Cancer, so is especially emotional. That it is opposite Saturn and Pluto in Capricorn indicates that emotions are high about the stern, serious, restrictive measures being taken to transform business and government.

On January 11, the master of change—Uranus—throws its weight into the proceedings as it turns direct in motion in the sign of Taurus. This means Uranus is working at full force to support change that is grounded and stable.

The big day is Sunday, January 12, when Saturn and Pluto are exactly conjunct at 22 Capricorn. At the same time, Mercury is at 22 Capricorn and the Sun is at 21 Capricorn. All four of these planets are working in concert, but the main stars are the heavyweight planets of Saturn and Pluto, who are together at the same point in the sky for the first time in 38 years.

Pluto recognizes that it leaves the sign of Capricorn in just four years and has to make good on its promise from 2008 when it entered the sign (and kicked off the global financial crisis) to transform business and government. Saturn is there to help make sure that happens. On January 12, they say: "Enough already. We have to got to make some tough decisions in order to transform governments and the way businesses operate. This is going to hurt and you won't like it, but you'll thank us later."

What makes January 12 even more interesting is its connection to the natal horoscope charts of the United States and the S&P 500 index:

1. The four-planet Capricorn stellium is opposite the USA natal Mercury, which could indicate a severe clamping down on freedom of the press or on commerce.
2. Transiting Mars is opposite the USA natal Uranus, an explosive combination. Also, it means that Mars is conjunct the sensitive degree area shared by the natal horoscope charts of the Dow Jones Industrial Average, the S&P 500 index and all three futures contracts derived from them. Be prepared for potential market explosions up or down.
3. Transiting Venus is conjunct the USA natal Sun, providing protection (and money) to the country and its leaders.

Interestingly, the very similar transits on January 13 point toward a potential low in the gold market.

FEBRUARY 2020

At mid-month, Mercury turns retrograde on February 17 and stays in reflective mode until March 20.

If you're into numbers, you'll like it when Jupiter makes a trine to Neptune on February 20—otherwise noted as 02/20/2020. Inflation could get a boost under this pair's influence. Also mark 02/20/2022 on your calendar. That's the day Pluto returns to where it was when the revolutionaries broke away from England by signing the Declaration of Independence in 1776. (More on this later in another publication I'll be working on, but it appears from an astrological perspective that the entire term of the U.S. president elected in 2020 will be focused on the country's Pluto return in 2022 and how to handle the revolutionary and transformative forces present during those four years.)

Watch for changes of trend in three markets from February 21 to 27. Astrological transits vs. first-trade horoscope charts indicate ripe conditions for either a high or a low in the S&P 500, a high in Euro FX, and a low in gold.

MARCH 2020

Mercury comes in like a lamb, remaining retrograde until it turns direct in motion on March 10.

The month goes out like a lion, however, as Mars and Saturn—considered the planetary malefics, i.e., bad guys—are aligned by conjunction at 0 degrees of Aquarius on March 31 and April 1, when Mars joins Saturn in the new sign. Saturn rules Aquarius, so the sign shift from Capricorn simply changes the planet's focus, not its strength. Watch for a tag-team effort to get something unusual started that was previously discarded as an idea that was ahead of its time.

APRIL 2020

Jupiter, Venus, and Pluto are working together on April 5 in what appears could be throwing a lot of money at a big problem. Jupiter expands whatever it touches, and it is touching Pluto exactly at the same degree of Capricorn. So, Pluto's effort to transform business and government is getting a big push from Jupiter. (Three weeks later, Pluto reconsiders a bit as it turns retrograde on April 25.)

To put an exclamation point on it, the two planets also are "parallel," meaning that they are at the same height in the sky as well as at the same degree of zodiacal longitude. They truly are tied together at the hip and working as in sync as is astrologically possible.

Venus, the money planet, is in a trine aspect to both Jupiter and Pluto. This aspect simply greases the skids to accomplish with funding whatever Jupiter and Pluto want to do.

In the first half of April, astrological transits set up for a potential low in the S&P 500 and crude oil markets and a high in 10-year T-notes.

MAY 2020

The astrological movement that occurs May 11-14 may be similar to what spawned the adage "sell in May and go away." Saturn turns retrograde on May 11; Venus turns retrograde on May 13; and Jupiter makes it a retrograde trio a day later, on May 14. What's more, the astrological transits for the S&P 500 market suggest a strong potential for a high on May 13.

Earlier in the month, on May 5, the Moon's North Node moves into the sign of Gemini. This ends its stay in the sign of Cancer and marks the end of what economist Louise McWhirter defined as the peak housing phase of the economic cycle. On the same day, the astrological transits set up for a potential high in the gold market.

JUNE-JULY 2020

Two lunar eclipses occur at the full moons in June and July and both are associated with the new moon/solar eclipse at the summer solstice on June 21—and all three are connected to the natal horoscope of the United States. Therefore, watch for game-changing news from June 5 to July 5. All three eclipses take their cue from the delineation of the solar eclipse, which warns of difficulty and being prone to misjudging the situation. Jumping on that theme is Saturn's retrograde movement back into Capricorn on July 1.

The first lunar eclipse, on June 5, is at 15 Sagittarius and is conjunct the USA's natal ascendant (using the Sibley horoscope). This eclipse may bring new insights into the country's outward persona as a sanctuary of freedom and champion of exploration.

The solar eclipse on June 21 occurs on the same day as the summer solstice, which bestows more than the ordinary significance. At 0 Cancer, the solar eclipse is conjunct the USA's natal Venus. Venus represents the heart and money, so this eclipse may see the United States in position to extend heartwarming amounts of monetary relief to those in need, but restricted from doing so because of the eclipse's energy that instills restraint, separation, and illusion.

The second lunar eclipse on July 5 is at 13 Capricorn and directly opposite the USA's natal Sun. Coming the day after the Independence Day holiday, the strength and identity of the country may be compromised in some way.

At month's end, Jupiter and Pluto are aligned for the second time this year. As both planets are in retrograde motion, look for a reprise and review of their first meeting on April 5.

Mercury is retrograde from June 18 to July 12 in Cancer, concurrent with the solar eclipse and the second lunar eclipse, making it more difficult to get news or communicate with accuracy.

In late June, Neptune turns retrograde on June 23, which increases fogginess and illusion generally, and can be bearish for the energy markets. Wait a month to see what happens, though. On July 20, astrological transits are ripe for a potential high in the crude oil market. Venus starts moving forward on June 25, which could give a boost to the stock market.

AUGUST 2020

In 1929, this was when the stock market topped—six months prior to the first waning (final) square of the Saturn/Uranus cycle from 1897 to 1932. In 2021, these two planets make an exact 90-degree aspect to each other three times—February 17, June 14, and December 24.

Be on alert through the last half of the month for sudden, trend-changing news, particularly as it concerns the United States and North Korea. Uranus kicks it off by turning retrograde on August 15. Then, Mercury and the Sun hit the degree of the Great American Eclipse on August 19 and August 21, respectively. On August 26, the astrological transits point to the potential for a high in the S&P 500 index as well as in soybeans.

SEPTEMBER 2020

Mars, which has been in its ruling sign of Aries since late June, turns retrograde on September 9. As a result, Mars will be in top form for feistiness, war, and aggression until January 2021. (Typically, Mars is in one sign for about two months, not six.)

Note that Mars is in Aries for likely both the Republican and Democratic national conventions, is retrograde for the U.S. presidential election, and moves into Taurus just when the new Congress convenes in January. Look for a tumultuous, contentious climax to the U.S. presidential campaign that continues even after the election.

On September 13, Jupiter turns direct in motion at 17 Capricorn and starts the march forward to meet up with Saturn at the same degree of the sign in December. Two weeks later, Saturn turns direct at 25 Capricorn on September 29. With these two powerhouses moving forward in the same sign, the discussion will turn toward increasing rules, regulations, and formalities for business and governments.

OCTOBER 2020

This is the month when you can legitimately claim "once in a blue moon." The full moon makes two appearances this month, on October 1 and on Halloween, October 31. Also on October 1, Venus hits the degree of the Great American Eclipse of 2017 while the Full Moon is in feisty Aries. Be on alert for more fireworks than normal on the first full moon. As for the latter, perhaps a Blue Moon costume party is in your future…

On October 4, Pluto turns direct in Capricorn so gets back into its focused ability to transform business and government in the last month of U.S. presidential campaigning. Ten days later, though, Mercury turns retrograde until the middle of Election Day, November 3, making late campaign promises misunderstood.

The bearish-leaning days based on the lunar calendar occur October 13-14, four days after astrological transits suggest a potential low in the S&P 500 market. At month's end, the transits see potential for a high in the 10-year T-note and soybean markets.

NOVEMBER 2020

Based on the economic paradigm shift coming in December, it would be best if the United States elected a president on November 3 who is aligned with the move toward valuing ideas, technology, and global community.

However, the astrological energy is difficult. For starters, Mercury turns direct at 12:50 pm (Eastern) on Election Day, so there may be problems with ballots cast in the morning or via early voting while Mercury was retrograde (since October 14). The following week, Jupiter and Pluto are conjunct in the same degree of Capricorn from November 8 to 12, with Saturn just 4 degrees away.

These three big planets are working as a team, without a doubt, to transform government. Is it because they want to make sure all the election's legal (Jupiter) rules (Saturn) are being followed? Or, is it because they want to support a heavy-handed, my-way-or-the-highway winner? Given this is the last of three Jupiter/Pluto conjunctions this year, it should have the flavor of what occurred in April, at the first one. The difference this time is that Saturn is in the mix, and Saturn insists on following the rules to the letter. Aggressor Mars turns direct in its own sign of Aries on November 14, adding impetus to the activities.

A week after the election, the astrological transits strongly suggest the potential for a low in the S&P 500 market on November 10, followed by a high in the gold market on November 11.

On November 29, Neptune turns direct, lifting the fog and confusion of the month. On the same day, look for a potential high in the Euro FX based on astrological transits.

On November 30, a full moon/lunar eclipse occurs in the sign of Gemini and is associated with the total solar eclipse two weeks later.

DECEMBER 2020

Before the eclipse, astrological transits point toward potential highs in crude oil and the S&P 500 with potential lows in Euro FX and soybeans during December 2-9. In the last week of the year, astrological transits are pointing toward lows in the Euro FX, 10-year T-note, and gold markets.

Mid-month, on December 14, a total solar eclipse at 23 Sagittarius is visible in Chile and Argentina. However, it is opposite the natal Mars of the United States, which only may exaggerate the eclipse's character of anger, lust, and frustration in that country. Relationships could end over money issues.

December 21, 2020 is perhaps the most important date in our lifetimes. Within eight hours on that day, the Sun will mark the winter solstice by entering the sign of Capricorn, and we will enter a new economic paradigm as Jupiter and Saturn conjoin at 0 degrees of Aquarius.

It would be important enough to mark the Jupiter/Saturn conjunction in any degree of Aquarius as the start of a new 20-year business cycle. But this conjunction is extraordinary in two other ways. First, the conjunction is at 0 degrees of Aquarius, the very first degree of the sign and a signal that what's to come has freshness and will start at the beginning.

Second—and the reason this has life-changing effects—is that Jupiter and Saturn are conjunct in an Air sign and will continue to make conjunctions in Air signs about every 20 years for the next 199 years. On this date, Jupiter and Saturn are closing the book on making conjunctions in Earth signs, which they have been doing since 1842. And, finally, the exclamation point is that the Air

Mutation, as astrologers call it, occurs on arguably the most important astrological day of the year—the winter solstice, when the Sun reaches its nadir and begins its own cycle anew.

EARTH VS. AIR ECONOMIES

Because the Jupiter/Saturn cycle is associated with business and the economy, their conjunctions in Earth signs since 1842 meant the economy valued material goods and physical things. Hence the Industrial Revolution and focus on money, banking and finances.

In Air signs until 2219, the Jupiter/Saturn cycle now declares that the economy will place value on ideas, intellectual property, technology, and collaboration. We got an early peek at what this economy might look like from 1981 to 2000 due to a quirk of planetary movement in which Jupiter and Saturn began that cycle in Libra (an Air sign), their only deviation from Earth conjunctions since 1842.

When Jupiter and Saturn were conjunct in Libra in March 1981, computers were just beginning to gain a foothold in homes; by the end of the cycle in 2000, the Internet had invaded nearly everyone's home. Online trading was all the rage, and new technology company listings made us wonder if indeed something had changed and that there was value in a stock that was still not much more than an idea. We got our answer in May 2000, just two months after the dot.com crash, when the planets made their final conjunction in an Earth sign and brought prices—and our ideas about how to price a stock—back down to earth and the prevailing economic reality that value lies in what can be seen and touched physically.

Starting at year-end 2020—and for the next 199 years—to have a physical presence will not be required in order to have economic value. We'll no doubt get a chance to figure that dot.com thing out. We likely will see movement toward a single, global, electronic-based currency, although I shudder to think of the economic chaos that may have to ensue for that to be seen as the viable option. And, if Dan Brown's novel, "Origin," provides foresight in that truth-is-stranger-than-fiction kind of way, we could see a melding of humans and technology by the mid-21st century.

The first 20 years of this new Air paradigm are in Aquarius, which values individuality and all things unique. The flip side to this brave, new world outlook is one in which individual rights are forsaken in the name of extreme collaboration, i.e., collectivism, where everything is produced for the good of the group. However, that is the extreme. The next Jupiter/Saturn conjunction will be in Libra, which values relationships, starting in October 2040.

CHAPTER 13

How to Introduce Astrology to Your Financial Toolbox

Because the over-achievers in the audience might have scanned the Table of Contents and come here first, I'm happy to give you all the big-picture overview on how to make practical use of the information in this book, whether you are a trader, an investor, or an astrologer with clients who have financial questions. And, because I'm a Capricorn sun sign, practical is always my key word, no matter what. So, here goes.

UNDERSTAND BIG ASTROLOGICAL TRENDS

What I love most about astrology is the ability to see far into the future. And I'm talking years and decades, not just months or weeks. Not that astrology can tell you what's going to happen in the future. It can't, and that's not the point of astrology. But, it can tell you about the character of the energy available at any given time, based on planetary positions published in any ephemeris or astrological software program.

Where I find that peek into the future most valuable is in providing a framework for where we're headed over the next several years, based on the large planetary-based economic cycles discussed in Chapter 5. In trader-speak, these big astrological trends are like looking at a monthly price chart. Both provide long-term perspective that sets the stage on which the shorter planetary cycles (or weekly/daily/intraday price charts) play out in terms of world events, news, and price action.

Beyond what I've written about the astrological economic cycles of Jupiter, Saturn, and Uranus in this book, I highly encourage you to read what I consider the best book of all in describing how these large, long-term planetary cycles have affected our lives for centuries—"Cosmos and Psyche," by Richard Tarnas, a cultural historian and professor of philosophy and depth psychology. As the book jacket says: "Based on thirty years of research, Cosmos and Psyche is the first book by a widely respected scholar to demonstrate the existence of a direct connection between planetary movements and the archetypal patterns of human experience."[77]

The insights and connections Tarnas derived about how we humans express the energy of our time are simply mind-blowing. For me, his book confirmed the beauty and orderliness of nature and the Universe. It also confirmed on an astrological level what I learned early on as a market reporter and observer—that the trend is your friend. Know what the biggest trend is and go with it. Buy dips in a big bull market. Sell rallies in a big bear market. You can do the same with astrological trends. Understand where we are in a current astrological cycle—like Jupiter/Saturn and Saturn/Uranus—and go with the flow. Read more about the current state of these big economic cycles in Chapter 5 and Chapter 12.

LEARN THE ASTROLOGICAL LANGUAGE

Astrology is a language of symbols and archetypes, and to use astrology in your financial toolbox, you simply have to learn the basics of the language—planets, signs, houses and aspects—and what they mean in words and graphic symbols, or glyphs.

---

77 Tarnas, Richard. Cosmos and Psyche. (New York: Viking Penguin, 2006).

I'm sure you've done something similar before in whatever industry you work in or whatever hobby you have explored. This is no different, and no more complicated. The astrological lingo just takes some focus and some practice. I've provided the basics in Chapter 1 and in the Astrology Glossary at the back of this book. If you want to dig deeper, check out the several-volume series under the titles "The Only Way to Learn Astrology," by Marion D. March & Joan McEvers. These books are considered classics, and are written so that everyone can understand them.

Once you're comfortable with the lingo, the next big step is to learn how to read an astrological chart, which is nothing more than an easy way to record the energy of a moment with the shorthand of symbolic glyphs. If you've learned to read a price chart or sheet music for choir, the piano or other musical instrument, those same skills are transferable and will help you learn to read an astrology chart. No pressure, though. It takes awhile and some concerted effort to get there.

PICK YOUR MARKET

Now that you've got the big picture in mind and have the astrological basics down, it's time to pick a single market as the first one you'll tackle. This book provides background, information, and outlook for six commodity futures markets, each one representing a major trading sector. One of these likely appeals to you the most, so pick that one and start there. At the very least, I think everyone can benefit from following the U.S. stock market via the S&P 500 futures market.

Certainly, you can pick a market not featured in this book. Indeed, I plan on continuing my research into first-trade data for commodity futures markets around the world and will be publishing supplements to this book as information is available.

If you trade stocks, I encourage you to start working with both the first-trade and incorporation natal horoscope charts of your favorites. In this arena, I have found great value in the work published by Bill Meridian (www.billmeridian.com) and Grace Morris (www.astroeconomics.com).

To take it a step further, I recommend comparing your personal natal horoscope with that of any market you want to trade. The more your two horoscope charts sync up, the more likely it is that you'll do well trading that market. In astrology lingo, this comparison is called a synastry chart, and I discuss how it works in Chapter 3. If you want to explore for yourself, you can contact me or work with any other trusted astrologer who does synastry work to see if you sync up with your market.

LEARN YOUR MARKET

The advice to learn your market from an astrological viewpoint is no different than what you likely already have done from a traditional fundamental and/or technical market analysis point of view.

Learn what the first-trade chart of that market looks like. Watch as the transiting planets move around the market's first-trade chart and see what happens when they trigger a natal planet or angle, particularly at conjunctions and oppositions, which are the strongest aspects. Go back in time, as I did in Chapters 6-11, to see which planets and which transits were activated at important turning points in your market. Then, go forward in time to see when those same transits will come around again, as I did in Chapter 12. And, finally, be sure to review the general astro trading tips at the end of Chapter 5.

LOOK FOR CONVERGING CLUES

Traders and astrologers would do well to heed the adage that one is a single and two is a pair…but three is a "collection." Astrologers like to see three indications in a chart that say something similar before opening their mouths about the potential for something to happen. Traders watching technical indicators do the same, waiting for a signal that is confirmed from a variety of directions.

Astrology excels at pinpointing potential timing in the markets because it can tell you to the minute when a transit's energy will be the strongest. But, in my opinion, astrology is not the end-all, be-all in terms of making a trading decision. Nor is any other single technical or fundamental indicator. Strength and confidence come from when at least three indicators are all pointing the same way.

TRADING IN SYNC

Because of astrology's unique ability to both provide long-term perspective and pinpoint short-term timing, I hope this book encourages you to find a place for it in your arsenal of trading tools.

Consider the astrological insight you've gotten here simply another indicator coming at the market from a different perspective. If the astrology helps you focus in on a particular time period, or a particular day or hour—great! If the astrological transits say there is the potential for a change of trend at the same time your other favorite technical indicators are flipping over, so much the better. And, finally, the cherry on top would be if your personal horoscope chart were also being activated in a way that helped you understand if you could anticipate a great outcome or should be cautious.

Put all three things together and you truly will be trading in sync.

Good luck!

APPENDIX

Dates of Potential Highs and Lows 2018-2020

The following tables show by chronological order the dates for all the potential high and low prices in the six markets covered in Chapter 6-11 from 2018 to 2020.

These dates are based on similar transits to those gleaned from researching previous significant highs and lows in each of these six markets over the last few decades. I have marked the ones I believe are the strongest contenders in boldface type.

2018

Potential Highs and Lows

Date	Soybeans	Crude Oil	Gold	Euro FX	S&P 500	10-year T-note
January 5			High			
January 16		High				
January 19				High		
February 5				Low		
February 18					High	
February 21			High			
March 12		Low				
March 21			High	High		
April 9						High
April 27			High or Low			
May 3				Low		
May 9	High					
May 11	Low					
May 15				High		
May 21						Low
May 22					High	
May 25			Low			
June 8		High		Low		
June 11		High				
June 13	High					
July 6		Low				
July 23					High	
July 25	Low					
August 7						Low
August 14		High or Low				
August 23					High or Low	
August 31	High					
September 6					Low	
September 11			Low			
September 14			High			

September 20							Low
September 24	Low						
October 5	High						
October 9					Low		
October 10				High			
October 15	Low						
October 18							Low
October 26					High		
November 5					Low		
November 7		Low					
November 8						High	
November 20		Low					
November 27						Low	
December 3		High					
December 10	Low						
December 17						Low	
December 19		High					
December 21		High or Low	High				

2019

Potential Highs and Lows

Date	Soybeans	Crude Oil	Gold	Euro FX	S&P 500	10-year T-note
January 2						**High**
January 11			Low			Low
January 14		High				
January 24						High
January 28						**Low**
February 5						High
February 19					High	
February 25				High		
February 26	Low					
March 15			High			
March 27				High		
April 2	Low					
April 5					High or Low	
April 9			High			
April 15		Low				
April 19						Low
April 29	High			Low		
May 3				Low		
May 9			High or Low			
May 10						Low
May 16			High			
May 17				High		
May 22						High
June 3	High					
June 7				High		
June 10						High
June 11			High			
June 13				Low		
June 19			High or Low			
July 22		High				

Date							
August 1		High or Low					
August 6		High					
August 15		High					
August 23					High		
August 30	High				High	High	
September 3				Low			
September 5							High
September 6				High or Low		High	
September 9	Low						
September 13							High
October 3	High						
October 7							High
October 10						Low	
October 18							Low
October 19		High or Low					
October 24				High			
October 29					High		
November 5					Low		
November 6						High	
November 20					High		
November 26							High
December 5							Low
December 10				High			
December 16		High					
December 20							High

2020

Potential Highs and Lows

Date	Soybeans	Crude Oil	Gold	Euro FX	S&P 500	10-year T-note
January 13			Low			
January 24						Low
February 21					High or Low	
February 23				High		
February 27			Low			
March 3					High	
March 9	Low					
March 20			High or Low			
March 26			Low			
March 31				High		
April 3					Low	
April 9						**High**
April 14		Low				
April 21				Low		
April 24	High					
April 28	Low					
May 1						Low
May 5			High			
May 13					High	
May 22	Low					
June 8	High					
June 15				Low		
July 13		High				
July 14		High				
July 20		High				
July 27					Low	
July 30				Low		
August 20	Low					
August 26	High					
September 8	Low					

September 14		High					
September 23							High
September 28		Low					
October 7	High						
October 9						Low	
October 15			Low				
October 20	Low						
October 28							High
October 29	High						
November 10						Low	
November 11			High or Low				
November 25						High	
November 27	Low						
November 29					High		
December 2		High					
December 4					Low	High	
December 9	Low						
December 21					Low		**Low**
December 28			Low				

Astrology Glossary

Ancient rulers—seven visible planets assigned as rulers of certain zodiac signs. Sun for Leo, Moon for Cancer, Mercury for Gemini and Virgo, Venus for Taurus and Libra, Mars for Aries and Scorpio, Jupiter for Sagittarius and Pisces, Saturn for Capricorn and Aquarius.

Angles—the horizontal and vertical axes of the horoscope chart that are considered most sensitive to natal or transiting planets close to them. The angles are the cusps of houses 1, 4, 7, and 10.

Applying—an aspect that is moving toward becoming exact.

Ascendant—1st house cusp; one of four angles of a horoscope chart.

Aspect—geometrical relationship between a transiting planet and a natal planet, or between two natal planets, or between two transiting planets.

Benefic—attribute ancient astrologers ascribed to planets thought to bring positive energy. Jupiter is the greater benefic; Venus is the lesser benefic.

Bi-wheel—two horoscope charts shown together, typically to see how transits (on the outside wheel) affect a natal chart (on the inside wheel).

Cardinal—the first zodiac sign of each season; has initiating quality: Aries, Cancer, Libra, Capricorn.

Combust—when a planet is within ± 17 zodiacal degrees of the Sun, making it unseen and weak.

Conjunction—aspect in which planets are near the same degree of the same zodiac sign.

Contraparallel—planets that are within 1 degree of opposite declination, i.e., one North, one South.

Cusp—the boundaries of an astrological house.

Declination—a planet's north/south distance in degrees from the celestial equator, i.e., the path of the Sun.

Descendant—7th house cusp; one of four angles of a horoscope chart.

Fixed—the second zodiac sign of each season; has staying power: Taurus, Leo, Scorpio, Aquarius.

Grand square—four planets that form a square formation in the sky, including two oppositions as well as each planet making a square (90-degree) aspect to the planet on either side of it.

IC—4th house cusp; stands for *Imum Coeli*, Latin for bottom of the sky; one of four angles of a horoscope chart.

Ingress—when a planet moves into a new zodiac sign.

Malefic—attribute ancient astrologers ascribed to planets thought to bring negative energy. Saturn is the greater malefic; Mars in the lesser malefic. Although not in the ancients' realm, Pluto is also considered a malefic planet.

Major aspects (Ptolemic aspects)—conjunction (0 degrees), opposition (180 degrees), square (90 degrees), trine (120 degrees), sextile (60 degrees).

MC—10th house cusp and midheaven; stands for *Medium Coeli*, Latin for middle of the sky.

Midheaven—see MC.

Minor aspects—any non-Ptolemic aspect, including semisextile (30 degrees), semisquare (45 degrees), quintile (72 degrees), sesquiquadrate (135 degrees), and quincunx (150 degrees).

Modern rulers—outer planets assigned co-rulership of certain zodiac signs. Uranus for Aquarius, Neptune for Pisces, and Pluto for Scorpio.

Mutable—the third zodiac sign of each season; easy to make changes: Gemini, Virgo, Sagittarius, Pisces.

Nodes—two points, exactly opposite one another, on the ecliptic where the

Moon (or any other planet) crosses the Sun's projected path.

Opposition—when planets are about 180 zodiacal degrees apart.

Orb—the number of degrees, plus or minus from exact, that define an aspect.

Out of bounds—when a planet's declination exceeds the Sun's maximum declination of 23 degrees, 26 minutes.

Parallel—planets that are within 1 degree of the same declination, either North or South.

Precession of the equinoxes—the moving backward in the zodiac of the degree and zodiac sign that appears on the eastern horizon at the spring equinox, beginning with 0 Aries in 2160 BCE and moving 1 degree every 72 years.

Quality—one of three designations assigned to a zodiac sign that take cues from the seasons: cardinal, fixed, mutable.

Retrograde—appearing to move backward in the sky.

Rulerships—associations between planets, zodiac signs, and horoscope houses in which the planet and/or zodiac sign is strongest. For example, Mars is the ruler of Aries; Mars and Aries rule the 1st house.

Saros Series—an identifier of eclipse families that have similar patterns over centuries.

Saturn return—when transiting Saturn returns to where it was in the natal horoscope; occurs at about ages 29, 59, and 89.

Sextile—when planets are about 60 zodiacal degrees apart.

Square—when planets are about 90 zodiacal degrees apart.

Separating—an aspect that is moving away from having been exact.

Station—when planets halt in motion as they move from direct to retrograde motion and vice versa.

Stellium—three or more planets close together in the same zodiac sign

Temperament—one of four elements assigned to a zodiac sign: fire, earth, air, or water.

Transit—when a planet in the sky comes into aspect with a planet in a natal chart.

Trine—when planets are about 120 zodiacal degrees apart.

Waning—aspects that occur in the last half of an astrological cycle, after the opposition.

Waxing—aspects that occur in the first half of an astrological cycle, before the opposition.

Yod—a triangle formation made by two planets that are sextile to one another, mutually connected to a third planet by 150-degree aspects. Called the "Finger of God" as fated events can occur by transit to the point of the triangle or the point opposite.

Bibliography

American Soybean Association. <u>1930s.</u> 24 Jan. 2017 https://soygrowers.com/about-asa/highlights/1930s/

Archer Daniels Midland. <u>History, 1920-1939.</u> 24 Jan. 2017 http://www.adm.com/en-US/company/history/Pages/1920-1939.aspx

Baer, Julius B. and Saxon, Olin Glenn. <u>Commodity Exchanges And Futures Trading Principles And Operating Methods.</u> New York: Harper & Brothers, 1949.

Bills, Rex E. <u>The Rulership Book.</u> Tempe, AZ: American Federation of Astrologers, Inc., 2007.

Brady, Bernadette. <u>Predictive Astrology.</u> San Francisco: Red Wheel/Weiser, LLC, 1999.

Buck, James E., ed. <u>The New York Stock Exchange: The First 200 Years.</u> Essex, Conn.: Greenwich Publishing Group, Inc., 1992.

Campion, Nicholas. <u>The Book of World Horoscopes.</u> Bournemouth: The Wessex Astrologer Ltd., 1999.

Carolan, Christopher. "Autumn Panics: A Calendar Phenomenon." 1998. http://spiralcalendar.com/wp-content/uploads/2016/09/autumn_panics.pdf

Carolan, Christopher. <u>The Spiral Calendar.</u> Gainesville, Ga: New Classics Library. 1993.

Chicago Board of Trade. <u>Act of Incorporation, Rules, By-Laws and Inspection Regulations of the Board of Trade of the City of Chicago.</u> Lawrence J. Gutter Collection of Chicagoana (University of Illinois at Chicago) ICIU, 1875.

Christino, Karen. Foreseeing the Future: Evangeline Adams and Astrology in America. Amherst, MA: One Reed Publications, 2002.

Clews, Henry. Fifty Years in Wall Street. Hoboken, N.J.: John Wiley & Sons, Inc., 2006.

Committee on Publicity, New York Stock Exchange. The New York Stock Exchange. New York: New York Stock Exchange, 1929.

Downey, Morgan. Oil 101. Wooden Table Press LLC, 2009.

Falloon, William D. Market Maker: A Sesquicentennial Look at the Chicago Board of Trade. Chicago: Board of Trade of the City of Chicago, 1998.

Gann, W.D. How to Make Profits Trading in Commodities. Pomeroy, Wash.: Lamber-Gann Publishing Co., Inc., 1951.

Gidel, Susan Abbott. Stock Index Futures & Options. New York: John Wiley & Sons, Inc., 2000.

Hieronymus, Thomas A. Economics of Futures Trading. New York: Commodity Research Bureau, Inc. 1976.

Howland, Ronald W. American Histrology. Tempe, AZ: American Federation of Astrologers, Inc., 2014.

Jones, Kathy; Camphausen, Lisa; and Sutphen, Leslie. "The Euro—Ready or Not. Trading Implications of the New Common Currency." Prudential Securities. Futures Research. Nov. 23, 1998.

Labuszewski, John W. and Aldinger, Lori. "Twenty Years of CME Globex." CME Group. June 21, 2012.

Lind-Waldock. The Complete Guide to Futures Trading. Hoboken, N.J.: John Wiley & Sons, Inc., 2005.

Lowell, Fred R. Profits in Soybeans. Kansas City: Keltner Statistical Service, Inc., 1966.

Lurie, Jonathan. The Chicago Board of Trade 1859-1905. Urbana, Ill.: University of Illinois Press. 1979.

Meridian, Bill. Planetary Stock Trading—IV. New York: Cycles Research LLC, 2013.

McWhirter, Louise M. Astrology and Stock Market Forecasting. New York: ASI Publishers, Inc., 1977.

Melamed, Leo and Tamarkin, Bob. Leo Melamed: Escape to the Futures. New York: John Wiley & Sons, Inc., 1996.

Michelsen, Neil F. Tables of Planetary Phenomena, Second Edition. San Diego: ACS Publications, 1995.

Michelsen, Neil F. and Pottenger, Rique. The American Ephemeris 1950-2050 at Midnight. Exeter, N.H.: ACS Publications, 2011.

Sandor, Richard L. Good Derivatives. Hoboken, N.J.: John Wiley & Sons, Inc., 2012.

Shurtleff, William, and Akiko Aoyagi. History of World Soy Production and Trade—Part 1. Soyfoods Center, 2004. 24 Jan. 2017. http://www.soyinfocenter.com/HSS/production_and_trade1.php

Stedman, Edmund Clarence. The New York Stock Exchange. New York: Stock Exchange Historical Company, 1905. (Reprinted by Forgotten Books, 2012.)

Tamarkin, Bob. The Merc. New York: HarperCollins Publishers, 1993.

Tarnas, Richard. Cosmos and Psyche. London: Viking Penguin, 2006

Taylor, Charles H., ed. History of the Board of Trade of the City of Chicago. Chicago: Robert O. Law Company, 1917.

U.S. Commodity Futures Trading Commission. Futures and Options Contracts Designated By the CFTC and its Predecessor Agencies, Backgrounder No. 3-91, Washington: CFTC Office of Public Affairs, December 1, 1993.

Williams, LCdr. David. Financial Astrology. Tempe, AZ: American Federation of Astrologers, Inc., 2004.

Resources

Please tap into the following resources that I have found helpful in understanding both the markets and astrology.

Barchart.com
https://www.barchart.com/

Robert F. Dieli
RDLB, Inc.
https://www.nospinforecast.com/

Benjamin Dykes
https://www.bendykes.com/

W.D. Gann, Inc.
https://www.wdgann.com/

Bill Meridian
www.billmeridian.com

Grace Morris
www.astroeconomics.com

International Academy of Astrology
www.astrocollege.org

NASA (eclipses)
https://eclipse.gsfc.nasa.gov/eclipse.html

Marie Schoeppel
https://www.globaltrendscycles.com/

Sirius v2.0
Cosmic Patterns Software
www.astrosoftware.com

Christeen Skinner
http://www.financialuniverse.co.uk/

"The Only Way to Learn Astrology" book series
By Marion D. March and Joan McEvers

University of Illinois at Chicago
Special Collections and Archives
https://library.uic.edu/special-collections-university-archives

Get in touch with Susan

Email:	susan@susangidel.com
Web:	www.susangidel.com
Facebook:	SusanGSays
Twitter:	@SusanGSays
LinkedIn:	Susan Abbott Gidel

Contribute first-trade date and time documentation to:

TeamCommodityTimes@yahoo.com.

www.ingramcontent.com/pod-product-compliance
Lightning Source LLC
Chambersburg PA
CBHW061441300426
44114CB00014B/1785